Contents

DAVID COHEN

PSYCHOLOGISTS
ON PSYCHOLOGY

Hodder & Stoughton

Orders: please contact Bookpoint Ltd, 130 Milton Park, Abingdon, Oxon OX14 4SB.
Telephone: (44) 01235 827720. Fax: (44) 01235 400454. Lines are open from 9.00–6.00,
Monday to Saturday, with a 24-hour message answering service. You can also
order through our website www.hodderheadline.co.uk.

British Library Cataloguing in Publication Data
A catalogue record for this title is available from the British Library

ISBN 0 340 81075 0

First Published 2004
Impression number   10 9 8 7 6 5 4 3 2 1
Year   2007 2006 2005 2004

Typeset by Servis Filmsetting Ltd, Manchester.
Printed in Great Britain for Hodder & Stoughton Educational, a division of
Hodder Headline, 338 Euston Road, London NW1 3BH by CPI Bath.

Introduction

The psychology of psychologists might seem an esoteric, even frivolous, subject. It shouldn't be. Psychology has become a very influential business. Psychologists like Oliver James in the UK and Philip Zimbardo in the United States are media personalities. The world clamours for their insights into new trends. Actually, that clamour is not so new. In 1927, John B. Watson, the founder of behaviourism, protested, dear Lord, that he was always being harassed by hacks who wanted a quote on the latest trends in sex, babies and motorcars. Psychopundits ruled even back then.

Today there's even more pressure. With God mostly dead in Western civilisation, we look to psychologists (and psychiatrists) to tell us what our lives really mean. Guru – be thou my guide and if the guru's got an -ology, all the more reason to trust him or her.

It is more than 25 years since the first edition of this book appeared – and psychology has changed considerably since then. The discipline's done well; there are more psychologists than ever before. In 1977, the membership of the British Psychological Society was just over 6000. Today it is over 35,000. The American Psychological Association has become so large, some members wonder if it's not too vast to be any use. You need a large airport to hold its convention. In Australia, South Africa and Japan tens of thousands of psychologists analyse and speculate. Even wack-wack countries like Rumania – and I'm part Rumanian so I can be rude about the place – have thousands of qualified psychologists.

Sheer numbers doesn't guarantee insight and progress. There have been many snipers in the last 30 years who have complained that while more of us than ever earn our beer and sushi by doing psychology, we may not, shame, shame, understand any better what makes humans tick.

When you challenge psychologists and ask what we actually know about how – and why – people behave, they often explain that one mustn't grumble. Psychology is, after all, a very young subject. You can't expect it to be as advanced as physics, chemistry or astronomy. That is true – and not so true. Psychology is younger than chemistry if you count the debut of psychology as the glorious moment in 1879, when the first laboratory devoted to the subject opened for business. That year Wilhelm Wundt founded his lab in Leipzig and William James founded his lab at Harvard. As of 2004, psychology is only 125 years old. How much can you expect? Astronomy dates back to Ptolemy and Copernicus, after all, and wasn't that Isaac Newton working in the 17th century? It'll soon be four centuries since the apple – and the penny – dropped leading him to invent gravity.

However, using 1879 as the start of psychology manages to ignore thinkers like Descartes, Berkeley, Hume and J.S. Mill who were interested in psychological problems from the 17th century on. Some Greeks like Aristotle even had a word to say on the psyche. Enough was known about melancholy by 1600 for Burton to write his massive treatise on a subject that sounds very much like depression. The great German physiologist Helmholtz was doing experiments on the psychology of sensation from the middle of the 19th century. Serious experiments on hypnosis were being carried out by Puysegur in France in the 1830s.

In the first edition, I reported there was much argument between, in the red corner, the sensible optimists who thought psychology was buzzing along quite nicely, thank you, building up fragments of knowledge; and, in the blue corner, the pessimists who thought the discipline had failed entirely. Paul Kline, one of Britain's authorities on psychological testing, wailed as late as 1990, that most psychology was pompously written-up common sense (*Psychology Exposed*, 1990). "Paul was going through a bad patch," Hans Eysenck countered back to me about his esteemed colleague. Both men are now sadly dead but I imagine them slugging it out in the after-life.

The first edition of this book also revealed one of the obsessions of psychologists. Please realise we are scientists. Don't confuse us with agony aunts. From the late sixties on, there had been great demand from students for psychology courses in the UK and the USA. Many of those I interviewed in the 1970s believed this was because students thought that by learning psychology, they would find out about life. A number of psychology's great and good sniped that this was a most unfortunate misconception. They were not quite sure how to define psychology but they were 100 per cent certain that it was only remotely connected with life. And better that way!

As governments all over the world prefer to back research that can yield practical results, fewer psychologists are ivory towered these days. Also, today, psychology offers a rather promising career – but the fledgling psychologist is expected to get his or her hands dirty. A degree in psychology can lead to a job in the health service or education or human resources. The 'human resource-nik' will design and administer the tests, which reveal whether you have what it takes to become an entrepreneur, a salesman or, even, a vicar. Nurses, social workers, teachers receive training in psychology as do policemen, magistrates and air stewardesses. "I will be handcuffing you with immense sensitivity, chummy", says the psycho-literate cop. In his interview, Zimbardo explains how he persuaded the Palo Alto police department to let him use rookie cops as subjects precisely to beef up their sensitivity – if sensitivity is something you beef up.

I'd like to say that the next Pope will be asked to take a psychological test before ascending the throne of St Peter's, but probably not. Politicians, however, might be required to submit to the psycho-probe if a recent story is true. It has been suggested MPs will have to undergo psychometric testing but they aren't likely to vote for this. As I write this, James Murdoch, son of Rupert, has had to agree to be psychometrically tested for the top job at BSkyB, his father's creation. Nepotists shudder at such impertinence but psychologists have persuaded the world that they have expertise that matters.

Yet psychologists have always been insecure. In this book I have included interviews with three psychologists who have won Nobel prizes. The truth is that there have only been five Nobel winning psychologists – Pavlov, Niko Tinbergen, Herbert Simon, Daniel Kahneman and Konrad Lorenz. Pavlov did not win for his work on learning and the conditioned reflex, but for his work on physiology. Freud never won the Nobel Prize nor did Burrhus Skinner, Noam Chomsky or Jean Piaget. Yet this quartet advanced knowledge and influenced life in the 20th century at least as much as most other winners of the Nobel.

When I started interviewing psychologists in the 1970s, I was struck by how little some psychologists thought of what they were doing. (Clinical psychologists diagnose this as lack of self esteem!) Nehemiah Jordan in his *Themes in Speculative Psychology* (1968) was the great Cassandra. He lamented:

"There can be no doubt about it, contemporary American scientific psychology is the sterile of the sterile. Years of arduous labour and the assiduous enterprise of hundreds of professors and thousands of students has yielded precisely nothing . . . In the fifty-three years that have passed since that 'momentous' occasion (J.B. Watson, 'Psychology as the behaviorist views it', 1913) can *one* positive contribution towards any increased knowledge of man be pointed to? None such can be found: no substantive contribution can be named. The canard that 'psychology is a new science' has long outlived its explanatory-away usefulness: the unpleasant and discouraging facts must be faced honestly."

Many psychologists rejected Jordan's view but it is telling that no physicist, chemist or biologist could have written an equivalent *J'accuse* of their discipline And even psychologists who believe the subject isn't doing badly work against that background. They have colleagues who believe psychology is puffed-up common sense, jumped-up jargon.

In the preface to the influential *The Structure of Scientific Revolutions* (1962) Thomas Kuhn wrote that the final stage of the work he was doing while he spent a year as a visiting fellow at the Center for Advanced Studies in the Behavioral Sciences at Stanford affected his ideas, he said (Preface, p. viii):

> ". . . spending the year in a community composed predominantly of social scientists confronted me with unanticipated problems about the differences between such communities and those of the natural scientists among whom I had been trained. Particularly, I was struck by the number and extent of overt disagreements between social scientists about the nature of legitimate scientific problems and methods. Both history and acquaintance made me doubt that the practitioners of the natural sciences possess permanent answers to such questions more than their colleagues in social science. Yet, somehow, the practice of astronomy, physics, chemistry or biology normally fails to evoke the controversies over fundamentals that today often seem endemic among, say, psychologists and sociologists."

I would argue that much of what Kuhn said still holds true today. No one can hope to understand the sprawling discipline that is psychology without understanding some of the old polemics.

The late Donald Broadbent gave me the best and most convincing statement of the modern behaviorist position and declared both in *Behaviour* (1961) and in *In Defence of Empirical Psychology* (1974) his commitment to traditional experimental methods. Near the end of *Behaviour*, in a section titled 'The Endless Search'. Broadbent wrote (pp. 200–1):

> "We end then upon a note of doubt, with no certainty about the beliefs which future psychologists will hold. This is as it should be. Nobody can grasp the nature of things from an armchair and until fresh experiments have been performed we do not know what their results will be. The confident dogmatists about human nature which fall so readily from pulpits, newspapers' editorials and school prize givings are not for us. Rather we must be prepared to live with an incomplete knowledge of behaviour but with confidence in the power of objective methods to give us that knowledge some day. These methods have proved themselves even in the past fifty years. Looking back we can see them destroying one over simplification after another, forcing us to reject Pavlov's theory or Hull's and bringing theoretical opponents together by the sheer weight of factual evidence. In this half century there has been recognizable progress in our understanding behaviour."

In this edition, I have left out the interviews with Broadbent who died in 1993 but the interview with Philip Zimbardo who was a student at Yale not long after Clark Hull died evokes the sheer confidence of those times.

In the UK, the most articulate critic of psychology was Liam Hudson who became famous very early in his career thanks to his studies of creative thinking in secondary schools. In *The Cult of the Fact* (1972), something like an intellectual autobiography, Hudson produced a damning summary (p. 111):

> "The discipline's health is suspect . . . it has failed to produce a coherent body of scientific law; and its fruits unmistakably have about them an air of triviality. Attempts to justify psychological research in terms of its social utility at present lead inexorably to bathos. There is little we have produced in the last fifty years that is, in any sense of that complex word, 'relevant.'"

Hudson ended his indictment with irony: "One might as well try to justify space exploration in terms of its technological spin-off, the non-stick flying pan" (ibid).

There are, crudely, two versions of the pessimist position. The 'hard' position suggests that psychology has succeeded in finding out almost nothing, which implies that we should see a total change in the kind of psychology that is done. The 'soft' position is that certain sorts of psychological problems and approaches have been seriously under-represented. If we are to achieve a more relevant, a more nearly complete psychology, there must be work using these less experimental, less behaviourist means.

Hudson wanted to see more work on normal people in normal environments, for example. (As with Broadbent I have not included his interview in this version simply for reasons of space.) Chomsky who is a linguist and still at the rigorous Massachusetts Institute of Technology, not the Polytechnic for Woolly Thinking, argued behaviourism had simply ignored too much about human beings. Chomsky did much to persuade psychologists that they had to start thinking about language and consciousness.

Critics like Chomsky and Hudson were appalled by the way in which behaviourism had conquered Anglo-American psychology when they were writing in the 1970s. Their special *bête noire* was Burrhus Skinner. Hudson sniped that Skinner had the mantle of a "demi god". In his interview, Chomsky provides some very interesting arguments for the success of Skinner's ideas.

The situation Kuhn described has become worse, if anything. Experimental psychologists now worry that the popularity of radical, humanist psychology will threaten sensible methods of studying human beings. Humanistic psychology was often linked to psychotherapy and various forms of analysis. Hans Eysenck regretted the fact that though the evidence showed that psychoanalysis was bunk and junk, people believed in it.

In a famous paper in 1952, Eysenck claimed to show that persons who underwent psychoanalytic treatment had less chance of recovering than if they did nothing at all. More people recovered spontaneously than were cured by psychoanalysis. Eysenck repeated, often, that Freud truly deserved the Goethe Prize for Literature, which he won in 1925. Freud was a great novelist but not a scientist. But most people didn't listen to the facts.

Donald Broadbent was no kinder to Freud. After writing that objective methods are 'generally accepted', he asks 'accepted by whom?' His answer is telling (1961, p. 35):

> "The answer to this question is, primarily, otiose people in the English-speaking countries who engage in pure academic research in psychology."

Broadbent's answer excluded many people the public sees as authorities on human nature. Among these were many psychiatrists without degrees in psychology. Broadbent admitted psychiatrists faced urgent clinical problems so they had to use any means available, including all too often "intuitive interpretations of their patients' difficulties". But that meant they were just guessing. Nothing Freud said had ever really been confirmed experimentally so it was hardly surprising his ideas "have been viewed with considerable scepticism by psychologists in the ivory towers of the universities".

I liked Broadbent very much but I couldn't miss his oh-so-polite put-downs of the unfortunate non-Anglo-Saxon who lacks a degree in academic psychology and perhaps has not been 'university-trained'. If he or she gets it wrong, it really isn't surprising given their sad lack of proper training.

Both Eysenck and Broadbent also distrusted experts who had a Messianic view of psychology. Psychology did not tell you how to live your life. They condemned not just Freud and Jung, but stars of humanistic psychology like Abraham Maslow, Viktor Frankl and Carl Rogers. Frankl tried hard in the interview in this book to seem humble but, frankly, it is not in his nature. These men had great faith in their own intuitions. Intuition is much less hard work than experimentation, Broadbent pointed out. It is, alas, usually wrong and if you do not conduct experiments to check your intuitions, you can never tell. You lock yourself into perpetual ignorance. You grant yourself the delusion of special knowledge. You never can know unless you bother to find out.

These battles were reflected in the 1960s, 1970s and 1980s in many books that explored what psychology ought to be more than what it was. I would include classics like Skinner's *Beyond Freedom and Dignity* (1972), as well as now largely forgotten books such as Isidor Chein's *The Science of Behaviour and the Image of Man* (1972). Other books on this theme were Hudson's *The Cult of the Fact* (1972) and *Human Beings* (1975), Taylor's *The Explanation of Behaviour* (1964) and Shotter's *Images of Man* (1975). Chomsky's *Language and Mind* (1968) contained a notable attack on behaviourism. Eysenck, in a contribution to a very useful set of confrontations, *Explanation in the Behavioural Sciences* (1970a), also treated the subject of what psychology ought to do and how it should set about it.

In 1977, I hoped that talking to 13 of the most influential psychologists in the world would explain the differences, and the assumptions behind those differences, in their approaches and beliefs. In 1993, for the second edition, I argued that the most important changes in psychology since had been the rise of cognitive psychology and more interesting work on artificial intelligence. I also included some major women psychologists like Sandra Bem and Patricia Churchland.

In the last ten years, we have seen more changes; the study of cognition and consciousness has become a major strand in psychology. But if psychology once felt inferior to physics, it now sees itself as infinitely less precise than molecular biology, which promises so much. Psychology has never had a breakthrough like the discovery of the double helix nature of DNA. It is there – and still in physics – that we find big ideas. And yet there is an obvious truth. Human beings are even more complex than stars or molecules.

The interviews in this new edition make it clear that one response from psychology has been to concentrate on smaller problems. As a result, today the discipline has become fragmented. Where once thinkers looked at what makes people tick and struggled to develop grand theories, we now have many studies of 'smaller', more answerable questions. Most science, of course, is not big science. Most biologists study molecule P or neurotransmitter Q, but they do so in the context of a discipline that is asking large questions about the nature and origins of life. Psychology seems to have retreated from such big questions. Even when it comes to the nature of consciousness, there is a tendency to say, "well, it's a bit of a myth". All that represents a change in the ambitions of psychology and psychologists.

The motives of psychologists

Another of my original aims was to try and see if there was any link between the theories advocated by a particular psychologist and his own personality and motivations. This proved only partially possible in 1977. Few of the psychologists were very forthcoming in discussing their own motivations. I did not think this was so much due to reticence as to the fact that it seemed an odd question for them. But the personality of psychologists is a very important area to investigate; for the relationship between a psychologist and his subject is curious, for the 'subject', to be candid, ought usually to be referred to as the object of the experiment. The so-called 'subjects' are persons. So is the psychologist a person. The nature of the experiment and of the hypothesis a psychologist offers usually implies a great deal about his image of human beings. A psychologist's personality must be reflected in some way in his or her theories about how human beings function.

It is interesting how little the personality of psychologists has been studied. A cynic might be forgiven for thinking they prefer to avoid the subject. Only two serious investigations seem to have been carried out – and both of these were as part of larger projects. Anne Roe (1953) published a series of monographs on the personalities of eminent scientists and, in the course of these, she discussed the personality of psychologists. At Harvard, a certain amount of research has been done into the personality of psychologists under the heading of work into the power motive. Apart from a few scattered papers, including some ideas on the subject by Hudson (1972), this appears to be the sum total of research into the issue.

In her studies on eminent scientists, Roe found some telling differences between biologists, physicists and psychologists. Biologists and physicists tended to be rather isolated during their childhood. Many theoretical physicists suffered from some serious disease so that they were left in bed, and to their own devices, for long periods. About a quarter of the biologists had lost either their mother or their father before they were ten. So as they grew up, biologists and physicists both tended to lay less stress on personal relations. Though many still respected their parents, few stayed or felt very close to them. One biologist told Roe, "My ties aren't that close."

Psychologists, on the other hand, tended to react to the difficulties of child-hood quite differently. They did not lose themselves in some intellectual pursuit, which allowed them to withdraw from personal relationships. It was also telling how late most psychologists came to psychology and how often the personal influence of some teacher seems to have been vital in deciding them to become psychologists.

Though many of the men Roe interviewed were in their forties and fifties, they still spoke with quite marked hostility of their parents. Many had been afraid of their fathers. One told Roe, "I was always in conflict with my mother"; another said, "I think family discipline was very strict", while a third admitted that he hated his "father overtly". Twenty years on they were still reacting with guilt and violence about their childhood and youth. In my biography of Carl Rogers, I traced much hostility to his father (Cohen, 1997). Many also admitted to Roe that they were conscious of being superior to others from their youth onwards. Roe suggested that while psychologists value human relationships very highly, they may not be very good at them.

At Harvard, Professor David McClelland (who did most of the original work on the achievement motive), believed that psychologists had a high need for power. In a paper on 'The two faces of power' (1973a), he argued that the essence of the need for power is to want to have a strong impact on others. This need could express itself in two ways. Students who had a high need for power tended to hold more offices in student bodies, and tended to drink more heavily. It was not the same students who did both. He summed it up:

"Men whose power thoughts centered on having impact for the sake of others tended to hold office, whereas those whose thoughts centered on personal dominance tended to drink heavily, or to 'act out' in college by attempting more sexual conquests or driving powerful cars" (1973a, p. 305).

McClelland argued that psychologists had a very high need for power. In the paper, he explained how when he had been involved in a project to develop achievement motivation among Indian businessmen, observers began to wonder if they were "psychological Machiavellians" who interfered with other people's lives by foisting achievement motivation on people who managed perfectly well without it. Imperialism of the mind is the ultimate imperialism. As the American psychologists tried to make the businessmen feel strong, competent and effective, they behaved throughout as "effective socialized leaders". McClelland noted a paradox that the effect of being exposed to leadership, even to charisma, is not to make an individual feel submissive to the Great Leader but to inspire him to be a leader himself. The psychologists succeeded in making the Indian businessmen leaders. They were doing a mental make-over. If people have a high need for power, they find that very satisfying.

McClelland thought he had a need for power himself and that this was one of the things that drew him to psychology. In the interviews that follow, psychologists do often reveal themselves to be combative and to seek both to influence and, occasionally, to control people.

One of the interesting points to emerge from the work on the power motive is the extent to which this makes psychologists seek arguments. They tend to become emotional and highly involved with their disagreements. They may, even, go further than this and parody the position of their opponents just to have the pleasure of demolishing it.

Eysenck was a prime example of the combative psychologist. He took delight in constantly attacking Freud and psychoanalysis. He was not the only one. Skinner rounded on the 'mentalists' as if mentalism were a kind of disease. He was not clear whether those who suffer from it were more to be condemned or pitied because of their pathetic need for self, and self-importance, that made them believe they ran their lives. Rather, their environments must have made them the vainglorious beings they were. Skinner once held a famous debate in

1957 with the humanist therapist Carl Rogers in which each man tried to blast the other man's ideas to oblivion.

The philosopher Charles Taylor accepted all this confusion 30 years ago, noting (Burger and Cioffi, 1970, p. 54):

> "One can describe the state of disarray and contention in which we find the sciences of man as arising from deep disagreements over the conceptual frameworks which are appropriate. Each of the above fields is the scene of several rival approaches, no one of which seems to be able to establish itself to the satisfaction of all workers in the field as the definitive framework."

Back in 1977, I argued that there was a tendency among psychologists to seek to polarize the subject. If you adopt one view – let us say a behaviorist one – it follows that you argue not that your approach is a valid approach to psychology, but that it is the only approach to psychology. However well-intentioned or clever what their ideological opponents are doing might be, it is clearly not psychology.

In a paper in which he criticised a romantic approach to the study of personality, Holt (1962) wrote: "In science, when we say we understand something, we mean that we can predict and control it". This is, of course, the precise aim of psychologists like Skinner. Holt contrasted this scientific sense of understanding with the romantic sense in which to understand is to identify, to feel absorbed by, to enjoy or suffer, empathise with a particular personality. Even today many psychologists feel that if psychology is to be defined as the study of human behaviour, it will confine itself merely to predicting and controlling how people behave in very artificial situations. On the other hand, definitions of psychology which involve less prediction and more understanding are usually, if not always, unacceptable to those who argue like Skinner and Holt.

Two studies by Mahoney (1976) have examined how psychologists reason. One experiment tested the reasoning skills of 15 psychologists, 15 scientists and 15 conservative Protestant ministers. There were few differences between the ministers and the psychologists which perhaps suggests how scientific psychologists are. In a second study, Mahoney asked 75 behavioural psychologists to review manuscripts on a controversial subject in psychology. The introduction and experimental procedures were identical in each manuscript but referees were given different results and discussion sections. In one group, results were 'positive' in that they supported the referees' known point of view. In another group, the results went against the referees' viewpoints. Additional groups were handed ambiguous results followed by discussions that either supported or went against their own previously taken positions. Mahoney expected these rational psychologists to evaluate the manuscripts purely in terms of logic and evidence.

Ambiguous manuscripts should get less support. Mahoney concluded: our scientific reviewers tended to recommend the article only when it reported evidence that supported their positions. When the data contradicted their position opinions, they criticised the article's method and interpretation, and they urged it be not published. Psychologists are less objective than they like to think.

Too little philosophy of psychology

Psychologists might have become more self-critical if contemporary philosophy of science had touched on their problems more. In 1970, Charles Taylor set out to attack in detail the behaviourist approach (ibid., pp. 61–2):

> "The behaviorist view of science is a kind of closed circle, a self-induced illusion of necessity. For there is no self-evidence to the proposition that the mental is the unobservable. In a perfectly valid sense, I can be said to observe another man's anger, sadness, his eagerness to please, his sense of his own dignity, uncertainty, love for a girl or whatever. I can find out these things about another sometimes by just observing him in the common sense of that term, sometimes by listening to what he says. But, in this latter case, I am not learning of some dubious and unspeakable 'introspection' on his part. For what people say about themselves is never in principle and rarely in practice unspeakable."

Taylor made his case against one particular, and extreme, form of behaviourism. First, he claimed that the mental is the unobservable. When many psychologists claim this, they place quite a narrow restriction on the 'mental'. They claim that mental states cannot be directly observed. For example, the only way I can know that you intend to do X is if you say so. You may be lying; you may be deceiving yourself. Many behaviourists like Broadbent were quite willing to listen to a person who says this, but they would not be willing to count it as the only evidence about the fact. For example, if a person who says he intends to go to New York is observed to be making arrangements such as packing, buying a plane ticket and so forth, it may be concluded that what he said was his intention is, indeed, his intention: on the other hand, if he says that he intends going to New York and is not, for years afterwards, observed to be making the slightest attempt to budge out of Streatham, we may decide that it was never really his intention in the first place.

Skinner told me he did not doubt that people have feelings, and actually admitted to having feelings himself. What he denied was that these feelings matter and cause behaviour. Taylor simply avoided the issues by depicting behaviourists as people who do not think you can observe a man being sad, a man being angry and so on. I argue instead that it is the meaning you put on these observations which matters and it was because the behaviourists placed little meaning on them, in the end, that they did not bother to carry the observations out.

One other factor has changed psychology – the rise and rise of psychological tests. They started becoming popular after the Second World War. Most used were IQ tests, and by the 1950s there were thousands of such tests. Many relied on subjects assessing what they thought, hoped and felt. Eysenck's own work on neuroticism and extraversion-introversion revealed a good deal about a person's tendency to be sad and his tendency to be uncertain. Eysenck relied on people filling in questionnaires about their feelings honestly and accurately. This is a kind of structured introspection. Some tests now include some open-ended questions where subjects are asked to add in their own words what they feel or think. Again, a kind of structured introspection.

Ironically while psychology has become less ambitious intellectually, it has become more ambitious in the public arena.

I'm a psychologist . . . give me a headline

The media adore psychology and psychologists have come to adore the media. Back in 1977, I wondered whether the sheer love of, and need for, argument didn't often lead psychologists to attribute positions that are far too extreme – not to say untenable – to their opponents. Some psychologists like Skinner prided themselves on writing for the press and, when they did so, they simplified. So Skinner stands for this and Laing for that, all their complexities gone. So power-mad psychologists often cling to their own theories with great conviction and blind themselves to the other's point of view.

But now we have media psychology everywhere giving most psychologists the chance to air their views and rain their expertise on the public. I do this myself quite often and I'd be lying if I didn't admit it gives me a certain pleasure. (I pund – this being the verb of 'pundit' – therefore I am.)

In 1977, Hudson argued that one might often think different psychologists were working in quite different disciplines. They did not share the same assumptions, the same language, the same idea of "what counts as a decent piece of research". Lacking such communal criteria, are they doing the same kind of thing? Doing my 13 interviews then made me share Hudson's view – no one school is willing to allow the other a right to exist as psychologists. That has changed but largely because of the growing fragmentation of the discipline. A psychologist who specialises in artificial intelligence seems to care rather less than before about what other psychologists are up to.

It's also important to realise that the way people become psychologists has changed out of recognition. Most of the men I interviewed in 1977 had not set out to be psychologists. They had graduated either before the Second World War or just after. Few universities offered degrees in psychology. Many of them took first and even second degrees in other fields, many had wanted to be something else. Skinner wanted to be a writer; Festinger wanted to be a chess player; Eysenck wanted to be a physicist; Hudson would have liked to be a philosopher. Others started out, and have remained, experts in other fields but find themselves embattled in psychology. Chomsky was, and is, a linguist; many psychologists wish he had remained that. Jouvet was, and is, a doctor and neurophysiologist; Laing was, and is, a doctor and psychiatrist; Leupold-Löwenthal was, and is, a doctor. Professor Tajfel, for example, did not actually get a degree in psychology till he was thirty-five. Some of that has changed.

The new interviews in this book reflect the fact that psychology has been popular in the interviews. Flavell and Damasio have both been interested in psychology since the start of their careers. That is also true of Daniel Kahneman. Of the new interviewees the only one who partly fits the earlier profile is Deborah Tannen. She made her name studying the different ways men and women speak. Like Chomsky she is part-linguist, part-psychologist. All this specialisation has made psychology more professional but, perhaps, in turn, less adventurous and less grand in its ambitions. I still think it's a lot of fun and I enjoyed talking to all the men and women in this book and thank them for their time. In the 1970 interviews, it was still common to use 'man' for men and women, I did not want to change what I said then and massage the text. In the later interviews I don't use the word.

Chapter 1: Sandra Bem

In the 1970s, Sandra Bem was a heroine of mine. It's sometimes hard to recapture the passion of the early 1970s when many radical, and angry, women were discovering feminism. Psychology was fairly slow to respond. Gender studies focused on the differences between boys and girls, men and women. Sandra Bem arrived with a fresh – and evangelical – perspective. She devised a theory of psychological androgyny.

In 'The measurement of psychological androgyny' (1974), Bem argued that women who were good at typically male tasks, like mending a car, were psychologically healthier than women who were stuck in gender stereotypes. Equally, men who could perform female tasks, like looking after babies, were also healthier mentally. Given these findings, Bem was being modest in her demands. Men did not have to change out of all recognition and abandon masculinity. Rather, they had to incorporate some aspects of the feminine into their personality. Combine the best of both sexes, Bem asked. The perfect, rounded person would hustle like a man and feel like a woman.

Bem comes from a working-class background. She was born in Pittsburgh and went to Carnegie Mellon University. She felt from very early on that she wanted to be a psychologist. But that meant her being some sort of counsellor or therapist. She did not dream of going into research.

When Bem met her future husband, Darryl Bem, everyone assumed her career would take second place. That depressed her and she almost wanted to call the marriage off. She had a fine academic record. She and her future husband did a deal. No one's job would take priority. It would be an equal marriage with equal opportunities for both.

Bem is a tiny woman who drives even though, she grins, she is almost blind. It's a handicap she uses nicely in her lectures when she discusses what she calls "biology in context". If she had been a Stone Age woman, she would have been killed off in her teens because her bad eyesight left her so vulnerable. In the brave new world of high-powered lenses, however, she can function as well as someone with 20/20 vision.

When I first met her, Bem was teaching at Cornell University in Ithaca in northern New York State. She gives an impression of thinking faster than she talks. Her sentences sometimes trip over themselves as she frames a new idea and, given the hostile reception that psychological androgyny had, she knows she needs to be very careful about how she sets out her ideas.

Bem was very courteous and came to meet me at the airport. She took me to lunch at an organic health bar. She obviously wanted some time to get a sense of what I was about. In the interview, Bem reveals a fascinating mix of how, in her career, the personal has been intertwined with the political. Psychology for her involves something that could be described as a personal crusade. She admits, as I have never heard a male scientist admit, that she wanted to arrive at empirical findings that would back up a personal vision – a vision in which the biological differences between the sexes dissolve as much as possible. Yet her positive, liberal theory soon got a hostile press from many feminists; they saw Bem's approach as a kind of betrayal. She found that both baffling and hurtful. It just didn't do to have a good word to say about men.

Bem's theory didn't just ignore the issues of violence and oppression (which Bem admits she did perhaps ignore a bit) but it suggested that progress in the battle of the sexes was through compromise and learning from each other. Psychological androgyny is not confrontational. Its aim is to use insight to let people grow, and often, grow with each other.

Bem's career has been orthodox. She has worked at elite American universities – Carnegie Mellon, Stanford and Cornell. She and her husband stuck to the bargain they made in their youth, so many universities have had to employ them as a couple. Bem says that while she has always seen herself as a feminist, she has always regarded her husband as her best friend – the person she could talk to about anything.

Bem spent some time as head of the department of women's studies at Cornell and enjoyed it. Unlike most well known American academics, she had not published a book when I first met her. In 1985, she got the idea for what turned out to be her first book, *The Lenses of Gender* (1993). She was very excited about it. The book argues a complex set of ideas about the role of biology. Some essentials will never change – women will be the ones who get pregnant – but Bem asks does it have to matter as much as we think it did in a society where technology and culture makes so much change possible? Bem still thinks it would be wonderful to dissolve sexual differences but, now, she argues, men and women are conditioned to view the world through the lenses of gender. She would like to remove those lenses.

Bem bubbled with enthusiasm for her new theory and stressed how useful her students found it. Useful both as an academic tool and also in their personal lives. For her, unlike most male psychologists, one reason for doing psychology is to understand – and change – the way we live.

When we had finished our lunch, she drove me to her house and we talked in the kitchen, a very appropriate setting in which to discuss sexism and biology in context.

• *Tell me a bit about the background that led you to do psychology. Why did you end up as an undergraduate interested in it?*

I come from a family that I don't think knew how to raise children very well. I think I was actually a psychologist in the sense of interested in human relationships, human thoughts, the determinants of behaviour, why people acted the way they did, I think for ever. I was born a psychologist at that level. There's a way in which I've always been the parent in my birth family and I think I thought when I was young that I would be sort of a child guidance clinical psychologist, and help people that didn't know how to deal with their children, and I would fix everything.

• *That sounds young and arrogant?*

Right, I think that's absolutely right. I think I was very young and arrogant, arrogant in the sense that young people think they know everything. I think it was that. I think I was just always a psychologist in the sense that I think I could see, or thought I could see, what people did wrong and why it screwed up their children.

• *When did you decide to be a formal psychologist as opposed to a birthright psychologist?*

I chose to major in psychology and liked it and when I was a senior in college, I took this course/seminar in research topics, which was something – we did a different thing every week.

For me, becoming a formal psychologist is very linked to making the decision about who I was going to marry. They're not that tied in everybody's life, but for me my husband, Darryl Bem, who's also a psychologist was a professor at the school at Carnegie Mellon where I was as an undergraduate. We met in my senior year. He made the field of psychology as a career, a discipline and a science, real to me, meaningful to me and so somehow that path just became my path.

• *When you went to graduate school what were you interested in?*

At first – it's not very well-defined when I think back, it's sort of funny – at first, I was still carrying over the clinical interest and there was an experimental psychologist at Michigan named David Birch who ended up being my adviser and was interested in this Russian stuff of Vygotsky and Luria. It was labelled verbal self-control and it was a question of what controls voluntary behaviour? But for me this, in some way, strange way, that I cannot reconstruct, connected to interest in things like: how do people get themselves to stop smoking? How do people get themselves to become more disciplined about things they're not being disciplined about? My interests were still vaguely clinical but I made some connection between these things and so started to work with him. David Birch gave me the sense that I had really good ideas. And so I think all I really got out of my graduate education was that I was creative and I could come up with experiments to address interesting things. They were my ideas, they were my experiments, I wasn't in an apprentice relationship to him, almost from the beginning. So, my career as a psychologist didn't pick up in any way on any of the things I studied or was trained in in graduate school.

You're not asking me this question yet, but to make any sense of a connection I have to go a slightly different route which is that – and it really has to come back to – sounds very gendered, but who I married and what else was going on then. I mean this was 1965. I married my husband, again as I said, a psychologist, in June of 1965. This was pre the Women's Movement, OK? What I became as a psychologist really arose out of that because the first time we went out, Darryl asked me: 'How do you – you're obviously a serious bright young woman – how are you going to co-ordinate career and family?' And I hadn't thought about that and I gave a good-girl answer. I said: 'I don't know, my husband's career will come first and I'll figure it out.' And we decided to get married just six weeks later and so a few days later I got very upset and I said to Darryl: 'It's off. I'm not getting married.' I said, I think about this for the first time, 'this means I have to – I mean you're already a professor, that would mean if you get a job, I would have to go with you. I'm not doing that.' So that got us both upset and so we started to think about what kind of decisions could we make and how could we make them and designed the skeleton of what was an egalitarian marriage. And so we did all that and then people would find out about it and think it was really weird and so we'd start talking about it. Out of this grew an interest in gender and a realization that: 'Here I am, this bright student, maybe the best psychology student Carnegie Mellon's had, they're all excited I'm getting into Harvard, I'm getting into Michigan and I say I'm getting married and they say: 'Oh you're going to go to the university of Pittsburgh then?' Well that's OK. And I say: 'Wait. Why do you think that? I wasn't doing that yesterday. Why are you making this assumption about me?' And so becoming a psychologist, becoming a wife, becoming a feminist, getting interested in issues of gender and seeing that the culture had an ideology that was going to have an impact, that was going to differentiate men's and women's lives came together. People started to make different assumptions about me just because I was married. That's sort of the adult-beginning base of where my psychology and my gender psychology came from. So it's not just a traditional path.

• *Did you do anything with that – obviously you did a lot with it in terms of your life, but did that quickly seep into your ideas or did it just kind of lie there?*
My ideas, but not my graduate training. It doesn't show up at all in graduate school in what I do as a psychologist. I have no courses in gender, I have no research in gender, nothing. But there on I start while in graduate school, giving speeches. There's a speech that becomes a part of a chapter in a little paperback called: *Police Attitudes in Human Affairs*, in 1970 I think it came out, but this is a speech that we started giving in about 1966 and we called it: 'Training the woman to know her place; the power of a non-conscious ideology'. Now we get all the way to 1993 and I see the new book as really about cultural ideology as related to gender. So there's a gigantic continuity here but when I'm graduating, what I'm saying is: Yes, it becomes ideas, it becomes intellectual, it becomes both intellectual, political and personal but not intellectual in the sense of yet being played out in what I'm doing, in what's formally called, my psychology.

• *So you went to Michigan and you worked around David Birch and then what did you do after that?*
I'll just be very specific, it's the only way I can do the links – Darryl had been a faculty member at Carnegie Mellon, when I got into Michigan, he took a leave of absence from his job at Carnegie Mellon and came to live with me at Michigan. As I was about to get my degree, my adviser sent letters around, you know: 'Here's this good student coming out, not in gender research but in developmental psychology. And by the way she has a husband.' There were no responses at all. I don't think people had any idea how to deal with couples, but Carnegie Mellon offered us both jobs, so we stayed there and I became assistant professor at Carnegie Mellon and Darryl stayed on.

And these first years of my being an assistant professor were sort of a transition for me. We'd go, give a talk and long-question-and-answer sessions and we did this for many, many years, probably until our first child was born in 1974. And I'm starting to teach and not doing research. I'm someone who does not like empirical work for its own sake. If I don't really have a good reason to want to know the answer, I just lose interest. I was young, I didn't know what alternative exactly I was envisioning, but I know I didn't know what to ask. You know, some people have index cards with the twenty-seven things they'd like to do and I've just never been like that. I didn't know what to do, so I had a professional identity crisis almost instantly. And I thought there was another local college in Pittsburgh, a women's college called Chatham where you just taught. You didn't do research. And I remember thinking for a while: 'Shall I do that?'

And then some day, I don't remember it as a sudden epiphany and I don't have a moment that I can point to but I know somewhere in there I got the idea that maybe there was a way to marry my political, personal and intellectual interests in what I'll just broadly call feminism and psychology. I think part of the form this took at the time was saying: here we are going around giving this talk called 'Training a woman to know her place', in which we're saying things like: 'As a pro-women's movement, as a pro-feminist kind of argument, the culture has taken these whole lovely, diverse, individually different human beings who come to us at birth and pushed them into these two separate channels and ends up with just two kinds of people rather than the multitudes'. And this is wrong, I'm saying. And the assumption is that people who don't fit the gender categories have something wrong with them. Maybe there's something constraining, imprisoning, problematic with people who fit the stereotypes. And I'm pushing this line and, at some point, I remember saying to myself and other people: 'Here I am shooting my mouth off with really not much data to back me up, would there be some way to do research in the service of these political, social-change and cultural-critique arguments?' I want to say, there's something wrong with the culture and psychology is a part of this somehow for segregating us, channelling us in these two moves. And so at some point at the very late 1960s, I thought: 'I'll try to do this.'

- *Well, did you meet a lot of opposition?*
Not right at the beginning. I don't know at what level to try to answer that question because that was a time of transition in a lot of ways. Just to continue the chronology for a minute, this was the late 1960s, the early 1970s. In 1970 we also moved, we moved to Stanford. Stanford was an interesting context for me in that I was thinking less about – I saw the environment as less saying: 'It's wrong to care about the outcome' than, 'it's really important to hit the ball out of the field. You want a home run.' So I think that what I heard my environment saying was: 'You might as well take a risk'. So the emphasis once I moved to Stanford was on the notion that you had to go for the gold, and that fits well with this idea of: 'I think this is important.' I mean, it's important to feminism and it's important politically. This idea doesn't exist in psychology. Androgyny is not a word in psychology. If I could put this word, this concept of a less gender-stereotyped way of thinking about the person, if I could get this idea introduced both into psychology and into the culture (I was clearly interested in both

things), this would be going for the gold, both in terms of my feminism – in terms of the women's movement – and in terms of what seemed to me like my profession.

• *And what began to give you the idea? Did you read Jung? Did you?*
No. Myself. No, it's all some merger of politics and intuition and – I don't really know how to put it. I never said that quite in that way before. What gave me the idea? I'm not sure that this is exactly the answer, but the first path I took obviously was to try to, the empirical way that I tried to deal with the idea was to say: 'Can I find evidence that people who are conventionally gender-stereotyped are in some way less good, have less good outcomes than people who are androgynous?' And then the question: 'What's androgynous? And how are we going to be able to measure it?' And one of the first ideas I had for measuring androgyny was like this . . . I was thinking what do I want to ask you to decide if *you're* androgynous? And the first question I thought of was something like: 'Well, describe yourself the way you are. Now how do you think you would be or would want to be, or could be or something, if you were the other sex?' So, in other words, how much does what sex you are feel like it's a central part of who you are or need to be? And the reason I'm saying that, when you say where did I get this idea – I think I was just very aware that I didn't feel my sex was that important, that just somehow I could have been a boy. I didn't think it would make me that different a person.

• *So you played with your adjectives and with your questions and what happened then?*
Well, there's a period of time, and we're talking from about 1970 to 1975–6, where that's a very empirical phase for me. Designing the inventory – there's a series of studies that are designed to try to ask the question: 'Is there some sense in which androgynous people are better off, healthier?' And this starts to become a language of mental health – healthier, better equipped to deal with more kinds of situations than gender-stereotyped people, and so there are studies that identify people as gender-stereotyped or androgynous and put them into different situations and look to see whether (this research by the way is very foreign to me now, it feels like an eternity ago), that asked the question: 'Is there any sense in which androgynous people are better off?' And we find that whereas masculine men and feminine women are more limited to the behaviour that the culture says is appropriate for their sex, androgynous people are better able to, or more willing, to produce both kinds of behaviour. So androgynous people are both independent and nurturing depending on the nature of the situation they're in.

Another study asks: 'Is it the case that the gender-stereotyped people are made uncomfortable by the possibility of having to do the gender-inappropriate thing?' And finding: 'Yes, they are.' So I always describe that as the behavioural correlates of androgyny. Then, a second phase that just goes further into this question about what's restricting the gender-stereotyped people. Why aren't they engaging in all this behaviour? And then comes research more focused on the gender-stereotyped people than on the androgynous people and saying: 'Is it the case that the gender stereotype when they look out at reality or they look at themselves, it's as if they see the world with the masculine and feminine filter over their eyes'. That instead of seeing – I mean, I see the world as this kaleido-scope that can be categorized and coded just in a multitude of ways. There's not some objective set of categories out there, I can say to my class: 'You know, I'm sitting in this – giving this lecture in this lecture hall. How are we going to describe this lecture hall? If you haven't had lunch yet you're going to be strik-ingly aware there's no food here, but that isn't normally how somebody describes the room.' It's true, all these things are reasonable interpretations. Somehow the gender-stereotyped people have put on these gender schemas, I called them then. Now I call it lenses and androgynous people. They have the information. They're able if you said to them: 'Is this a masculine way to behave or feminine way to behave?' They can tell you. It's not that they're dumb or ignorant or haven't been socialized by the culture to have this gender knowledge, but it isn't something they spontaneously or as readily use.

So there start to be a set of studies on what I call the cognitive antecedents or correlates or causes of sex typing and androgyny. Then, we start to find evidence that the gender-stereotyped people have a gender schema that is more accessible, that they're using it more and that that is presumably even part of why they describe themselves as gender stereotypes in the first place on the *Bem Sex Role Inventory*. Here's this set of 60 items, they're all mixed up, they don't have little 'ms' and 'fs' next to them but when they look at that list they fall into those cat-egories for them in some way. Not necessarily consciously. That's just not how they're coding things.

• *What you're describing is, in a sense, more a sophisticated description rather than an explanation. Did you ever get below that to what differentiated them? What in terms of background, personality, upbringing, differentiated your gender-stereotyped people from your androgynous people?*
No. And here's where it starts to be clear that I was never interested in the diff-erences really between these people. I think my interest was always cultural cri-tique. What I want to be saying is: 'Look, America, you're really pushing this gender category stuff over and over and it's not necessary. Don't you see there are

gender categories here? How can I show you that there are gender categories here? Let me show you some people who don't seem to use them as much.' That makes the possibility of not using them rise to consciousness. 'How can we begin to show you some alternatives, America and psychology, to the unstated, non-conscious assumption that somehow it's just the given that everything's going to fall into these gender categories. Let's find some people who don't.'

The questions I started to ask were perfectly reasonable questions, but it was never: 'Did I go deeper and find out the differences between the people?' Where I went was to say: 'Why do people, not which people, but in general, why do people have these gender lenses?' Because the culture inculcates them. You see the culture does things like have pink for girls and blue for boys. Does it need to do that? The culture has dresses for girls – whether you're talking about very simple things like that, or deeper and more subtle things. My interest instantly stepped out into the culture and said: 'Let's look at what the culture does to raise its children to have these lenses'.

• *So presumably that choice of question was more related to your, initial if you like, political interest?*
I think so – both the political interest that emerged with feminism and then the deeper interest which is personal, intellectual and political. This notion that categories are constructed and that the culture constructs our categories, I mean that's not, I don't want to call it – I don't want to say it's not political because certainly there are thousands of political contexts in which you can take it, you can say we have these big categories now. You have to be heterosexual or homosexual. Are those really the only two categories? Are those natural categories? Or is that the way America, western culture, looks at it? There are societies in which those aren't the two sexual categories. What about male/female? There are cultures – we take all these kids who are born with what we called anomalous genitalia and we say there's something wrong with them, we have to force them and do surgical correction and put them into one of two categories.

• *One of the things that I remember, I must have read some of your papers in the 1970s, and what I thought was extremely interesting was the fact that, unlike most feminist writers, you didn't seem to have a particular down on men and it seemed to be part of your wish to improve, not just to redress, if you like, the situation of women, but to also redress the situation of men. Is that a fair comment?*
Yes, I think, absolutely. If anything, I think that I had a very naive understanding of the ways in which women, in particular, have a problem, or are oppressed, or have a special need for redress as opposed to that both sexes are being strait-

jacketed. Let me put it this way. In the kind of language I use now, there are a lot of different ways you can talk about what androgyny is. You can say: 'The culture and the person shouldn't pay any attention to gender at all', and ask 'Why should things like behaviours have gender or sex?' That we ought just not to think of these as human things, human possibilities and that's sort of a deep moral of androgyny, asking what is this artificial divide that says some things belong to male, masculine, some things belong to female, feminine. Again, notice it's all anti-category, it's always anti-category.

There's nothing in that that says that the society or history has done anything particularly bad to women so there'd be no blaming of men because men are – in the language of that day – just as unable to cry and feel dependent or express their vulnerabilities as women are unable to be athletic or leaders, etc. So it's totally symmetrical with respect to men and women. In the language of the book, the language in which I currently talk, this is about gender polarization, this is about imposing a male/female dichotomy onto things that don't have to have that male/female dichotomy imposed on them. But whether in the language of androgyny from 1970 or the language of gender polarization from 1993, it is still me saying the same thing. It's all symmetric with respect to men and women. Over the years since then, as feminism got more alive in the culture and started to impact – and again androgyny didn't come out of feminism for me – I increasingly came to realize that I'm not saying anything at all about the special problems that society imposes on women and those need to be addressed. I mean, yes, men can't cry but men have money and men have power and women don't. But that's a different concept and a different issue and in the book so now we're talking androgyny and gender polarization as I see it and I say: 'Here's humanity and it's been split into these two male and female parts, or masculine and feminine parts and it's not just people but traits and clothes, etc; anything you want to name, sexual desire, anything, ways of expressing emotion. But when you pull them apart in the context of androgyny or gender polarization, they're still more or less – they're still equal.'

But that is not what the world is like. The world does something else. It creates inequality. It raises the male one and lowers the female one. So men end up with money. Masculine behaviours end up good, until we end up with inequality and hierarchy. In the book, I talk about them in the context of androcentrism or male-centredness, the notion that whatever is male is going to be better. And that's sort of like a separate notion and I think our world has both. That means that you could as a feminist in principle at least imagine getting rid of androcentrism, that is still having masculinity and femininity completely pulled apart, but now let's start to value the female things too. So that you could, in principle, get rid of androcentricism but still be left with gender polarization. For me, I want to say: 'Yes, but that's not my utopia. My utopia gets rid of gender polarization, too.' Now how is that a response to your question?

• *The other thing I was going to ask you is, presumably the idea of addressing the oppression of women is something which came to you later?*
Well in a way that's right, I mean in a way it's where it began because it really was important to me that those professors of mine at Carnegie Mellon, they didn't say to my husband: 'Oh so you're going to give up your job and follow your wife.' They said to me: 'Oh you're going to give up your chance to go to Harvard or Michigan and go to the university down the block.' So even there, there was an asymmetry directed at women and I did think about the assumptions about wives and somehow that wasn't where my pull was. For me, having said that, it's still true that when I then started to theorize about it, and intuit about it or whatever I was doing, right it wasn't about the oppression of women in particular.

• *I remember reading some critique of your papers which suggested that most of the resulting androgyny could actually be accounted for in terms of high masculinity and I'm not sure that I've remembered right but does that ring a bell with you?*
Yes. I'm thinking about the correlations with self-esteem. That's what that brings up for me – that it was that masculine and androgynous people had higher self-esteem. This really does become the point where I know I'm not an empiricist. When I look at the self-esteem scales and what kinds of items are on them, and I look at the masculinity scales, there's a lot of sharing of items that don't look that different and so maybe I want to say, maybe there isn't even two things being measured, I don't know. I'm not sure what to conclude from that at the empirical level and, then, I'm right off into another place and I find myself saying: 'Yes, but masculinity's what the culture values, of course – things are going to work out better for masculine people because they have what the culture likes.' To the extent that androgynous people are in any way deviant from the culture at any particular historical moment in time, I'd never be necessarily predicting that they're happier, better, have more self-esteem. Because if the culture doesn't like them, I can't necessarily predict that they would be better.

• *What kind of response did you get from feminists in the 1970s who presumably were pleased but not totally pleased with the response?*
There's a big shift in the 1970s. In the context of psychology, androgyny – notoriously – was loved at first, just loved. Here was this feminist idea, a new idea, a

way of patching both theoretically and empirically a critique. In the early 1970s there starts to be a lot of critique both of the culture and psychology. Feminism enters psychology. You have a couple of landmark articles that stand out to me. You have this article by a whole bunch of names, the first two being the Brovermans, that show that they interviewed psychiatrists, clinical psychologists and social workers about their definition of mental *health* and they find that in all those groups those clinicians all consider you more mentally *healthy* if you match your sex and that sort of notion. Then, there's an article by Ann Constantinople that critiques previous sex-role or gender inventories. Anyway there's a lot of deconstructing of the gender stereotypes in psychology and in the culture, and androgynous stuff fits right into that. There's a concept and there's a test, and lots of interest came around it.

But then two things happened very quickly within psychology. For me, what I remember more, because it was more salient to me – and I can't believe I was as narrow as I was, but androgyny had become an idea of interest outside of psychology, in other fields, like in the humanities, before it did in psychology. And by the time I was introducing androgyny in psychology – losing favour outside of psychology. When you say what happened to it I sort of got trapped in that moment personally. So suddenly it got very big in psychology but, of course, I'm connected to feminist *scholarship* outside of psychology too, and was increasingly becoming so and I didn't understand at first at all, this sort of crosscurrent that I got caught in. Suddenly androgyny became this idea that feminists didn't like at all. I sort of reeled from that for a while. The name I most associate with this problem is Adrienne Rich, who's a poet. In the earlier 1970s, she's writing a poem – it's in the book. She's writing a poem in favour of androgyny and by 1976 or 1978 she's saying things like: 'There are words I can never speak again and androgyny and humanism are two of them.' Because now she's becoming much more focused on women and inequality. So the very fact that androgyny doesn't in any way focus on what's happening to women and treats men and women as if equivalent things are happening to them, as if the oppression of them is symmetric, creates hostility. Androgyny gets very caught up in this. It becomes a dirty word very fast among feminists.

And feminism moves into what I see it becoming by the 1980s which is – and I think of people like Carol Gilligan – feminism becomes very caught up in revaluing in women and femininity and what androcentrism has forever devalued, things like caring, connectedness and relationships. The emphasis is not any longer on minimizing the differences between men and women and, to use the language of polarization, depolarizing the sexes, but is instead on taking what has been considered female or feminine and revaluing it and engaging in a critique of masculinity, maleness and male institutions. So androgyny maybe had a longer honeymoon outside of psychology. Inside psychology it was very short, the honeymoon. Very quickly the feminist tide turned in the direction of wanting to celebrate female difference. And androgyny's just not consistent with that at all.

• *And what did that leave you feeling?*
Devastated. I didn't understand it at the time at all. I just felt caught in some sort of whirlpool. I just didn't understand. I remember when I first came here, in 1978, I think psychologists are relatively narrowly read by and large. I think they mostly read other psychologists and they read biology or at least some do and computer – cognitive science. They're not widely read in the humanities. And I wasn't. It's not suggested that you read in those 'softer fields'. So when I came to Cornell very shortly after – Cornell has a programme called the A.D. White Professor-At-Large Program, where they invite distinguished people to come in. They have a five-year term and they'll come for a few weeks every year and Adrienne Rich was one within a year or so after I was here – and I found myself in discussions where, whenever the word androgyny came up, it was clearly like a dirty word. And I just didn't understand it – I don't know whether I was younger, less secure, I don't know. It was just very confusing to me and it took me a while to figure out what these currents were.

• *No, my question's whether it's basically the reaction that you had that changed you.*
I had already in my own way shifted past androgyny before I knew any of this. I mean my ideas are always evolving. So by the time, probably even before the androgyny research found its way to a journal, I think I was already saying things like: 'Yeah, but that's not quite it. That's not quite what I meant to be saying.' I didn't mean to be asking, are you both nurturant and aggressive or assertive? That's not what I mean by androgyny. It's not being both, it's having, not even thinking of, the category. That's not how androgyny's gotten – it's not how I ended up operationalizing androgyny. The focus is wrong here and so I'll shift to gender schematicity as I called it then, which is the idea that for the gender-stereotyped person they hear a set of words and divide them into masculine and feminine things and androgynous people don't. Here is the notion that they're not using the same lens. That's somehow getting closer to it. By the time this public critique of androgyny, was emerging, which I didn't understand and I found devastating emotionally – because I was identified with androgyny in my own intellectual evolution – I was already past it anyway. I was already struggling for new and better ways to express what my basic ideas had been to start with anyway. Do you see what I'm saying?

• *So OK, you're moving past that point presumably also at a time settling in England where I suppose I think of the late 1970s as the hung point of that particular kind of feminist critique. I remember I was married to someone who was very feminist and there were endless things that were just for women. But presumably at this time here you had as well a very successful feminist movement.*
Earlier I think. And you see what's interesting is I'm not really part of that. I've never been in a women's group. I've always been in a best-friend relationship with my husband. He's a feminist too. I'm not saying that's an inappropriate aspect of feminism. It just was never part of my politics, my own particular personal politics.

• *Can you describe what you said in the book?.*
In 1985 I think there's a paper in the *Nebraska Symposium* called: 'Androgyny and gender schema theory: a conceptual and empirical (or empirical and conceptual) integration'. So I try to put those two things together and some new ideas, you know, sneak in there. There's a paper in *Science* around that same time but nothing too much happens. Then, there is a really interesting moment and it's just funny. I remember this vividly. I'm sitting in my office at Cornell and I'm – not being Director of Women's Studies any more so I'm reading without knowing exactly where I'm going to go and I'm reading this article by an anthropologist, Richard Schwader, called: 'Anthropology's romantic rebellion against enlightenment'. But anyway, I read this article and it's sort of about the cultural construction of, in my language, it's about the cultural construction of lenses. It's about how different cultures have different lenses, ideologies, worldviews and I'm reading this article and I call Darryl and I say: 'I've just read the best article in my life. I mean, I just love this article.' This is related to me and nothing I've ever read in psychology felt like it was related to me. Now what happens after that? There's a slow development of, a kind of repositioning of what my work's been about in a sort of different historical tradition, but it isn't very articulatable yet. Now I guess I'd call it something like social constructionism. So slowly there begins to emerge the sense that maybe there's an intellectual context into which my work fits that isn't just about gender. Anyway, I don't know that I can be much more specific than that. In 1987 we took a leave and spent a year at Harvard. I can't remember exactly what was swimming around in my mind but one of the things I wanted to do was answer the question that year: 'Is there a book in my head?'

I just went to Harvard Square and bought books by the hundreds and read them. About March I sat down with Darryl and said: 'See if I can just make an outline. What would my chapters look like?' And somehow there were those chapters. I saw myself as saying – in a way I said: 'I've been teaching and thinking about gender for twenty years'. I like to be able to hold things in my hand. I like big ideas, but I like 'em simple. That doesn't mean deep or dumb but simple. I wanted a way to see for myself really, if I could, just as a sort of intellectual challenge, sort of hold it all together. I had the feeling I could be saying something that was very distinctive, that would really express what is my view of gender. That's how the book evolved and I came up with an outline and started doing it.

• *Take me through these three basic lenses, what each of them is.*
OK. I want to read you the first para from the book because that'll help me. It says: 'Throughout the history of western culture three beliefs about women and men have prevailed. That they have fundamentally different psychological and sexual natures. So we have this idea of difference. That men are inherently the dominant or superior sex. So we have this notion of inequality. And that both male/female difference and male dominance are natural. Those are the traditional views. Until the mid-nineteenth century this naturalness was typically conceived in religious terms as part of God's grand creation. Since then it's typically been conceived in scientific terms as part of biology's or evolution's grand creation.'

I'm sort of taking those three traditional ideas: there is difference, there is inequality, and that's natural, and turning them on their heads and saying: 'No, there's nothing natural here.' What we have is a cultural assumption that is androcentric. A cultural assumption that says: 'Man is better.' Or not actually better but somehow the norm, the baseline, the prototypical exemplar of the human species and woman is just something other, something different. It doesn't matter as much, whatever she is, she's defined in relation to man. You asked me the question about the lenses, I'll start with that question.

So that's the first idea and it's not something natural. Quite the contrary, it's an organizing principle. That's another way that I think of as a lens, an organizing principle upon which our culture is built and, hence, ultimately upon which our psyches are built. We get our psyches from our culture. So the first lens is androcentrism. The second idea was difference. The second lens is gender polarization. The difference isn't natural either. What we do is we take humanity, and all things connected to humanity, and we impose a male/female dichotomy on it. Instead of seeing it as a multitudinous kaleidoscope, we see it as dichotomous categories. So that's gender polarization. And the way in which I get sexual – issues about sexuality in this is to say – and we do that to things like about the way sexual desire is experienced, too. And we say, this is imposed gender – we say men and women are different – men like women and women like men. But no, I'm saying, we impose a sexual dichotomy, a male/female dichotomy on sexual desire. And the third lens is biological essentialism, which is the notion that these things are natural.

• *And when you raise an argument with students or with colleagues, what kind of response do you get? Are you being met with the sort of hostility that androgyny very soon was met with?*
My students love it, OK? My students absolutely love it. My students share my excitement. I'm a very enthusiastic excitement-filled lecturer generally and, my God, now they have the feeling that they are participating in some phenomenal event here with me. I think the thing that my students most say, and again, they are emerging feminists, both men and women, or they wouldn't be in my class, they say that they find themselves always in a world where they don't know how to respond to people when people are saying conventional things in any way related to gender. They say that the book gives them tools for knowing how to respond. But it hasn't been out there. There's a way in which I can't answer the question: 'What's the reaction?'

• *Sure. Are you nervous about it?*
As I've been writing the book the people that I have been most nervous about are feminists. In a way because they're the audience I care about the most and in a way because again, throughout the 1980s, the dominant voice of feminism has been difference-centred, gender maximizers rather than minimizers. I've been nervous about them and that ebbs and flows. But I think that the culture, I think feminism and America are sort of at a turning point. I've had the feeling that the pendulum had gone perhaps very far in the direction of really emphasizing male/female differences and that maybe, hopefully, by the time my book would come out, I wouldn't be such an anomaly in the context of American feminism. And I think that's true. This might seem like an odd thing to point to, but I notice when I look down shelves in bookstores there's more books on bisexuality now. Well, there hasn't been anything on bisexuality for years. Lesbian/gay/bisexual studies is starting to be a big thing. I think a lot of the difference-centred feminism that really focused on female difference, the links between what's the underlying politics of feminism and how does that tie to gay liberation has gotten a little lost because it's not been about gender and those who deviate from gender norms and the constraints of the gender categories, but it's been about just the oppression of women. What does that say about gay men? I've seen myself at least as tied to gay men as I am to women, I'm not saying I don't feel tied to women, but my politics and theorizing is about both of those. I think that just, as partly out of the AIDS travesty and tragedy, lesbians and gay men have linked back together, I think a lot of the splits between

men and women's issues – I just think the pendulum's swinging a little bit the other direction. There's the rebirth of activism, feminism in America.

• *It's interesting because I think in England there's been a very British response, for instance, to the men's movement and yet people like Robert Bly's books sell a great deal.*
So, British psychology knows more about my book than American psychology because of my trip there, and because of Sheila Kitzinger – it's hard for me to think of another psychologist, with whom I feel as much kinship in terms of the critique of psychology and the connection of feminism and issues of sexual orientation. I feel that the underlying intellectual theory and politics of this book are more in line with her than with almost anybody else I know. And so that's part of why the interview was so good. I mean, she was able to use me. She knew what questions she wanted to ask me. That's very unlike any other interview with a psychologist. And so it was a good merger and so she's promoted the book, so there's more play there than here so far.

• *You talked earlier of how celebration of difference was not the kind of utopia you saw. I mean, do you have a vision of the kind of utopia that you see . . . ?*
Yes, but I don't know what it really is like. I have – I'll read you the last paragraph of the book. The last chapter, the two main headings are called, well, there's something on the conundrum of difference. It talks about how the focus on difference has been dead, ending in a lot of ways, and then it's called: 'Core gender neutrality, eradicating androcentrism' and then the last section is called: 'Toward utopia, eradicating gender polarisation' and the last two paragraphs read:
[At this point, Bem fetched her copy, spread it on the kitchen table and read. I reproduce her paragraph.]
'Ultimately gender depolarisation would require even more than the social revolution involved in rearranging social institutions and refraining cultural discourses. Gender depolarisation would also require a psychological revolution in our most profound sense of who, and what, we are as males and females, a profound alteration in our feelings about the meaning of our biological sex and its relation to our psyche and our sexuality. Simply put, this psychological revolution would have us begin to view the biological fact of being male or female in much the same way as we now view the biological fact of being human, rather than seeing our sex as so authentically who we are that it needs to be elaborated, or so tenuous that it needs to be bolstered, or so limiting that it needs to be traded in for another model. We would instead view our sex as so completely given by nature, so capable of exerting its influence automatically and so limited

in its sphere of influence to those domains where it really does matter biologically, like whether you have a baby, that it could safely be tucked away in the backs of our minds and left to its own devices. In other words, biological sex would no longer be at the core of individual identity and sexuality.'

Now that's my view of utopia. In other words break the links between – at the moment, I see culture and history as having forged just innumerable historically constructed links between sex and everything in the culture and just cut them, let them be gone. But I don't know what that really looks like. So you ask me: do I have a vision of utopia? I have a principle of utopia, not a vision of utopia exactly.

• *Presumably what that then, in a quite different way, is about is the celebration of individuals as being different?*
And people are always asking me: 'But the human mind requires categories. What would we put in its place?' That's why I don't have a vision. What would we think like? I don't know. But that's so far away that we're not building that yet. That's not a pragmatic vision of utopia. Of course the mind needs categories, I agree with that. And you see that's the sense in which I am all the way back at my beginning. That's what I thought when I began and I've been saying that the – and I can quibble with the metaphor, I know how to argue against it, but the metaphor of having our sex be like our human-ness, in that, obviously, the fact that you are a human being shapes many things about you. You walk on two legs rather than four, thousands of things, but you don't do them on purpose. I mean you don't think about: 'I'm a human, therefore I will walk on two legs.' I assume that what sex we are probably shapes things about us, just as our species identity does, but it doesn't require our participation in a voluntarily, conscious, culturally constructed way.

• *One of the things which is certainly strange and I think needs to be accounted, is that it does seem that within almost all cultures across the world you do get this androcentredness, so do you have any way of accounting for that?*
Yes. But it's only a once-upon-a-time story. In the second chapter [of *The Lenses of Gender* (1993 op. cit.)] in 'Biological essentialism' I do two kinds of things. One, I critique the ways in which scientific theories of both male/female difference and male/female inequality since the mid- to late 19th century have been biologically essentialist. By which I mean simply, overemphasizing biology and underemphasising about the historical or cultural context. But then the second thing I do in the chapter is to say: 'Well one of the reasons a theory like sociobiology is so seductive is that it seems to so easily explain something that we feel as if it needs explaining, which is, that when you look around the world, and

you see male power. You see male dominance. You see males in charge. Why was it learned everywhere?

And I said, 'Well, OK. Well, I'll put a once upon-a-time story up the same as, which is all I think socio-biology does. I feel that we need an account that would say something like this. There obviously are, and were, biological differences between the sexes with men bigger and stronger on the average and women pregnant and nursing most of their adult lives. Once upon a time, however, there were also certain indisputable truths about the environment. Like that there was no substitute for mother's milk. Work was primarily physical rather than mental; there were no technological instruments for extending the strength of the human body. And I suggest that then, back in our pre-history, the interaction between biology and culture or biology and environment, was virtually decisive, that there almost had to be a sexual division of labour. There had to be a gender polarization in terms of who did what when. For no other reason than women almost always had babies in them or on them, and I'm less clear on this, that somehow there also needed to emerge perhaps, males in power. Whether that's because of the need to defend the group, whether that's because by virtue of their greater size and strength and women being pregnant or nursing, men got to be warriors and, then, because they were warriors, they felt they had to or it came to be believed that they needed to control other decisions.

Somehow our biology ended up leading to both a division of labour, which is gender polarization, and some sort of hierarchy. So I begin with biology in a certain context and I say – and once in power and we have to get to men in power, but once in power, then, and I don't even see this as anti-men, I mean I think it's still consistent with the notion that I don't see myself as anti-men. I see a system developing that, once in power, males built institutions. I see males as having been responsible for building most of our institutions and cultural ideologies. They were the ones in control. They saw things from their own perspective. They were at the centre of the world, they were making decisions. Women seemed peripheral, women seemed other. And men built institutions and cultural discourses that ended up systematically maintaining the status quo and reproducing male power and that's the argument this book makes and it says ultimately that story about how it all began is just one version and it's not a very complete version of what it might look like. But whatever the answer's going to look like, it's going to be something about biology and context.

For me, as both an intellectual and a feminist, I don't think anything's ever just biology. I am virtually blind. That would have killed me off in the year 500 AD. Biology matters, but in how it matters depends on the context.

If eyeglasses, if lenses didn't get invented till the year 5000, I'd be useless until then, but then it would be OK. And I just use simple examples like that. It's the nature of the human organism not to be able to fly but we invented airplanes, so now we can fly. So it's just very much a notion of biology in context. And one of the points I make is that this simplistic story I made up is not meant to be something I think is true. It's to give you a model of what biology in context might look like. And the important point is that according to the institutional and cultural reproduction of power that I'm talking about in the book, it doesn't matter what the origin was. We can be interested in the origin but once established, the system reproduces itself. And so you don't ultimately have to know: is that story right? You might want to know intellectually, but in order to think about social change, you don't have to know about what it was doing then. Anyway, that's how I think about those questions and it's very important to me.

There are just people all over the place who have been incredibly obsessed with the question of difference, as if knowing the answer to this question is somehow urgent. And in the context of the oppression of women, let's just say, I don't think discussion is the least bit urgent. The reason people think it's urgent is it's as if feminists had been saying for a hundred years we have to change things to make women more equal and anti-feminists are saying wait, we have to find out about biology because biology is this sort of bedrock beyond which change is impossible. So let's see whether the kind of world you're envisioning is even a biological possibility and I say they don't under . . .

- *You were going to say: who don't understand.*
Right. Falsely as – you know this bedrock idea is wrong – biology varies with context and what we have to see about the context now, is that it's an androcentric context that turns whatever women's differences are into women's disadvantage. So why don't women become senators? Is it because there's something about women? It's often said in the United States that short people can't be fire fighters because they're not big enough or strong enough to wield the ladders and hoses, so I say imagine a village of short people, like me. Do you think all our houses would burn down? And the answer is yes, if we had to use the ladders and hoses that tall people built. But no, if we could design lighter ladders and hoses that tall people and short people could use. It's not about biology. It's about biology and context and if we have to live with social institutions that don't work for us.

What is perhaps most striking about the interview with Bem is that she comes closer than most psychologists to admitting that psychology is not just about finding out facts but an expression of personal style and concerns. It is, as she knows, a dangerous admission to make. Always evolving, Bem is now working as a clinical psychologist.

Chapter 2: Noam Chomsky

Noam Chomsky did not choose to become a psychologist; he did not train to become one. He found his work in linguistics was making a psychologist out of him. Many psychologists who are very impressed by Chomsky's linguistic work say they regret the fact that he dabbles in psychology. He does not know the subject. Two ironies can be found in this. First, Chomsky argues that many of these psychologists, obsessed with the desire to be scientists, are no better than pseudo-scientists, creating a dogma whose origins they barely understand. Secondly, Chomsky himself does not regard himself as a professional linguist. As he points out in the interview, he does not know many of the things a linguist should. His work is the product of working in a number of disciplines.

Until 1957, when Chomsky published *Syntactic Structures* (1957), his first book, and a book that radically changed linguistics, he was having difficulty in getting his papers published and even getting a job. Chomsky very nearly dropped out of college in 1948. After two years at the University of Pennsylvania, he lost all his proper Jewish enthusiasm for academic work. He decided to go to Israel and seek out a radical Arab/Jewish working-class movement. The disillusioned young idealist then met Zellig Harris, professor of linguistics at Pennsylvania who not only shared his radical views but turned Chomsky to the study of linguistics.

When Chomsky met him, Harris had just finished writing his *Structural Linguistics* (1949). Harris was trying to achieve an empirical and almost behaviourist approach to linguistics. He was trying to formulate principles of phonological and syntactic analysis of language without any reference to meaning. Until 1955, Chomsky worked very hard and loyally to make Harris's system work. He tried to refine it; he tried to formalise it. It was a long time – and, I suspect, a measure of Harris's influence over Chomsky – before he dropped that and developed his own account of a generative grammar. He had been toying with that as a kind of hobby, much less important at first than making Harris's system work.

Chomsky was well qualified to try to formalise Harris's work. After Pennsylvania, he worked under the philosopher, Nelson Goodman. Goodman recommended him for a junior fellowship in the Society of Fellows at Harvard. There, Chomsky studied mathematics, formal logic and algebra. He liked working with symbolism. This mathematical influence on Chomsky was important for his work: I suspect it is also important in defining the attitudes of psychologists to it. For four years, there was no pressure on Chomsky to specialise in any particular branch of a particular subject to 'deserve' his fellowship. Chomsky believes he was very lucky. In the early fifties, too, it was not yet necessary for American academics to publish or be damned to dull jobs. He believes it was the freedom to pursue odd topics like formal logic that allowed him to play around with the ideas that led to *Syntactic Structures*.

Chomsky has described himself as having grown up in the radical Jewish community in New York. His father was a Hebrew scholar of some distinction. From an early age, Chomsky picked up a body of informal knowledge about the structure and history of the Semitic languages. He had some idea of what linguistics might be about historically, studying how a word had evolved so that, at a particular time, it had a particular meaning. The task of the linguist was to explain why it had come to have this meaning at this time. Chomsky did some of his early work in modern Hebrew.

Chomsky then developed a theory of language with three key parts. There is the 'surface structure' of the language, which corresponds to the actual sentences that we hear. There is the 'deep structure' which is composed of meanings. For example, the surface structure 'a wise man is honest' emerges from the deep structure 'a man who is wise is honest'. The actual sentence emerges by a series of transformations. Chomsky himself described his theory as follows in a contribution to a symposium on *Explanation in the Behavioural Sciences* (1970, p. 429):

"The general framework that seems most appropriate for the study of problems of language and mind was developed as part of the rationalist psychology of the seventeenth and eighteenth centuries, and then largely forgotten as attention shifted to different matters. According to this traditional conception, a system of propositions expressing the meaning of a sentence is produced in the mind as the sentence is revised as a physical signal, the two being related by certain formal operations which, in current terminology, we may call *grammatical transformations*. Continuing with current terminology, we can thus distinguish the surface structure of the sentence, its organization into categories and phrases as a physical signal, from the underlying deep structure, also a system of categories and phrases but with a more abstract character. Thus, the surface structure of the sentence 'a wise man is honest' might analyse it into the subject 'a wise man' and the predicate 'is honest'. The deep structure, however, will be rather different. It will, in particular, extract from the complex idea that constitutes the subject of the surface structure an underlying proposition with the subject 'man' and the predicate 'be wise'. In fact, the deep structure, in the traditionalized, is a system of two propositions neither of which is asserted but which interrelate in such a way as to express the meaning of the sentence 'a wise nun is honest'."

Chomsky analysed the necessary constituents of the deep structure and the transformations through which this deep structure is turned into the surface structure we recognise and use as sentences. He claims that our knowledge of language is based upon this deep structure, a structure that we cannot guess or divine just from speaking, and upon the necessary transformations.

Chomsky's work is formal and depends a great deal on symbolism. Psychologists tend to be poor at such work. Zimbardo admitted, for example, his maths was just not good enough. I suspect Chomsky may have scared psychologists because he understood how to use mathematical symbolism properly. Worse he does work in an institution that is devoted to hard science. And even worse, he condemns most psychologists for being pseudo-scientists.

As a graduate at Harvard, he read Skinner's *Science and Human Behaviour* in manuscript. It was being passed around the campus. He found it empty then, he claims. Only two years after *Syntactic Structures* appeared, Chomsky wrote a famous, long and bitterly hostile review of Skinner's *Verbal Behaviour*. Already, he was arguing that you could not account for the way children learn language on any behaviourist model. Children did not learn the habit of saying particular words, phrases or sentences: it was not a question of language being reinforced by parental attention. The essential point is that our use of language is creative. Nearly every sentence we speak has not been spoken before by the speaker. Yet the speaker can speak it; the listener can understand it. Any model of language learning must be able to explain this fact.

Early in his career Chomsky saw the psychological implications of his work in linguistics. In *Cartesian Linguistics* (1966) and *Language and Mind* (1968), he reintroduced the mind, then a taboo topic, into psychology. Chomsky claimed that we have failed to understand some of the more valuable points rationalist philosophers made in the 17th and 18th centuries. The English philosopher John Locke, for example, attacked the doctrine of innate ideas on the ground that if a child grew up never hearing speech he would not speak. No philosopher of any consequence has argued for this extreme form of innate ideas. Stick a child in total silence where she or he can't even hear speech and, yes, that child will be dumb. That does not prove much. Chomsky believes that language learning depends on innate biological schemata whose sole purpose is to allow the child to learn language. Normal toddlers quickly learn to extract the very complex rules of grammar and you can observe them trying out various rules. A five-year-old speaks very nearly like an adult and can generate thousands of new sentences. Behaviorism can't explain that or explain the fact that in every culture children learn to speak. To speak is human. It helps, of course, if the child is encouraged or coached but only marginally. Talk all you like to an ape, however, and it will only grunt back.

Later Chomsky argued that thinking and the use of our imagination may also be part of our biological specialization. Again, he snipes, the empirical tradition in psychology has prevented the development of a serious scientific attitude. People may acquire knowledge in more ways than behaviourists and learning theorists dream of. To refuse to tackle such questions, to beg such questions, is the sign of an unscientific attitude.

In the interview, Chomsky expands at length on his critique of behaviourism. One point however that he barely touches on is introspection. Behaviourists have always attacked those who sought to reintroduce the mind into psychology on the grounds that they want to return to the chaos which introspection produced in the early 1900s. Chomsky is hostile to introspection, however. There may be innate principles of mind but he sees no reason to think that we can, by thinking about how we think, discover these principles. Rationalist philosophers, of course, did believe that by scrupulous introspection, they could find the principles of mind.

Chomsky, personally, is also interesting because science is not his only major interest. He remains torn between research and radical politics. He describes himself as 'schizophrenic': and he has been in that state for a long while. Visiting his office at MIT is bizarre. For MIT seems a temple of hard, aggressive science. You wander through corridors with signs that warn of danger. Notices suggest you are not far from work on radioactivity or war programmes. Chomsky's office is decorated with revolutionary posters. Since 1965, he has been one of the most persistent critics of US foreign policy first in Vietnam and now in Iraq. He encouraged draft dodgers and risked prison by refusing to pay half his taxes as a protest against the Vietnam war. He has been involved in radical politics since the age of 14. It is not something he came to when it became fashionable.

In the last 20 years Chomsky has devoted far more time to his radical political views than to research. He has become a critic of the American Empire and he recently said that the current state of politics made him feel not depressed but agitated. "A lot of adrenaline flowing. It may not show, but a lot of anger. But there are things that just have to be done. I think the world is better than it was 30 years ago, our behaviour is better than it was, but it's got a long way to go." He blames American presidents – Reagan, Clinton, the Bushes – for "every kind of hideous terror that you can imagine". Nearly always it is Washington backing monstrous regimes. I have not pursued this in talking to Chomsky since this is a book about psychology and he remains one of the giants who forced psychology to abandon crude behaviourism. Yet it is interesting that like Skinner, like Zimbardo, like Frankl, he has very strong political views. In one way his politics and his science come together. He has been one of the sharpest critics of behaviourism, not just because he thinks it is theoretically wrong but because he thinks it socially dangerous. He is very careful to distinguish between what Skinner hoped his work might do and the way Skinner's work was and still is being used. Skinner championed ideas which are either empty or are only popular because they are useful to American society.

As a scientist, however, Chomsky remains quite conventional. He told me:

"Of course it is always exciting to pursue an interesting idea and to find out it works. My main frustration, I guess, is that I never seem to have the time to follow up in detail since some other demand intervenes. Hence, often, the satisfaction is vicarious, in that it is a matter of seeing how students follow up and work out a half-baked but intriguing idea, or, often, to see how someone I do not or barely know comes up with something that provides real illumination into problems that interest me. As for frustrations, when research doesn't go, it is annoying, naturally, but there generally are enough promising lines of investigation open at any one time that I find it easy to simply abandon (I hope, temporarily) a line of inquiry that seems to be getting nowhere hoping it will fall into place later on, on the basis of some new insight or understanding. Hence that kind of failure is not much a source of frustration. Much more frustrating is the discovery that an idea that seemed really nice (or a principle that suggested something deep) doesn't work out or is false i.e. that the world is less elegant than one might have hoped. Again, there always seem to be enough intriguing alternatives to compensate."

I find this love of elegance interesting because it is more typical of hard scientists than of those who try to deal with the all too messy data human beings provide. Chomsky would say that without a formal system, you could make little sense of all these heaps of observations.

• *Could I ask you one or two things about your career before you became a linguist? You have often spoken about the rules of rational science and it strikes me as strange that one of the most humanist of contemporary workers in psychology should be at MIT. Were you trained as a scientist?*
No, I had no scientific training to speak of other than what I learned at school. The reason I'm at MIT is very simple. The work I was doing as a graduate student was considered too esoteric and too outlandish that it didn't belong to any recognised field. I didn't get much work published and I certainly had no job offers when I finished graduate school at Harvard. The reason I'm at MIT is, first, that I had a very close friend here, Maurice Halle – who is a real professional linguist in the sense in which I'm not – who was interested in what I was

doing and tried to arrange a niche into which I could fit. The second reason is that the research lab of electronics was, at that stage, a pretty wide-open institution. It had all sorts of strange things going on – neurophysiology, automata theory, communications theory. Gary Weissner who was then head of it felt they could tolerate another strange creature so that they could see what was coming from any of this stuff. That's why I'm here.

• *What was your early training in?*
Well, my undergraduate work was in linguistics at the University of Pennsylvania with Zellig Harris. Then, I did a year or two at Penn of graduate work with Harris and Nelson Goodman who was a philosopher. Goodman nominated me for the graduate fellowship in an organization called the Society of Fellows at Harvard, which is a small graduate research institute where they give you three years. I got one of those and I stayed four years. I got a renewal. I was doing mostly my own work on linguistic theory and also studying philosophy, logic and mathematics. It was really a marvellous structure to do graduate research. There were no formal conditions. I could study anything I wanted. I could spend as much time on my own work as I wanted and take it in any direction awaited. I didn't have, fortunately for me, the structure of a graduate programme imposed on me. I did what I felt like. The result was that the work I did not belong to any recognised field, so I was not professionally qualified when I finished in any field. I mean I'm not really a professional linguist. There are a lot of things a linguist ought to know which I don't know and I'm not interested in. I'm not criticising anyone for not offering me a job as a linguist. They were perfectly within their rights. But it had the advantage that I could go my own way. It worked pretty well. It's a good system but it carries the risk that you won't be employed or published. The major work that I did in this field was a very extensive book completed in 1955, which still isn't published.

• *What were the early influences on you or were you going your own way so much that there weren't any major influences?*
Can I give you my version of that? Which I'm not sure is accurate. What I'm aware of, certainly, was . . . in the first place there were negative and positive influences. Harris was an enormous influence in that I tried very hard for many years to make his kind of system work the kind of way he believed it could work. Nelson Goodman who was a philosopher who didn't know Harris but who worked along the same lines was, intellectually, rather similar to him too. He was interested in developing constructional systems. I was a student of his at a time when he wrote a really important book called *The Structure of Experience* which was an effort to build up in quite a systematic way an account of the

nature of our organization of our experiences on the basis of primary, primitive perceptions of qualities. I was very much influenced by a lot of the methods that he developed. Ultimately, I came to believe this was the wrong approach but the experience of trying to work through it, with it, was extremely valuable and I'm sure carried into a lot of work I've done in another way.

At the same time, it was very helpful to have studied modern logic, mostly at Harris's suggestion and, again at Harris's suggestion, modern mathematics and mathematical logic, the foundations of algebra. I don't know that I derived some specific conclusion but it was a way of thinking I found congenial and which could be easily put to use in my own interest. Somebody like Quine, too, at Harvard had a very great influence on how I came to think, though in the end I came to disagree sharply with him about many things. My original work in generative grammar was influenced as much as anything by the knowledge I picked up as a child about Semitic grammar. My father was a Semitic scholar. I knew as a kid just something about the history of the Semitic languages and when I came to do my own work in generative grammar, I sort of carried over one very important principle of historical, traditional grammar, namely, that one is trying to give an explanation for a particular stage of the language on the basis of a layering with historically successive things that have taken place. That's to say, we know certain things about biblical Hebrew and we might try to explain why the language is that way by assuming a series of changes, successive particular changes till it ended up that way. Well that kind of model is very easy to transfer to an explanatory theory of the stage of the language. And that seems as much of an influence as any.

• *Professor McClelland believes that many of the people who went into psychology did so in reaction to a very strict religious upbringing. Was that so in your case?*
No, quite the contrary in fact. I was very much involved in radical politics. Involved is a funny word. I was never part of an organised movement. I was very much a loner in that respect. That was my main interest in life by the time I was 13 or so. I had convinced myself that all of the organised movements, namely, the Communist Party, the Trotskyites, were quite reactionary basically. And, at a kind of 14-year-old level, I had worked myself into a left-wing Marxist or Marxist-anarchist position which was critical of any authoritarian tendency and regarded them as, basically, reactionaries of some sort who had taken on a kind of socialist terminology. And I had no particular place to go with this belief when I met Harris. And I met him . . . he was a very acute social critic. He's never written about it but a lot of people have been influenced by him politically. Surprising people, who passed through his influence at some formative

stage in their lives. And I was one. I met him at a time when I was planning to drop out of college, which seemed a stupid waste of time. I had no interest in anything I was doing in college. I was planning at that point – it was 1947 – to go off to the Middle East and to work on an Arab/Jewish working-class movement of a sort that I dreamed at that time, whether it existed or not, and I'd live in a kibbutz which, incidentally, I later did. Though I had entered college with a great deal of enthusiasm, by the time I'd had two years, I'd had all the enthusiasm knocked out of me. Every course I took convinced me it was completely boring, and not for me. It wasn't till I met Harris that I found anything intellectually stimulating, though my contact with him was originally through radical politics. So that's the actual background. I mean there may be subtler things . . .

• *More unconscious ones? That was the conscious background. How did you come to be interested in psychology?*
Well, I think it would be more accurate to say that I became interested in linguistics and came to feel that what I was doing in linguistics was psychology by any rational definition of the field. There is a tendency to define psychology in what strikes me as a curious and, basically, unscientific way, as having to do only with behaviour or only with processing of information or only with certain low-level types of interaction with the environment or whatever, and to exclude from psychology the study of what I call competence. And this is what just seems to me to leave a discipline that has no rationale. That is, I would assume that if psychology is to be a comprehensive and, in any sense deep investigation of its subject matter, it would also have to take into account in a fundamental way an investigation of what kinds of cognitive structures an organism – that is a human in this case – acquires and comes to use. And language is one of those. So I would assume that by being a linguist I am automatically a psychologist.

• *At what point when you were doing your linguistic work did you feel that what you were doing was, by any other name, psychology?*
Almost at the very beginning, when I was a graduate student, as far back as I can remember. I came to Harvard in 1950 as a graduate student. That was shortly after Skinner's William James Lectures had been delivered. They were being passed around in manuscript and hadn't yet appeared as a book. I had friends who were students of his. The whole thing was in the air and rather influential at the time. And it struck me at once as a curious sort of mysticism, for just the reasons I mentioned. It was very foreign to the spirit of the sciences and rather empty when you looked at it. I couldn't understand the interest and why anyone would conceive of psychology, of putting psychology in that weird straitjacket

instead of using the standard approach of the sciences. It always seemed to me obvious that investigating cognitive structures, whether they have been acquired by the organism, and investigating language must be psychology. If psychology is going to have any hope of coming to terms with its subject matter, it's going to have to deal with this central problem.

• *How did your early work develop?*
How much detail do you want me to go into?

• *As much as you need.*
I worked first as a student of Harris's at the University of Pennsylvania. In fact, my introduction to linguistics was in my sophomore year. I happened to meet Harris through common political connections but I got interested in his work and I liked him a lot. I read his book *Structural Linguistics* that was then in manuscript and that was my introduction to the field. I then took some of his courses, and he suggested that I did some work on a language I knew. I picked modern Hebrew, which I knew quite well. I tried for a while to use the methods of linguistics on Hebrew but it was just very clear that it was unilluminating and it wasn't getting anywhere and then I sort of abandoned it and said, 'What would be the rational way of approaching this question?' And I saw that the only rationality to approach it would be to try and construct a generative grammar: that is, a system of rules that would characterize the infinite classes of structures of the sense of the language and gives a base for interpreting them. So, I dropped all that and just went on with that. I didn't regard that as linguistics, I just regarded that as my private hobby. In fact, for a number of years, I was leading a schizophrenic existence until about 1953. I was working along two lines. On the one hand I was trying to sharpen and clarify the methods of structural linguistics which is an inductive approach in some ways like behavioural psychology. It was alleged that one could arrive at a class of observations, which would characterize the language. I was completely convinced that must be possible and, therefore, worked very hard at it. I thought the reasons it was obviously failing had to do with the lack of formality of the methods – or, some gap. At the same time, I was working, first in Hebrew and then in English, on the problems of generative grammar. I was following these two quite independent lines of work. One an effort to refine the methods of structural linguistics more or less on the lines of Harris and, secondly, my own private interest in generative grammar. It became obvious to me at some point, partly because of the results I was obtaining and partly because of the prodding of a few friends, that there was a good reason why the effort to refine the methods of structural linguistics wasn't working – namely,

that it was intrinsically the wrong approach. There was no reason to expect an inductive step-by-step procedure, no matter how sharpened and refined, to give an, or the, enlightening, or true, grammar of the language, the one that is acquired by the person who bas learned the language. Because there is no reason to accept the *a priori* assumption that that's how it's done by the organism. In fact, there's another good reason why the other approach I was taking was, in fact, giving rather interesting results, explanations of complicated phenomena – namely, that they did reflect the way the system came into existence and was used.

• *Did you do this in parallel? I mean did you begin describing the rules of generative grammar and becoming aware that this could reflect the way language is actually learned at the same time? One frequent criticism of you is that, though you are a fantastic linguist and however obese may be the rules, there is no reason to suppose these are actually psychologically or physiologically coded in that way.* The question is whether I took a realist interpretation of the system of grammar and did I assume it reflected the structure of the organism. And the answer is that, at first, it did not. I assumed, I took for granted, the approach to structural linguistics which was close in spirit to much of behaviourist psychology – namely, that took for granted that the way the system really works is that people apply these inductive procedures and by applying them to the data they experience, they arrive at systems of classification which are their grammar. But, gradually, it became obvious there were fundamental difficulties in working out these inductive approaches. It also became obvious that the other approach, that didn't raise any questions about how these principles were developed but simply investigated their consequences, was leading to what I thought were some pretty dramatic successes. It gradually dawned on me that it was wholly unscientific to take the realist approach with respect to *a priori* assumptions that were involved in the behavioural approach and to refuse to take the realist assumptions for a system that seemed to be working and giving, approximately, a satisfactory explanatory theory. Once that realization dawned, it was an elementary step and a correct step to abandon the *a priori* commitment to data-processing, inductive procedures as simply a metaphysics that could be thrown out of the window. It seemed unreasonable to accept it. And reasonable to assume that, if a system of principles seemed to be giving insight, explanations and predictions and so on, to take a reasonable approach and postulate, yes, this does reflect the structure of the organism.

Now, in this case, as we don't know anything about how such structures might be represented neurologically – but that's beside the point. If a scientist were unable to break into a machine that he was investigating, he wouldn't hesitate for a moment to postulate that the structure of the machine was in accord with the principles of organization that he'd postulated, if these principles, in fact, meet conditions of providing insight, explanation and so on. Well, let me make this clear. In investigating the adult organism, one is only determining the steady state, the final state that is achieved at the point at which further acquisition of language is either marginal or non-existent. The analogy I mentioned before I meant to be taken pretty seriously. There is, in the case of language learning, a radical change through one period of life, and then you reach a pretty much steady state. You may learn new words but nothing fundamental changes. In studying the adult's speech we're trying to find something out about the steady state. That does not tell us anything in itself about how the steady state is achieved. If all we knew was how adults behaved, the null hypothesis might be that adults were born speaking English. If a Martian scientist were to come here, that might be his first assumption. It might be a reasonable assumption – to assume that the system has evolved or even changes through time? Of course, we know that that's not true because people aren't born speaking English. So, by an investigation of the range of the evidence, by looking at the similarities of final states achieved by speakers of the same language, by investigation of the similarities of the final states achieved by speakers of different languages, by studies of different languages, we can begin to make some pretty plausible suggestions about what must have been the initial state that made it possible to acquire those particular systems. For instance, if we discover that, then in the case of English grammar, some very abstract principle is operating. And if those conditions are well confirmed – they do explain things – then we have to face the question of how do the conditions of knowledge of those principles arise? On the basis of what sort of evidence does the organism determine that those principles are to be operative. And, in fact, in many cases, there is no evidence to the language learner, or marginal evidence at the most, that these are the operative principles. Nevertheless, they are applied at once – and uniformly. Given that kind of observation, it would be most rational to postulate that they are part of an original schematism that the organism simply brings to bear on the acquisition of these systems. This is the approach. If it were not human beings that were involved, if it were some other organism, that would be taken without question. No one would dream of showing that a bird learns to fly through association. You just assume that the kind of complex structure is simply in the nature of the organism and has developed through evolution – not through learning. In the case of humans, their special characteristic, I suppose, is a certain type of intellectual structure. I see no reason to take a different approach to the study in the case of humans, or a machine, for that matter.

• *Your schematism still has to be triggered. How do you relate the role of the environment? Is it just negative so that if certain things don't happen, then your innate capacity, your schematism, just withers away?*

Well, I don't believe there's enough evidence to answer that question. The possibility you suggest does exist. In fact, it is known, I believe, that's the way some intrinsic structures do seem to operate. Deprivation experiments seem to show that some of the highly organised perceptual structures do wither away if they're not set into operation at a certain early stage. It's quite conceivable that the same is true of the special structures that determine the nature of language system and systems of thought, representation, of symbolization and so on. But, of course, we have no really serious evidence for that. We don't do deprivation experiments on humans, obviously. There are a few examples that have been discovered of children who were apparently subjected to very serious sensory deprivation. And some of these been investigated, but they don't give very sharp evidence. That's certainly plausible. But, I mean, there's no doubt there are effects of the environment, of experience, on the language you learn. That's certainly true. How extensive that influence is an open question. How much evidence does a child have to have to acquire a language? Well – remarkably little. Very complicated structures are set into motion in very specific, highly articulated ways on the basis of very rudimentary evidence. And, what's more, it's done uniformly by all children. This indicates that there are very specialized, highly developed schemata that are presupposed in the acquisition of knowledge. It does even more than that. It directs us to what some of these principles might be.

• *How do you deal with the study that shows if you read to a child for thirty minutes each day his vocabulary, his verbal skill is improved? Are your schemata the basic element on which almost Skinnerian principles act?*

Well, I don't know there's any reason to assume there's any role for Skinnerian principles in particular. There is learning, undoubtedly but there's no reason to suppose it's based on those principles. I'm quite sure that if you pay a lot of attention to a child you can increase its vocabulary and its linguistic skill, quite substantially. But, still looking at it from the Martian point of view, from the outside, I think that a scientist would be very much struck by how minute are the differences between individuals who are given radically different training and treatment as compared with the enormous similarities. I mean a child who just picked language up off the streets, to whom no one pays much attention, still has acquired an extensive, complex, intricate system. He may not be using the same vocabulary as a child who's been force-fed but, still there is no child, apart from one who is severely disabled, who fails to acquire an enormously rich linguistic system – very much like that of anyone else. For this reason, I would assume that special training procedures like reading don't really affect the acquisition of the basic structure of the language. They may add some frills.

• *How do you deal with the* Pygmalion *situation? Did Eliza in* My Fair Lady *pick up an entirely novel set of rules?*
Well, the *Pygmalion* situation is a bit different. It doesn't have anything to do with the acquisition of language really. It has to do with the acquisition of a certain system of cultural snobbery. That is, Eliza, before they got hold of her, was still speaking as rich and as complicated a language as she did after the transformation. It was a different one. It wasn't the language of the British upper classes. It was rather the language she had acquired in her natural fashion. So, I think, there are no reasons to assume there is a difference in the richness or expressive power between the language of, say, upper-class snobbish and the language of the streets. Obviously, they have their differences. But, just in so far as we know, there are no differences between the languages of so-called primitive societies and those of, say, technological situation societies, apart from the kinds of things they talk about. There are probably forms of cultural richness in, say, Australian bush society reflected in their use of language that we don't bother with and, conversely.

• *But these are refinements to the basic structure for the acquisition of language?*
Well, you can train people to speak with a British accent like you can train people to distinguish different kinds of wine or to behave with the proper manners at an academic dinner or something of that sort. However, I don't think that that kind of training ought to be confused with the acquisition of fundamental human traits such as the ability to eat, take in cultural patterns or the ability to acquire the very complex and not yet fully understood system of cultural patterns that anyone who grows up in a society internalizes and uses.

• *Is language the most fundamental, most basic of all our higher-level skills?*
Well, it's often been speculated and I think it's a reasonable speculation. But we have to be very careful about it because the difficulty is that the question has often been raised by psychologists and by philosophers as to whether these linguistic abilities are a unique faculty of mind, let's say, to use some old-fashioned terminology, or, whether they're simply a reflection of much more general capacities. We'll only have an answer to that when other areas of intellectual achievement are investigated in much the same way as language. If, for example, people learn a great many things other than language: they learn something of,

they develop a theory about, the physical world. They develop a theory of social relations, they develop the ability to analyse personality structures on the basis of a very small amount of evidence once again. All sorts of systems are developed by human beings in the course of their normal growth and maturation. If other systems are investigated, if grammars of them are constructed, we will then be able to ask the question if they have the same or analogous properties to those of the faculty of mind. Frankly, I don't see any reason to suppose that they do. It would be surprising if they did, but that's an open question.

• *You have been credited with reintroducing the mind, or innate abilities and capacities into philosophy and psychology. Do you really feel that the work you have been doing bears any relation to that long tradition of rationalism, Leibniz and Spinoza, for instance?*
I think it bears a very close relationship. I think so and I've tried to show in a number of books that there is a close relation and, further, that the classical tradition has been misunderstood. People paid attention to certain parts of it and omitted consideration of other parts of it. For example, there's a good deal of attention now to the classical rationalist theory of innate ideas as a contribution to the foundations of necessary knowledge and necessary truths. And that's certainly one part of it. But there's another part that I find much more interesting, personally, and on which I've focused. That was the attempt to develop a rationalist psychology that had nothing to do with necessary truths, but which had simply to do with organizing principles in perception which had to do with a basic schematic framework that is an essential part of mind, that determines the preconditions for experiences and determines the system of knowledge that's acquired on the basis of experience. That's a point of view more naturally associated with Kant. But one finds a lot of interesting things in the 17th century, in Descartes, in Cudworth, in the minor Cartesians and, in particular, in the grammarians who developed under their influence. In fact, there are great similarities between many of the things they were attempting to do and many of the things I am trying to do.

There are also quite a number of differences for, I think, Descartes and Leibniz seem to have taken for granted that the contents of the mind were in principle open to introspection, that is, if you thought hard you could find, introspect into, the principles by which you're functioning mentally. That assumption was quite common to classical rationalism and empiricism. It was everybody's assumption. And that assumption is very implausible because there's no reason to believe it to be true. There's no reason to believe that by mere introspection you can discover the principles of the operation of the mind. Why should that be the code? They had a reason. They didn't just arbitrarily make it up. We can discover what their reason was but we don't have to accept their reason. Similarly, they, Descartes, had an argument favouring dualism, for thinking that mind was a substance not reducible to physics and chemistry. Nevertheless, we don't have to accept that argument. There are flaws in it. There are other ways of looking at the matter. His concept of physics was far too narrow. Everybody knows that now.

So, we're not forced to follow a Cartesian line of reasoning that leads to dualism and, similarly, Descartes's argument in favour of the necessity of the phenomena of Nature has enormous logical flaws in it. It's based on the assumption – he thought he'd proved it but it's clearly unproven – that there is a God who cannot deceive us. Well, OK, that's a pretty bad argument. In that respect, it'd be absurd to try to pursue classical rational framework as it saw itself. Still, I think there are many striking and interesting respects in which these developments were important precursors and suggest what ought to be undertaken.

• *What are the necessary preconditions of experience that you see other than language?*
Well, I think it's hard to be specific because no other domain of human intelligence, to our knowledge, has been studied in a similar manner. It's just obvious or superficial thinking, in the view of our experience, they interact. With people, in the main we're putting to use a system of very complicated beliefs. I don't know what the system is. We have to try and find out what the system is. It seems to me clear, qualitatively, that the situation is not so very different from the one sketched in the analogy earlier – we find different people, say you or I, are employing very similar patterns of beliefs. That's why we can communicate, why we can predict one another's behaviour intuitively, why we know the way we behave in the physical environment around is more or less fixed. We have acquired quite complicated systems of belief, which is a matter that we can't introspect into. We can't find out what they are like by thinking about them. However we acquired them, they are quite comparable. There is a great deal of shared belief in the fact that we have very little evidence for the system or of the structure of these systems, which must be similar. I don't see how we can go beyond that except by carrying out an inquiry and investigation comparable and analogous in many ways to the one which has been carried out into language and trying to make explicit just what those systems are and how they are put into action. In doing that, we may find principles quite analogous to the principles that appear to govern our linguistic behaviour.

• *Do you think that one of the reasons why many psychologists have so stubbornly refused to go into this kind of area of the mindful for so long is that they didn't feel that they were able to do it in a serious, sound way?*

Well, I think there are a lot of historical reasons why psychology took the turn it did, some no doubt valid at the time. Objections to rather empty introspection, objections to rather empty feudalistic approaches, for example. I think there are really much deeper reasons. I think one has to go into why the study of humans since the origins of British empiricism has been so remarkably remote from the mainstream of science. There are certain dogmatic elements in association and empiricist psychology, which mark it as extremely hostile to the spirit of the sciences. For instance, that certain modes of learning must be postulated without any investigation of whether such postulations, such modes of learning, will, in fact, account for the systems of belief that are in fact, acquired. This is a remarkably unscientific approach. I mean this is the approach one would expect from some branch of theology, quite distinct from the approach of the sciences. I think the tendency of much of modern psychology to pursue a line of approach that is remarkable in its hostility to the scientific method is, perhaps, an outgrowth of that in part.

- *That is strange. Many psychologists say that it is precisely because they are so enamoured of the scientific method that they have to leave out the sort of work you are interested in.*

Let's forget about studying humans. Suppose we were to become interested in some organism or machine. Suppose some machine is placed in front of us. We find lots of examples of it and for some reason, we're interested in discovering how it works. Here is a problem of science, of engineering almost.

The natural approach any scientist would take – we assume we have evidence that this machine changes through time and that it interacts with its environment and that, in certain respects, it's acting differently from the way it did at the beginning. Suppose we discover that much to be the case and suppose the scientist is interested in the questions what is the nature of the machine, how is it changing through time, how are other machines like it? The way that any scientist would approach this question would be to try and characterize two basic states of the machine, its initial state and its final state. Let's add one assumption – that, at a certain point, the modifications in the way the machine acts are marginal as compared with the changes that have taken place up to that point. It's kind of hit a steady state, in which slight modifications take place. Given such a wealth of qualitative observations, what the scientist would attempt to do is to characterize by any complex system of inquiries he could try, the steady state of the machine and he would search for uniformities among these machines in the kind of final states that they achieved. He would also try to characterize their initial stages. Then, having developed some form of hypothesis about the final state of the machine, he would try to ask himself a developmental question. He would say: 'What must I presuppose about the initial state, given my knowledge of the interaction with the environment the machine has undergone, given a hypothesis about the final state, given its adequacy and given whatever experiments I've been able to conduct and given my observations of interaction. What must I postulate about the initial state to be able to account for these changes.'

And these second-order postulations about the initial state of the machine would be the theory of learning for this machine. Now, if you then went on to discover that there are great similarities between the machines as to their final states that would be evidence as to what the possible initial states would be. So you would proceed.

Suppose, on the other hand, some sort of pseudo-scientist were to approach the same qualitative observations but were to approach them as follows: 'Look, I don't care what the final state is, I'm not even going to look at that. I'm just going to postulate *a priori* that the modes by which this machine interacts with the environment are such and such. It forms associations, it generalises in terms of certain physical dimensions which I specify. It constructs probabilistic habit structures.' I mean this sort of pseudo-scientist picks out a number of such techniques and whatever they are saying I simply postulate that these are the ways in which the machine interacts with the environment. And suppose we get him to abandon entirely the question of whether by postulating these properties he could explain the final state of the machine which he would consign to some kind of mysticism, and suppose he were simply to conduct experiments on the ways in which these *a priori* procedures could be made use of by the device – no doubt he could make up a subject – it could be that the methods he picks actually have virtually nothing to do with the way the machine interacts with the environment. Nevertheless, he could evolve a long subject, have many PhD theses and so on investigating this *a priori* selection of principles by which one supposes learning takes place.

Now, I find this view characteristic of psychology. Psychology through British empiricism and modern behaviourism has never seen an effort to show that the methods of learning which are postulated do, in fact, succeed and did succeed in attaining the final state which is postulated as being true of the machine. To carry out the scientific approach one would try to determine the systems of belief, the cognitive structures, the competence or whatever that the organism has, in fact, attained. It's precisely this problem that, traditionally, large domains of psychology have excised as being outside their concerns. These branches of psychology are theological about it, almost.

• *What do you say to the psychologist who says there just are not the techniques to cope with such problems? That psychology is the art of the possible and that all*

I can now do is to build up little bricks here and there? Then, someday in the future, an Einstein will come along and give us a more total, rounded psychology?
First of all, it's not correct. There are many things we can discover about the systems of knowledge and belief that a person has. And then, I think that investigating it would give us a lot of insight into the system, into what may be the modes of coming to terms with the environment. But if someone were to take the position you attributed to Broadbent I would consider it pointless but not irrational. But, on the other hand, I don't think that is the position psychologists are taking very often. They're not saying, 'Look, it's premature to discuss, to study the adequacy of the methods that we postulated *a priori*'. It's not that. What we're saying is that psychology is defined by the investigation of these methods. Psychology is defined by the study of S–R connections, by habit structures, by stimulus sampling theory and so on.

• *Ever since your work became so influential, there's been a tendency to try and construct a grammar of non-linguistic kinds of human interaction. Is it likely that the model of language will turn out not to be a unique model?*
Well, it depends. I think myself – and this is speculating – we don't have the results or the knowledge at this point. But I think it's very likely that the grammar of the system of language does reflect a special faculty of the mind. I think it would be surprising if there were striking or strong analogies between our innate capacities to acquire linguistic systems and our innate capacities to acquire an understanding of social reality or the physical world. There's no particular reason why they should be modelled on the same set of principles. But, at a certain high enough level of abstraction, the systems will of course observe similar principles and be in some way interrelated. However, I think I wouldn't suggest if someone is interested in social interaction that they should try to apply the model of transformational grammar. But what I'd do is to approach the problem in the same manner, which is borrowed from the physical sciences – namely to ask. What is the system, what is the system of belief that governs the behaviour we are observing? Let us discover the competence that underlies the behaviour of a person in a social situation if that is the topic. And having developed an understanding of that competence, that internal system of beliefs and knowledge, then we have first to ask the question, what is it that's learned? Let us discover as scientifically as we can what we can about the system that's been acquired and call it the grammar, if you like it. Then having, to the extent that we can, answered that question, we can sensibly raise the question of learning for the first time. The question of learning is the question of how that postulated system arises. On the basis of interaction with the environment, the question about learning can't be asked except to the extent that we already have some

picture, some postulate, some concept as to the acquiring of the system. So, in this respect, I would think that any approach to psychology ought to follow the model of linguistics or, I hasten to say, it's not the model of linguistics but the model of any rational endeavour. And the fact that psychologists regard that as strange and curious is just a comment on how remote that kind of psychology is from rational endeavour and from the sciences in particular.

• *Do you think that stems from the American preference for studying actions rather than thought?*
Well, now you've raised the question of why behaviourist psychology has such an enormous vogue, particularly in the United States. And I'm not sure what the answer to that is. I think, in part, it had to do with the very erroneous idea that by keeping close to observation of data, to manipulation, it was somehow being scientific. That belief is a grotesque caricature and distortion of science but there's no doubt that many people did have that belief. I suppose, if you want to go deeper into the question, one would have to give a sociological analysis of the use of American psychology for manipulation, for advertising, for control. A large part of the vogue for behaviourist psychology has to do with its ideological role. Behaviourist psychology is pretty empty as a intellectual pursuit, in my opinion. But it does have an important ideological role. For example, it's considered not nice to treat human beings by the techniques of the police state. It's not nice to coerce people or to control them or to train machine guns on them. But, on the other hand, if you have a mass of people you want to control and you can claim you are not doing anything ugly like that but just applying the methods of science which, as everyone knows, are neutral and good and benevolent and achieve the same result, that's much more palatable. Much more acceptable. So one finds, let's say, in total institutions, in institutions in which masses of people are placed subject to external controls, like prisons, schools and mental hospitals, not quite even that behaviourist psychology is in vogue but that it provides support. It may even sharpen and refine the methods, which are known intuitively to anyone who has to control masses of people. It provides a kind of palatable ideology for the application of these techniques of coercion.

• *Skinner, in fact, says that one of the reasons why he feels badly misunderstood is that people think he advocates greater controls. What he's been trying to do is to show people the way they were and could be controlled so they could guard against it. Is that fair do you think? Or does it go against the whole trend of his thought as you see it?*
I think one has to distinguish what Skinner himself may be trying to do from something quite different – namely, the question of why it has such appeal.

These may be very different things. As to what he may be trying to do, I can't say. I don't have any idea of what he's trying to do. I've looked at his work pretty carefully and I have never been able to discover or tried to impute to him any motives in particular. I don't know what they might be. It seems to me that when he gets away from the investigation of partial reinforcement – when he does things like one finds in *Beyond Freedom and Dignity* – it's basically trivial and wouldn't be taken seriously by anyone if it weren't for the fact that it fills a certain role for those who are accepting the system. Now, the role it fills for them may be very different from anything he intended. So, my point is when one gives anything like a close analysis to the system Skinner proposes – and I'm not talking now of his detailed studies of conditioning and reinforcement, they are what they are, but I am talking about what he calls his extrapolations in which he's showing people how they are controlled, what the system of controls is and trying to build up a social philosophy – well, that second Skinner, as far as I can see, is almost entirely empty. You cannot find a substantive thesis that's even worth discussing, let alone refuting. And therefore no serious person would pay the slightest attention to it on the basis of its actual intellectual content. Yet people do pay enormous attention to it and it's enormously influential. The reasons may have nothing to do with content or with what Skinner's intentions may be, which I know nothing about. All I'm saying is that the appeal and the acceptance has to do with other matters: namely, that the system, though quite vacuous, does provide a kind of aura of acceptability for techniques of control and coercion that are very naturally sought in situations where people have to be controlled, coerced and guided. Now I'm not imputing to Skinner that intent. That's my point.

- *How does your concept of competence work?*

Well, I used the word 'competence' because I didn't want to get into pointless arguments with philosophers about whether one should call unconscious true belief knowledge. A lot of people don't like to use the word 'knowledge' where the beliefs are unconscious. OK. I think it's a kind of pointless argument but I didn't feel like getting into it so I invented a technical term, but it turns out, as usual, to be more misleading than the original. By competence I just mean that system of internal principles and structures that we use for our behaviour. I would be perfectly happy with the term knowledge. What I mean by compe-tence is our knowledge of language but my only hesitancy is that the knowledge here is plainly unconscious. We don't have, we couldn't have, conscious know-ledge of these principles. I find it difficult to say we know the principles. By competence, I just mean that system of knowledge that we put to use. There's no principle of competence. I thinks if I use those machines I was talking about, I would have no hesitancy in assigning to those machines a system of competence, namely, a system of organization and principles and structures and interaction that I am led to postulate can effectively explain what they do – the characterization of their mental states, if you like. The characterization of the steady state achieved by these machines would be what I'd call their competence.

• *Do your views about Man hint at some kind of sympathy with a man like Laing who sees many mystical elements in Man, that are maybe too random to be encompassed by science?*
I would look at it differently, I think. I would just take it for granted that a human being is a biological organism like any other. It's a biological organism with a very unique intellectual capacity that we are only barely beginning to understand. I think our intellectual capacities are very highly structured. They are our biological specialization. These biological structures enable us to construct extremely rich, very penetrating systems, scientific theories if you like. Some of them are common sense. Some of them are articulated, which allows us to understand things rather deeply far beyond any evidence that's available to us. However, these same principles, which give such enormous range to our system of understanding, also limit its scope. There facts are very closely linked together. Any sort of limited data also is likely to limit the class of possible theories that you can attain. Now it may very well be that among the theories that we are not able to attain is included the theory of mind. In that case, it will appear that human beings have mystical, unintelligible properties because we as biological organisms will not have within our range (which is obviously a finite range) the theory that would, in fact, explain it. There's nothing inconsistent about that. We are biological organisms. We are capable of constructing certain systems and understanding certain scientific theories. It's an open question as to whether those scientific theories happen to include the true theory of some domain that happens to interest us. It may or it may not. If it does not, that domain all appear to be mystical. It will only be a higher organism or a differently endowed organism that will understand it. But I think that's about all that can be said.

• *So you think it is finite? Some have told me that they thought psychology is so finite it about reached the end of the road. Presumably you see a time when it will have reached the end of the road.*
I think human intelligence will reach the end of the road except for details. We'll always be able to learn more details, more specific facts. I think it's quite possible that, at some point, we will have exhausted our intellectual capacities in some domain. And, I suppose, at every stage of history that seemed to have hap-

pened, it turned out to be false. I think one could build a kind of case, a mildly persuasive case, that we have reached a stage not in psychology but in many other domains. A very striking fact about 20th century modernism is the move in one area after another, in art, in poetry, in music, in certain parts of science, into a kind of unintelligibility. I think there's probably no period in this brief history of Western civilization in which the creative achievements of artists were so remote from the common consciousness and understanding of non-artists. I think it's conceivable that this does indicate a reaching the limit or approaching the limit in certain domains of intellectual and creative achievement.

- *Is that true of psychology?*
Frankly I don't think it's in any sense true of psychology. Psychology has barely come into existence, It's just barely beginning to ask some of the questions that might lead to a future science. But someday it will happen.

Activities connected with Vietnam, with US foreign policy, with civil liberty issues. I've tried to maintain throughout this an ongoing commitment to both areas and, of course, both have suffered. But I've recently completed a long study on the conditions of these rules and I've got other work on these lines going. But it's a rather schizophrenic existence again.

Chapter 3: Antonio Damasio

Most of the psychologists interviewed in this book come from an Anglo-Saxon background. Antonio Damasio who teaches at the University of Iowa, however, was born in Portugal and started his career there. He graduated from Lisbon University and qualified as a neurosurgeon. When I rang to make an appointment with him in Iowa, the first assumption was that I was trying to make an appointment because I had a neurological problem. Damasio fits in with a very long and honourable tradition of doctors who speculate on the human condition. He has not yet had one of his books turned into a Hollywood movie or into an opera, as his fellow neurologist Oliver Sacks has had, and he may not because his works are a little more theoretical.

Europe has marked Damasio. Two of the titles of his books refer to great European philosophers – Rene Descartes and Bento Spinoza. Damasio seems rather fond of Spinoza who got himself excommunicated by the Jewish community in Amsterdam because he could not stomach an orthodox, personal God. Some of the book describes Damasio wandering through the city of canals in search of his hero and the message Spinoza still holds for us today.

In Bento Spinoza's day the brain was utterly mysterious but he nevertheless did come to understand that body and mind are linked. Spinoza also grasped the role of emotions in human survival and culture.

Damasio first became well known through his book *Descartes' Error*. Descartes is famous for his elegant axiom '*Cogito ergo sum*'. I think, therefore, I am. As an undergraduate one of my tutors set me an essay to discuss whether it would have been more appropriate if Descartes had written '*Dubito ergo sum*' – I doubt therefore I am. Descartes was claiming that we could doubt everything we saw or thought but the one thing we could not doubt was the process of 'thinking'. But all his thoughts were doubts.

Damasio offered in *Descartes' Error* a very different version of this classic. There, he argued that western culture and western science has tended to over emphasise the role of thinking and reasoning – and that we will only understand how the brain works by focusing at least as much on emotions. It is not a totally new idea. In the 1960s we became familiar with the left brain versus right brain debate. The left hemisphere of the brain controlled language and logic – in right-handers at least. The right hemisphere was much more intuitive, poetic, all about feelings rather than thought.

Then in *The Feeling of What Happens* Damasio attacked one of the most unknottable knots of science today: how the brain gives rise to consciousness. He offered a novel theory of that. The primacy of the emotions is also a theme of *Looking for Spinoza* whose full title is *Joy and Sorrow in the Brain*.

Damasio is a man with a sense of history and he knows that the mid-19th century was a key moment in brain science. In the 1830s, the fashionable thinking was based on phrenology, the science of the bumps of the brain. Intelligent men suggested that if you had a pronounced bump or curve in the skull two inches from your left ear that would correlate with what the brain inside was like. And that bump showed you were likely to be highly emotional. Today we dismiss that as nonsense. One of the reasons we do that is that from 1860s onwards, neuroscientists like the Frenchman Broca were able to associate damage to particular areas of the brain with strange behaviour. Broca found when he conducted post-mortems on patients who had lost the ability to speak that many of them had damage to certain areas of the temporal lobe. There is, as Damasio acknowledges, a link between Broca and the extraordinary developments in brain science of the last 20 years. Today doctors and researchers can see the brain in action through new techniques such as Magnetic Resonance Imaging. These make it possible to see which areas of the brain 'light up' into action as we perform certain tasks. This was not one of the key reasons why psychology became interested in consciousness again in the 1970s but since then it has fuelled many interesting studies. The problem is, as Damasio, admits that we are still a long way from solving the problem of consciousness.

Eysenck once said of Freud that he deserved the Goethe Prize for fiction because his case histories made such fascinating reading. Damasio is always ready to delve into his casebook, which is full of the histories of individuals who have brain damage.

Damasio suggests we have three different kinds of self and two of them somehow weave the pattern of our consciousness. He is very aware that the brain changes from moment to moment and he argues that we have, first, a *proto-self*, an interconnected and temporarily coherent collection of neural patterns. This represents the moment-by-moment state of the organism at different levels of the brain. I don't find it hard to imagine this self, which alters from moment to moment, but usually the proto-self is unconscious. I can't really access it. I may be able to hold an image of my neural cells whizzing as I write this in the middle of the night but I can't really access my proto-self.

The next level is the conscious and Damasio calls that the *core self*. The core self does not change much throughout our lifetime, and we are conscious of it. Hence we can speak of core consciousness. Damasio is hardly the first person to wonder at how it is that when we wake up we tend to think we are the same person as the self who nodded off to sleep eight hours earlier. He has come up with the interesting idea that core consciousness is continually regenerated in a series of pulses. The pulses are, of course, electrical and chemical activity in the brain. It shows how little we still know about the brain that Damasio cannot define them too precisely. These pulses somehow blend together to give a continuous 'stream of consciousness'.

With his sense of history, Damasio links his notions of core consciousness with those of earlier thinkers especially the philosophers John Locke and Immanuel Kant, as did Freud and William James who first used the phrase the stream of consciousness.

The third self is the *autobiographical self*, which is based on memory and on anticipating of the future. There have been many studies of how children start to develop a sense of their own history. Damasio suggests that this autobiographical self develops gradually through life. If you do not have a core self you cannot acquire an autobiographical self, but the opposite is not true. As a teaser out of how brain damage affects – and can radically change the personality of individuals – Damasio offers many cases in which people lose their autobiographical self, temporarily or permanently, while they still have their core consciousness.

Being aware of the past and the future does distinguish the human from the kangaroo and even lesser forms of life such as the crocodile or the amoeba. We will assume that none of these species have the brain resources to sustain an autobiographical self or the existence of a much richer form of consciousness, which Damasio calls extended consciousness.

But Damasio also attaches great importance to the role of emotion. To make it easier to understand some of the interview, it may be useful to explain how Damasio uses some very common language. By 'emotion', Damasio does not mean a psychological state; instead and – here he follows William James – Damasio uses 'emotion' to refer to internal changes in body state (chemical, visceral, muscular). All these changes are accompanied by changes in the nervous system. As a result, emotions are not conscious – just like the proto-self is not conscious. This goes against the way we think because we constantly talk about emotions and feelings. Damasio carefully distinguishes between emotions and feelings. Imagine you see an old lover licking an ice cream cone with her new lover. There are certainly internal changes in your body state. But there are also feelings. You feel jealous because she is with a new man, you feel sad because you remember the good times, you feel . . . oops . . . guilty because after all it was your fault happiness ended when you snogged her best friend at the faculty party. Such feelings often motivate action. Your sadness may lead to you avoiding situations – you slink off round the corner and cry, for example. Or you may decide that what you feel most is the waste of it and you decide that you will ring her up and try to get back together again. If you are in a prolonged feeling state that, Damasio says, constitutes a mood.

William James worried about the question of whether feelings are conscious. Damasio suggests – not very controversially – that they are and they aren't. It seems that sometimes they are and sometimes they are not. As we tend to suffer from Descartes' error, we tend to think that feelings must always be conscious, but Damasio thinks an organism may "represent in neural and mental patterns" the state that we call a feeling without ever knowing that the feeling is taking place. For example, we may suddenly find ourselves feeling anxious, or pleased, or relaxed, without knowing why; in such cases the physical state that gave rise to the feeling must have begun some time previously.

It is because we do rather often know that we have a feeling that we have to speak of a third level of development, that of conscious knowledge of feeling. Damasio suggests that organisms who knew all this had an evolutionary advantage. It made it easier to plan and to negotiate the conflicts in groups. Species who are unable to go in for counselling – such as deer – have to resolve difficulties simply by locking horns. Since we can access a vocabulary of feelings, we do better.

Pleasure and pain are the bedrocks of humanity, Damasio has said. He places emotions (unconscious in the body), feelings (usually conscious in human beings), and consciousness itself (allowing reflections on feelings) along a continuum – and in a way that is Damasio's most profound idea. Most serious psychological theories have suggested that there is much less of a link between the way we think and the way we feel. And the notion that our ability to feel and to understand our feelings was key in the development of consciousness is also deeply interesting.

Damasio also claims that there are some animals that exhibit emotions and may well have feelings, but they don't know they have them. The dog Zak may feel sad or happy because his owner has or has not thrown a slipper for him to fetch, but Zak cannot explain why he feels sad or bad. There is no word to name "feelings that are not conscious", Damasio suggests, but perhaps there should be if we are to become more self-aware and more able to control our lives.

In his work, Damasio finds himself coming face-to-face with patients with various kinds of localised brain damage. Sometimes they cannot feel happiness or sadness in the way that they had been able to before they suffered brain injury. This leads him to think that different brain systems control different feelings. As a doctor he has found that patients who have lost the ability to experience certain feelings can still reveal signs of the corresponding emotion. Damasio asks himself whether emotion was born first and feeling second.

The lack of a good vocabulary to describe his ideas is indeed something of a problem for Damasio. In one book he offers what is rather apologetically called 'A Glosssary of Sorts'. As Damasio acknowledges at the outset, he does not deal with an old problem that his ideas lead up to – how do the processes in our brain produce the subjective experience of the blueness of the sky or the sound of a piano? He believes that this question can be approached through neurology. That is an optimistic position because the enormous success of brain science in the last 20 years has been very much in the detail rather than in understanding the grand totality of the brain. As Chomsky said the brain may not be able to understand the brain. But Damasio clearly does not believe that. He asked me to submit questions in advance, and this explains our first exchange.

• *I feel it's not a question of looking for Spinoza but looking for Damasio.*
Very good. You have a question here that says there's a French website that refers to me as the Toscanini of psychology.

• *Does it amuse you?*
Yes, very much, although I remember the first time that I was told that, I said, 'Well, I really don't think that Toscanini is my favourite conductor' but that's fine. I get the point. OK. Very good. The question here: 'Did you have teachers who were an important influence?' The answer is yes. At many levels. I always remember the teacher of philosophy in the Gymnasium . . . I had a teacher of philosophy who was a very bright person, who had an enormous influence on my life at a time when I was uncertain about a lot of things. I knew I had a great interest in the mind and I wanted to study issues that had to do with human behaviour and I thought I might want to be a philosopher. And he said, 'No, what you really want to become is a neurologist.' He was the person who opened my eyes to the possibility of studying the brain in order to get to the mind. So I think that was a great influence.

• *And who was this person?*
A person by the name of Joel Serrao and he was a philosopher himself. One great thing in those days with education in places like Portugal was that actually the teachers we had, to be fair, were generally people who could not be in universities because there were so few universities. So you had absolutely superb professors who were themselves investigators of some kind or philosophers in this case. So that was a great influence and I had numerous important influences

in my early career, some in Portugal and some in the United States. In the United States, the main one is Norman Geschwind, who was a professor of neurology.

• *I did a degree at Oxford in psychology and philosophy. We had to study Geschwind and Gazzaniga.*
Geschwind was a very early influence on me. That's a more mature influence in the sense that I was already in medical school and I learned about Geschwind. Then he was a very strong determinant because, had I not read and met Geschwind, I might have done neuro-physiology, which was what I was beginning to do. Geschwind allowed me to combine my interest in human beings with my interest in science in one fell swoop, and that was very important to me.

• *Did you go to Iowa or somewhere else?*
Actually my research career started with a fellowship with Norman Geschwind in Boston. That was 1967, which will date me horribly but that's the truth.

• *But you look very youthful in the photograph on the cover of* Looking for Spinoza.
Well, I try to look youthful.

• *You obviously remain, by the standards of Anglo-Saxon science, very influenced by European philosophers. I mean, you've written* Descartes' Error *and* Looking for Spinoza.
I don't know if it has to do with my European background. Let's put it this way. First of all, I think that an interest in philosophy is a very important one for the very simple reason that the questions that we are interested in today as scientists, especially in the science of the mind, are questions that have been part of the agenda of philosophy for two thousand years. So I think it's very important for one to try to go back as often as possible to early thinkers and try to measure up what you're doing against what they were trying to do. It's a very general interest. It's like a discipline for what you should be doing, things that you should be reminded of. The interest in Descartes arose very naturally because Descartes is a constant reference in neuro-science. He is, in fact, almost the only reference to philosophy in neuro-science. At the time, I had no idea that I would ever write something that embraced Spinoza. That came later on. It's interesting because most people believe that I had this incredible game plan ten years ago or 12 years ago that would allow me to start with Descartes and end with Spinoza. There was no such thing. Spinoza arose very organically and he arose by my realizing that Spinoza is the philosopher that in outline is closest to what I think

on the issue of mind–body relationships and the issue of emotions. And the fact is he is not a reference in neuro-science.

• *I was taught Spinoza by a very distinguished philosopher by the name of Anthony Quinton. I don't know if the name means anything to you.*
When were you at Oxford?

• *I left in 1968, so that dates me too.*
I know that Stewart Hampshire who wrote his book on Spinoza in the early sixties was a rather unusual figure in that he really talked about Spinoza. I don't think people were that interested. Certainly, in the United States, people had no interest in Spinoza. I'm told now that it's changing. On the continent, it's different, I think. The French, the Germans and Italians, the Dutch, of course, have always been very interested in Spinoza. That tells me why I was very interested. So your next question. 'How much have technical advances in the methods of brain research like M.R.I. helped change ideas about the brain, about feelings and consciousness?' I think they have helped. I think that it would be impossible to have the evolution of ideas that we have had without some of the facts that came out of research using those technologies. On the other hand, I don't think that technology is the only motor. I think that facts lead to changes in the neurological perspective and those are just as important. So you really have very good new facts that come out of new technology, which you would not get otherwise. And then there's a theoretical process that visits and revises former ideas and thus produces something by itself. What I'm trying to say is that it's not the facts alone. It's the facts digested and interpreted by a theoretical perspective that are the engine of our scientific progress. So, without a doubt, the new technologies have been very important. Perhaps the most important has been the availability of structural imaging of the brain, then the functional imaging. I think this tends to be a little bit lost because there are so many pretty pictures that are published in science pages everywhere that come out of the current functional imaging. The fact is that the real leap forward came from the ability to image the living brain with things like the CT-scanner and then the MR-scanner. And it was studies done with lesions that permitted us to get the first ground map of brain systems in relation to different mental functions.

• *So did the structural images therefore make it possible to pinpoint the lesions?*
Yes. In the old days . . . It's very interesting because the lesion method dates back to the 19th century.

- *M. Broca?*

M. Broca and Mr Wernicke. Of course, those were always studies done at autopsy. And what became completely novel – it's quite amazing because this is only in the late '70s – was the possibility of finding out where a lesion is, in the life of the patient, and doing concurrent experimental studies of the individual and knowing where the lesion is at that time. So, literally, more than a hundred years have to go by until we get the proper facilities.

- *Whatever happened to Wilder Penfield's work?*

It's very interesting work and I use it all the time. As you probably saw from my books, I cite him all the time. It's like a burst of energy that occurs in the late forties and early fifties, curiously very much together with a desire to understand consciousness. And then the whole thing tapers out. I think it was one of those approaches that was so tied with the energy of a single man that once he retired, the entire thing collapsed. Curiously, it's now coming back in a new version. So the same way you can say that the lesion method was rescued by Geschwind in the sixties and then miraculously revitalized by the new technologies of brain imaging, you can say that Penfield disappeared for a short period and now there are new techniques of recording from the human brain, there are a handful of neurological surgeons who are following in his footsteps. For example, we have a wonderful neurosurgeon here in Iowa, a man called Matthew Howard, who is doing very beautiful recordings in living patients. But, of course, this is now done with incredible sophistication with the full participation of the patients. And the setting is still the same: studying patients who are being evaluated for epilepsy surgery. The big difference is in the techniques. It's not so much the stimulation side as in Penfield but the recordings of potentials from the cerebral cortex from different nuclei with very remarkable sophistication.

- *What made you interested in Phineas Gage?*

There is a little background in philosophy here. Both my wife and I became interested in Phineas Gage because he represents the first case in which we can find a relationship between a disturbance of social behaviour and one specific area of the brain. The damage was, of course extremely gross and one has to use anecdotal evidence to get evidence of the changes he suffered. But after the crowbar went through his skull and frontal lobes the man was no longer Phineas Gage. He changed from being responsible and upstanding to being rather lax. The man who described Phineas Gage was John Martyn Harlow and he was very perceptive and put two and two together. He called attention to the fact that there was a connection between the brain and social behaviour. It has to be said that there are plenty of Phineas Gages walking around today and being studied.

• *Where are we in terms of thinking about the frontal lobes?*
I have never thought of my research in terms of lobes, but in terms of themes. And there are two or three important themes linked to frontal lobes. One is that of the emotional . . . a section of the frontal lobes is critical for the development of social skills. The frontal lobes are also critical for reasoning, decision making and creativity. So the research on frontal lobes is taking us to an understanding of decision making and the interaction of emotions and decision making and creativity.

• *I was surprised to find that lobotomy, the removal of the frontal lobes, was not mentioned in* Looking for Spinoza?
There are references to that in *Descartes' Error*. My view is that lobotomy was a very objectionable version of an operation called prefrontal leucotomy, which was developed by Moniz. Moniz won the Nobel Prize in 1935, but his contribution was more than prefrontal leucotomy. He also developed cerebral angiography, which was the critical diagnostic method for understanding what was going on in the brain for 80 years. Leucotomy was in a way a stroke of genius and way ahead of its time and way ahead of the technology, because it was a stroke of genius to believe you could intervene on the brain to relieve human suffering. But the methods available then were too gross to allow the method to succeed. You have to remember that at the time there were no antipsychotic drugs. Patients used to be restrained in straitjackets. You had incredible methods of dealing with the deeply disturbed such as insulin shock. The treatments that were available were crude and cruel. Against that background you have to accept that Moniz brought profound relief to a number of people who suffered from psychosis and from obsessive-compulsive disorder.

• *But the lobotomy story was not so noble perhaps?*
From Moniz to the United States where the business is business. Freeman and Watts developed a much grosser operation than prefrontal leucotomy. This was a gross operation using an ice pick of a knife that was used in an indiscriminate manner. The result was that an intervention, which had been careful though bold, became something of a runaway business. That gave it a bad name. In the perspective of time it did still succeed in some cases. And there is another question. Admittedly these operations did cause damage to the brain but we have no idea of the damage that is being caused by drugs. To imagine that you can take Prozac, say, for 20 years and that this causes no damage or changes to the brain is innocent. The prefrontal leucotomy and even the lobotomy to some extent was ahead of its time. I would be very surprised if in the next few years we did not see very selective intervention. Something very similar is happening in the

treatment of Parkinson's with the making of small lesions and the placing of electrodes in the brain that act as a kind of pace maker. My prediction is that we will see in the next few years more and more interventions of the same type as Moniz pioneered with prefrontal leucotomy.

• *You seem to have been deeply influenced by William James? His theory of the emotions if I remember right was that the brain notices how the body is respond-ing – say adrenaline is pulsing – and it concludes I'm happy or sad . . .*
Until I brought Spinoza into the equation he was my hero and he continues to be my hero. Why? Because he saw that feeling is our take on what happens in the body. William James is not complete however – and why should he be when he was working 100 years ago. What I have done with William James is to create some alternative paths, the 'as if' body loop. This allows the body to be bypassed, if you like but for messages to still be generated 'as if' the body had been involved. The simple William James story is too basic. My contribution is to say what you feel is the result of perceiving what is in the brain's body maps. Happiness, sorrow and other emotions can be simulated from within the brain. You don't need to go through the body.

• *Can you explain how you distinguish between feelings and emotions?*
When I try to make a distinction between feelings and emotions, it is not a pedantic distinction but it is something I need as a research strategy. Once I have a hypothesis, I need to have this distance between the process where the brain evaluates a stimulus and the body maps. Emotions are public phenomena that are quantifiable and measurable in theory at least.

• *Because you can measure the physiological changes in the body?*
Then the next phase is the brain's perceptions of those changes and also of the object or stimulus that caused them. And that is the body map. But the distinc-tion is that even all that does not allow us to experience the feeling. It is even possible that in the next few years we will be able to look at a pattern of brain activity and say that the pattern is happiness but that will not mean that I can experience the happiness you feel. Feelings remain private and inaccessible to anyone else.

• *Can you explain what a somatic marker means and how it functions in terms of your thinking?*
Perhaps the best instance of what I mean by a somatic marker is when you think of having a gut feeling. You are thinking of how to go next, when you are rea-soning or trying to make a choice, there is a signal which you prefer one choice

or another. In making that kind of choice you have reasoning and you have the past and you have your formal analysis but we also have an automated system that guides in one direction or another. That allows us to operate faster – not better – because we often make wrong decisions when we use this system. But this mechanism of the somatic marker helps with the process.

• *And even with the processing? I mean of information . . .*
Our decisions are the results not only of knowledge and reason but also of past emotional history. This is an impulse that is not conscious – like the gut feeling which tells us not to do something.

• *Is this very like Robert Zajonc's notion of hot cognitions, which for example show that what we feel about someone happens very fast and then goes on to affect how we judge them?*
Zajonc was pointing to something like that, yes.

• *Does that mean we should replace Descartes' cogito ergo sum with I* feel *therefore I exist.*
Yes indeed.

• *Did you meet much resistance to your work because it does mark a departure from classic Anglo-American attitudes?*
It was not a question of resistance. Not at all. My wife and I started doing a lot of work on language and memory and that was very well received. I have no complaints and it was received pretty much the same way in Europe as in America. In the 1980s I made a shift towards studying the frontal lobe and the links with emotions. I felt I had to. To develop the somatic marker hypothesis I had to immerse myself in emotions. People thought I was crazy to be studying the frontal lobes and the emotions. They felt I was going off the deep end but then when I published my work, the reaction was extremely positive. Neuroscience had turned round to the emotions after a long period of neglect. People in other fields are interested in emotions. I have had some contact with economists who are very interested in the question of how emotions affect investment.

• *I did once write a book called* Fear, Greed and Panic – the psychology of the stock market *and it is hard to shift people from those three as explanations for all stock market behaviour.*
That seems rather stupid. [Damasio laughed and asked if I would send him a copy of the book.]

• *Can I return to the question of resistance?*

The more productive people are the more they know how little they know. Our knowledge of the brain is pathetically inadequate given the complexity of the brain. You're not there. We're not there. To think we should not be pretty humble is strange indeed.

Chapter 4: Hans Eysenck

The first time I interviewed the late Hans Eysenck – rated No. 4 in the list of all time psychology greats according to the British Psychological Society poll – I was writing a profile of him for *Penthouse*. In 1972, *Penthouse* did porn with pretension. They were interested in Eysenck's controversial views on race, IQ and sex.

Over the years I interviewed Eysenck a number of times. He was always very polite in a way I found familiar. My mother's family came from central Europe too and oozed that same, sometimes slightly unctuous, politeness. But Eysenck was very different in one way. My central European relatives were usually timid. It wouldn't do to upset the British or the authorities who had so kindly allowed them into the Sceptred Isle. Displease the Queen and she could have you back in Dracula-land before you could say sorry. Eysenck had none of this deference.

In 1992, Eysenck had retired and I went to see him in his office, a flat on a grim grey estate close to the Institute of Psychiatry. Wryly – and he liked wry – he said this was the less than gracious way English institutions treated their old professors!

Eysenck has always been something of an ideological issue in himself. He was said to be very cold. I found him friendly but distant. He talked about his work, his ideas, his critics but little about himself. When I first asked him about his feelings when research went well, there was a flicker of surprise as if it were odd to be asked so personal a question.

In the last 20 years of his life Eysenck changed. He published an autobiography, *Rebel with a Cause* (1990), a typically belligerent title. In many ways, the autobiography turned out to be more revealing than expected. Eysenck tried hard to explain his motives and was honest. Yet, when I had finished it, I felt he hadn't revealed either what motivated him or, perhaps the most interesting of all, what often made him a formidable controversialist, sometimes for unpopular causes.

Escaping from Germany, Eysenck argued, made him hostile to any kind of censorship. His experiences under real fascism made him despise the agitprop left in the 1960s and 1970s who called British or American Conservatives fascists. Eysenck had seen real fascists at work. The Nazis killed ideological opponents. And the pain was very personal. He could not bear to see films that deal with the concentration camps. His grandmother died in one.

Eysenck could be funny about being a foreigner in Britain. In 1938, the Hungarian humourist George Mikes described, in *How to Be an Alien*, how the Brits thought all foreigners mad, bad and dangerous to know. Mikes added that Continentals have a sex life while the British have hot-water bottles. The young Eysenck was a true Continental. He had a lot of girlfriends. Eysenck was once accused of having lascivious thoughts because he flirted with a fellow student. If he had been an English student, he was told, he would have been expelled from London University. But he was a foreigner and they let him off, telling him he had not had the benefit of a proper upbringing with, presumably, lashings of hot-water bottles!

Eysenck's England was not kind to him. At the start of the war he was classed as an enemy alien. The only work he could get was as an air-raid warden. After six months, he was sent for by Sir Aubrey Lewis who worked at the Maudsley Hospital. Lewis wanted to develop clinical psychology and recruited Eysenck.

Even here, Eysenck was combative: he disagreed with the powerful Sir Aubrey. He argued psychologists should do more than just assess patients for psychiatrists. This led to bitter quarrels, especially when Eysenck developed some of the ideas about behaviour therapy which implied psychologists should treat patients. Total impertinence, barked Sir Aubrey and the psychiatrists. In the end, Eysenck won and he was right. Psychiatry is too complex to be left just to psychiatrists!

Eysenck could be marvellously cool at surveying his opponents with amused, but a little condescending, reasonableness. A nice example was the way he remained bewildered by psychoanalysts. Why did they cling so stubbornly to their faith in a technique that didn't work? He explained to me that it was a psychoanalyst, Alexander Herzberg, who first gave him the idea for behaviour therapy. Herzberg had used some techniques very like those that became behaviour therapy to speed up analysis but did not ask if it wasn't these techniques themselves which healed – and not analysis itself. Eysenck seemed startled when I suggested that maybe life-long womb-to-tomb analysts just could not ask themselves that question.

Eysenck could always turn in a good wounding phrase, so his sweet reasonableness could be infuriating. Eysenck explained the hostility he aroused differently. As a personality theorist he upset most experimental psychologists who perform experiments on perception, memory, verbal skills, learning, not to mention dart throwing, without ever considering whether personality might affect the results. All humans should behave in the same way. Just like molecules.

But extroverts and introverts learn and even throw darts very differently, Eysenck argued.

Eysenck believed he also offended the oh-so-sensitive romantic personality theorists. Personality was, for him, a matter of data, statistics and factor analysis, of performing complex operations on the data. He had little truck with understanding, in some grandiose sense, the personality of other people. Theorists like Carl Rogers offended him because they suffered from delusions of insight. They lacked rigour, he said. They biffed back he was insensitive or superficial, or plain wrong.

In debate Eysenck could be savage. He believed people did not want to find out the truth in a reasonable way. They preferred to think they knew it all, or to guess, or to just go on as they always did. Not a scientific attitude. In the ten years before his death, however, Eysenck fought for what seem to be some strange research results – studies of astrology, sunspots and vitamin C – but on exactly the same grounds.

The war changed Eysenck's career. As a young man he wanted to be a physicist. When he had to leave Germany for London, he found that impossible. A series of accidents then forced him into psychology. One of his main aims, he insisted, was to make psychologists realise that unless they adopted the model of the natural sciences, psychology was doomed. The truth may be uncomfortable as in the case of race, IQ and heredity but you must discover what it is before you can take remedial action. Too many of his fellow psychologists were too willing to skive away from the truth and preferred to avoid the risk of finding it out.

Eysenck claimed the race and IQ controversy of the 1970s made him "a devil for our times" and the topic was an example of where psychologists preferred not to find out. When Arthur Jensen published his results showing black Americans had lower IQs, Eysenck supported him. Eysenck always claimed that it was wrong to pillory Jensen. They were merely reporting the data. Eysenck stressed, however, he never supported William Shockley who wanted to see those with inferior IQ sterilized. Eysenck told me that he had been privately supported by many geneticists who were scared of speaking out in public.

But Eysenck never confronted one fact. Those who see themselves as the discoverers – and defenders – of unpopular truths sometimes revel in it. Arthur Jensen had a certain tendency to cast himself as Galileo persecuted by the politically correct. Nevertheless Eysenck defended Jensen totally.

Eysenck also had to deal in the 1970s with the Cyril Burt scandal. In the interview, Eysenck reveals it's likely that Burt did make up some of the data on twins and intelligence. But he thinks there is now so much other data supporting the hypothesis that identical twins have much more similar IQs than fraternal twins that Burt's forgeries do not really matter.

In the late 1970s and 1980s Eysenck took up two unlikely causes. The first was the work of Michel Gauquelin. He was a French psychologist and statistician who argued an extraordinary hypothesis with some effect. Gauquelin studied the position of the planets at birth and correlated these positions with famous and less famous people in various professions. Famous sportsmen tended to be born when Mars had either just risen above the horizon or was at its high point in the sky. The statistical correlation was amazing. In most psychology studies, if there is one chance in a hundred that the correlations might be obtained by chance, it is a strong result. With the Mars effect, there was one chance in 5 million the results might be due to chance. There were also correlations between birth when Jupiter and Saturn were in those positions and success in other professions like politics, medicine and acting.

Scientists were outraged by Gauquelin as just another occult conman and then increasingly tried to discredit his data. Eysenck checked his data, found they stood up and joined in various efforts to pursue this puzzle. I knew Gauquelin well and he spoke very highly of the support that Eysenck gave him and his wife. It wasn't easy to do that. Many organizations, like the Committee for the Investigation of Paranormal Phenomena, did their best to prove the Gauquelins made up their data. "But the results could be replicated", Eysenck told me. It needed to be studied.

Eysenck did his most original work on behaviour therapy, which derives its techniques from learning theory and in the mapping of the three dimensions of personality, *extraversion–introversion, neuroticism* and *psychoticism*. The dimensions he used were put forward since the time of Galen in the 2nd century AD. But Eysenck argued he made these dimensions rigorous. He studied large samples and used sophisticated analysis. The dimensions made connections between various kinds of traits of behaviour or personality and, crucially, they allowed predictions to be made: they promoted not just psychological research but research in other scientific disciplines. "Most psychological problems transcend psychology", as Eysenck has put it. Psychology is not pure.

Eysenck wrote (1970a, p. 406): "Genetics, physiology, neurology, anatomy and biochemistry are all implicated in our attempt to account for individual differences in neuroticism and extraversion. It will be clear that this is not the end of the chain." He added that "the distinctions between psychology, physiology, genetics and other biological specialities are man-made to serve administrative and other practical purposes, but have no counterpart in nature."

As a would-be physicist and a psychologist, it is not surprising that Eysenck should believe psychology has to be scientific. But he also argued psychologists were naive innocents, they had an idealized notion of how the physical sciences worked. He described the discovery of the planet Neptune as "a mixture of genuine deduction from established scientific law, chance, error, luck and farce". The discovery depended on the fact that at the time the astronomers looked for it, Neptune was in a part of its orbit where the quite erroneous calculations predicted it would be. But, the textbooks usually describe its discovery as a model of logical scientific deduction after the orbit of Uranus turned out to have perturbations in it. Real research wasn't so neat.

Eysenck, also rather surprisingly, derided the mania for prediction. Often, he said, an experiment in which the predictions fail does not mean that work is useless. Newton himself had failures of deduction and, in places, found it necessary to invoke the interference of God in order to rescue his theory. That probably wouldn't carry much weight with the editor of the *Journal of Experimental Psychology* but trying to ape physics could be damaging. Psychology threw out good new ideas too easily.

Eysenck always felt obliged to do some research which would be useful rather than interesting to himself. Behaviour therapy is for him the chief example of that. He did the work in order to repay his debt to a society that gave him the time and money to "pursue his fancies". The phrase "pursue his fancies" does suggest more of a curiosity about human behaviour than he ever explicitly admitted. It is also interesting that he should admit great surprise when any of his predictions do happen to work out. But, as he pointed out, he made no claim to insight. He suspected those who rely on their self-declared insight. At precisely the intuitive level that he would condemn, this seems to fit in with one of the remarks in the interview when he explains that when his research goes well, he feels, most sensually, like the cat who has had the cream and, as he does when he listens to Brahms' Violin Concerto and knows "this is good".

The change in political mood since the 1960s and 1970s made Eysenck much less of a demon figure to students. Nevertheless, he continued to have his difficulties with the media. In 1990, he was involved with Nobel Laureate Linus Pauling in what should have been unexceptional research on the effects of diet on IQ, which looked at the effect of giving a supplement of vitamins and minerals to children. The children in the study were given vitamins and minerals for three months and their IQ improved quite dramatically; a year on the results held.

Eysenck was surprised it proved impossible to get the funding to pursue these findings. No one seemed interested in trying to give these vitamin and mineral supplements to "poor children from deprived inner-city areas". They couldn't raise the funds for what seemed an obvious idea. Proof again that many people don't really want to know.

In his autobiography Eysenck warned the reader not to be too disappointed by his lack of insight. It's unfair to expect psychologists to know and explain themselves better than other people. Policemen and prostitutes, Eysenck laments, are often better at psychology in the heat of the moment. It's a curious modesty. You spend your life trying to understand what makes people behave in a certain way and, yet, faced with the muddles and conflicts of the everyday, you shrug and say "Actually cops and whores do it better".

• *How did you become a psychologist?*
It was an accident really. I had really always been interested in becoming a research physicist. When I had to leave Germany, I tried to get into the University of London and I was told I would have to sit an examination. The subjects it was easiest for me to do were Latin, French, German, English and maths and when I presented myself to register for the physics courses, I was told I had taken the wrong subjects for that. The University of London was terribly bureaucratic. I asked what I could do about it. They said I could come back next year and present the right subjects. But I didn't have the money to do that, so I asked if there wasn't any scientific subject that I could take. 'Yes', they said, 'psychology'. And I said, 'What on earth is psychology?' I'd never heard of it. So I became a psychologist. It took me a long time to get over the shock.

• *In much of your work you criticize the unscientific approach of much psychology. Would you have preferred to deal with the certainties of physics?*
In many ways, yes, I would have preferred that. On the other hand, I think that my particular gifts are more needed, shall we say, in psychology than in physics. There are a lot of very good physicists but few psychologists who have the proper scientific background. In psychology, one finds that one has to spend half one's time making it clear to people that problems should be attacked in a scientific manner rather than in a political, social or philosophical or existential manner or whatever. And that is very time-consuming.

• *Professor David McClelland told me that he thinks many psychologists turned to psychology in reaction to a very fundamental religious upbringing. Did you have such an upbringing?*
No. Religion was not much mentioned. My father was a Lutheran but pretty sceptical about it. My mother was a Catholic who never did much about it. My grandmother, who was the person who really brought me up, later became a very devout Catholic and died in a concentration camp which shows, of course, how strong religious feelings can be. But that was not true of the way I was brought up.

• *Were there any major influences on you as you worked towards becoming a psychologist?*

Cyril Burt was my professor. He was a very important influence. I think he was probably the most intelligent person I ever met – very knowledgeable. I was very fortunate to be in his department because it was the only department that really laid stress on the mathematics, statistics and psychometrics that were needed for a scientific approach. Burt had a great influence. People say that I am just his pupil and so go on with the same kind of stuff. But this is quite untrue. My natural reaction to anybody is to try and oppose it, to find the weaknesses in it. It is because I couldn't find the weaknesses in it, in his general theory – I found many weaknesses in particular but the general teaching he gave is, I think, pretty invulnerable – that I took it over. Not because I was his student, but in spite of being his student.

Spearman was another influence. I met him at some lectures. I found his book *The Abilities of Man* (1927) just the kind of thing I was looking for, the application of proper scientific methods to psychological material. The other person was Pavlov, whom I never met, of course, but who showed me there is a way to attack these problems biologically. Neither Burt nor Spearman were very biologically oriented. I found Pavlov's approach refreshing. It was these two general directions – the psychometric and the biological – that were the most important.

• *What was your early work in?*

I did quite a lot of things at the beginning on different lines. I did some work on the effects of hypnosis. The problem that interested me was this. People had claimed, and there seemed to be experimental evidence, that under hypnosis people can do things way above what they can do usually. Perception was said to be better. People could do muscular work better and for longer. I found that all hypnosis could do was abolish pain and the sense of pain. So, you could abolish the sense of pain, the sense of muscular fatigue and get people to carry on longer. But the hypnotized subjects did no better than a well-motivated, non-hypnotized one on a whole set of tasks.

• *You were also interested in aesthetics, weren't you?*

Yes, especially the degree to which people agree in their assessment of the beauty and attractiveness of certain things. I made some statistical investigations and I found that you can get a more precise judgement by asking more people. If you ask one person to rank a hundred pictures in terms of which is more beautiful, he won't be very accurate. But if you ask a hundred people, then their average order of rank of beauty will be very similar to that of another group of a hundred people. And I devised a formula which indicates how many judges you need to produce agreement between groups of judges. I was also interested in the sense of humour idea. You know how all nationalities – the French, the British, the German, the Americans – boast of their own particular sense of humour, as something very special. Well, I discovered that this very national view just didn't stand up.

• *Does this early work you did bear any relation to the work you later did on personality and IQ or was it just a question of using similar techniques again?*
I did things that interested me. It didn't concern my later work because that also came about by accident.

• *How did you, from studying aesthetics, hypnosis and humour, get into the field of clinical psychology?*
I was an enemy alien here in Britain and no one wanted to give me a job or take me into the army, though I tried very hard. Then I was appointed research psychologist at Mill Hill Emergency Hospital. It was highly fortuitous. A friend of mine, Philip Vernon, recommended me and I was accepted. I had no particular interest in mental abnormality or personality. I was more inclined, in fact, to psychometrics and learning theory, in the experimental study of various things rather than in such a nebulous area but . . . one has to live and I made a living by going into psychiatry.

• *Was your paper in 1952 in which you argued against the efficacy of psychotherapy and, particularly, psychoanalysis your first controversial one?*
Yes, my previous papers were quite well received, I think. But as they weren't controversial, there was nothing in them to really excite people. But when I came into this field of mental abnormality, I found a large number of things wrong in it. I have already mentioned the unreliability of diagnoses. When I looked into treatment I found there was no evidence for the efficacy of treatment either. In the war, I got a job at a psychiatric clinic dealing with people who had war neuroses. One of the things that needed doing was to prepare tests that would distinguish between different diagnostic categories. So, it was important to know how reliably these diagnostic categories were assessed by the psychiatrists. So, I went to the head of the Unit and asked to check what the diagnoses had been for patients who had been treated by different doctors at different times. I wanted to compare these. He took me aside in a fatherly fashion and asked if there weren't any more important things to do or that I wanted to do. Everything possible was done to discourage, and even stop, me. When I looked into treatment I found there was no evidence for the efficacy of treatment either. This was just accepted on personal hearsay, on what people

believed or had been taught – but not on any evidence. And when I looked at
the kinds of test that were used to assess psychiatric patients' state of mind, like
Rorschach tests and projection tests, I found there was no evidence you could
do anything with such tests. I took a sample of 50 highly neurotic patients and
50 normals who were alike in terms of age, sex, class and so on. They were all
given a Rorschach test by one expert and then their Rorschachs were sent to
another expert. All I asked him to do was to sort them out into which had been
done by normals and which by neurotic patients. I found that he could do no
better than chance. The same went for another Rorschach expert. Now, if you
can't even find out from such a test whether a person is severely neurotic or
normal, what can you do with it? That was very controversial then, but it is
widely recognised now.

Then Professor Aubrey Lewis, chief professor of psychiatry at the Maudsley,
wanted to start a profession of clinical psychology in this country and wanted
me to do it. So, I went to the USA to see what American practices were like and
I became very disenchanted. I had to decide what needed to be done and it
seemed to me that one needed to have a proper clinical psychology based, not on
psychoanalysis, but on experimental psychology which would give us a proper
system of diagnosis, a proper system of mental assessment, a proper system of
therapy. The first stage was to write a series of critical papers like the 1952 one.
At the same time, I was working towards the more positive aspects, creating a set
of tests that could be used for personality assessment in psychiatric testing and
developing adequate methods of treatment which I called behaviour therapy.

• *You know, of course, that there have been a number of criticisms of your 1952
paper such as that spontaneous remission is a myth you invented and that the
statistics you based your case on came from life insurance companies. Did you
ever feel you had to modify your conclusions?*
If you look at the criticisms, I think you will find that most of them, a dozen or
so, didn't criticize what I said at all but what they might have liked me to have
said. What I said in that paper was that there was no evidence that psychotherapy of any kind produced any effects greater than those of spontaneous remission. What they criticized was a statement I never made, namely, that
psychoanalysis and psychotherapy were ineffective. I never said that. You can't
demonstrate a negative. I never claimed that. But the evidence for efficacy is
poor, the statistics are poor and the descriptions are insufficient. One would not
normally deal with evidence of that kind but as it was all the evidence there was,
it didn't prove anything whatsoever. Most of the criticisms rather viciously
attacked the material I had collected but I said I was aware of its insufficiency
but it was all there. So that if you accept these criticisms, my general conclusion

still stands, there isn't anything like evidence of the effects of psychotherapy because the evidence is not sufficient.

• *And what about spontaneous remission? Is that a myth?*
As regards the question of spontaneous remission, one or two people have credited me with creating a myth which is without any truth. The evidence for it is now much better than in 1952. It has been reviewed by S. Rachman in his book on the effects of psychotherapy where he comes to the conclusion, after very carefully looking at the evidence, that my original conclusions both as to the effect of psychotherapy and to the existence of spontaneous remission cannot be modified. Later evidence supports what I argued. So, I would say, it is still true and better supported now.

• *Why do you think that psychology is so unscientific in its general approach?*
There are a number of reasons. In the first place, people have always been interested in psychological problems, problems of motivation, problems of attitude, problems of changing people's behaviour and, round all these problems, a number of disciplines have grown up. Penologists, educationalists, psychiatrists, who all, without any scientific background, have accumulated what they consider to be expertise. So they think they know the answers where, in fact, they know nothing at all. So, they vehemently oppose anyone who wishes to study the subject on a scientific basis. Take what I described happened to me when I was a raw young experimental psychologist who wanted to look at diagnostic consistency. After that and my 1952 paper, people were terribly upset and I was practically shunned and exorcised in psychiatric and clinical circles. Now the message has got through and many will accept my criticisms as true statements of fact. Many people even want to do something about it. And there are now experiments that show that behaviour therapy does better than spontaneous remission or psychotherapy. So, there has been a change.

But, in education for instance, there has not been much of a change. You still get these silly swings from one enthusiasm to another, without any demonstration that what you're doing now is any better than what you did before. Often, people don't even try to document what they are doing so that later it might be possible to say if it was or wasn't effective. People seem to be afraid to put their ideas to the test. And that, of course, is just what the scientist wants to do.

• *When you work as a scientist on a problem, do you use your intuition or do you proceed in a very mechanical way, step by step?*
It's a difficult question to answer because I'm not sure what you mean by intuition or how one would recognize it. I would put it this way. That one of the

traits in my make-up that has helped me to do work in science is an ability to recognize important problems. I take in what many people just let go as unimportant or irrelevant.

• *Do you feel that this ability to isolate the problem is a very key one – especially with so much information and experimentation being produced now?*
I think it is. We have over two hundred PhD students here. The thing that impresses me even about the very bright ones is that they're very good at applying the methods they have learned. Many of them know more statistics than I do and many of them are very good at manipulating apparatus and writing programs for the computer. The thing they fall down on is looking for the right question to ask. They go for the things that are popular and are considered interesting but that are really of no importance at all. The same is true of most of the papers that I read in the journals. In ten years' time no one will remember them because they are not addressing themselves to important questions.

• *But can you define what it is that makes you see a problem as important?*
I try to define it in seminars and I try to do it by giving students examples, by telling them what kind of thing to look out for. It's really the unexpected, the odd, that you can't explain within a framework easily. For instance, I got started in behaviour therapy in that way. I was not concerned with that problem at all. I had just finished my degree and I met a German psychiatrist, Alexander Herzberg, who was writing a book on active psychotherapy. He was Freudian, very Freudian. But he was impressed with the fact that Freudian analysis was slow and he wanted to speed it up because that was the only way to make it accessible to many people. What he did was set his patients tasks. For instance, if someone was homebound and afraid to go out, he would give treatment as an analyst and say then, 'Go to the door and look out, then go two steps to the right, two steps to the left and then back again.' Next time, it would be five steps. And so on. And he found when he did this that his patients did get better much more quickly than before. He allowed me to sit in at meetings which he had with other refugee German psychiatrists who discussed their cases. They all agreed it was a useful method. The thing that occurred to me immediately was that there was no evidence that psychoanalysis played any part at all in this. Was it not possible that the tasks by themselves produced the improvement? There was evidence that analysis helped. You could account for the improvement in learning theory terms through extinction. So that was the beginning of my notion of behaviour therapy. It was typical that none of the others saw in this anything, except a slightly useful adjunct to analysis, whereas it was important because here you had a comparison of psychoanalysis with tasks and psycho-

analysis without tasks. It was much better with the tasks and there was no evidence it was any use without the tasks.

• *But, of course, you could allow yourself to see that. You were not committed to psychoanalysis.*
No – and that reason is, of course, very important. These people had spent their lives training and working in it. It was their livelihood. I can see that.

• *How did you become interested in problems of personality?*
I had been interested in personality from the time I came into the psychometric field. It seemed obvious that it was a central area and it raised a number of problems. For instance, are the differences between normal and neurotic people differences of category, are they different in some fundamental way or are they simply differences of degree so that neurotics are simply more neurotic, farther along a dimension which 'normals' also share. I became interested in the statistical aspects of the problem.

• *And did the idea for your dimension of extraversion–introversion also come by isolating a particular problem as important?*
It's a theory that goes back a long way to Galen and Hippocrates and the theory of the humours. In various ways, quite a large number of people have put it forward. I was impressed with many of them but none of them used a method which could prove it. Consequently, you had a great variety of people saying something similar but you could not make a choice between them because there was no evidence. They were just saying it. From very good observation, no doubt, but you could not do much with it. Similarly with Jung, who relied on very good observation but had no idea of the implications of some of the things that he was saying. For instance, he said that at one end hysterics are inclined to be psychotics and also that extreme introverts were inclined to be psychotics. But that immediately implied a second dimension where the extremes are identical in some sense, a dimension different from neurotic. It was the kind of thing that is akin to the cycloid or schizoid put forward by Kretschmer. If at both extremes there were psychotic groups, then that implied there must be another dimension where these groups would find themselves at the same end. You had to turn the graphs round, so to speak. So I set about investigating the dimension of this field.

• *Do you believe that the dimensions of personality you have postulated are enough?*
I have no doubt there are more dimensions. It's just the very elementary beginning. We are working on psychoticism, the third dimension which I proposed

in 1952. I think these dimensions are, if not unique, at least different from other dimensions that have been put forward because they are so closely linked with physiological systems. Neuroticism is linked with the reticular formation and psychoticism with the androgen/oestrogen balance and endocrine balance but I'm sure that these three dimensions are not enough to encompass the whole of personality. I've never suggested this and I wouldn't believe it for a moment.

• *Is it difficult to explore personality from this point of view? You said once that you were left in the middle between the S–R psychologists, who ignored what goes on inside the organisms, and the murky depths of psychoanalysis, as you might call them. Do you still feel that?*
Very much so. On the one hand, you have experimental psychologists who go about their tasks in what they think is a functional way, and who traditionally look at what goes into the organism – the stimulus – and at what goes out – the response – without paying any attention to the actual organism. And on the other hand, you have the so-called 'depth' psychoanalysts who devote all their attention to the personality but do so in a completely unscientific way. Take, for example, the way that alcohol affects performance.

In some people it makes a difference; in others, it doesn't. When you average the whole, you must have a hypothesis that links the experiment with personality. And you must bear in mind the nature of the organism in any experiment, Without that, the whole thing is meaningless. Another example is the mouse because mice, too, have personality. Suppose you ask the question 'Is the activity of the mouse affected by alcoholic fumes?' It sounds a reasonable question but it is meaningless unless you specify what kind of mouse. This experiment has been done on six strains of mice. For two strains, it didn't make any difference. For two strains, it made them more active. For two strains, it made them much less active. How will you average out these results? They become meaningless.

• *Surely this raises a very difficult problem in psychology in general. If you have only a vast range of individual differences, how can you ever arrive at general laws? Will you not be left with laws about individual cases?*
I think you could make the same point about physics. There are now over 92 elements. Really, what it amounts to is that you can have a general law but you must recognize there are different types. The problem is not insoluble but it must be recognized. Psychology, experimental psychology, has not recognized it in the past but it is beginning to recognize it now. Kenneth Spence was one of the few psychologists to work along these lines but, outside this department, no one else is doing much. So I feel that, though I am an experimental psycholo-

gist, I look at it in a rather different way from most. I insist that we must introduce the organism into the general picture. On the other hand, I disagree completely with the usual personality theorists like the existentialists because they try to create a personality psychology that is not based on scientific evidence and that again is wrong. What we have to do is to look again at the concepts of experimental psychology and use these concepts as parameters to study individual differences in; for instance, one could do this with reactive inhibition, a leading concept in Hullian theory. What I have been trying to do is to combine personality and experimental psychology, which means sitting between two stools, which means you tend to get clobbered by both sides. But things are looking up. People are beginning to recognize the need for approaching problems this way.

• *You have been one of the great popularisers of IQ. So, you still feel that IQ is the only reliable guide to measure of general intelligence?*
Essentially, what I think is that the theory put forward by Burt in 1910 is right. Burt argued one was dealing with a hierarchical system at the top of which you have general intelligence and this comes into every intellectual activity. Below that, you have a number of specific factors, numerical, verbal, visual and so on, which involve general intelligence and a specific ability. This view goes beyond Spearman and is in line with Thurstone's later view. I know of no evidence to contradict it.

• *So, presumably, if you are satisfied with the status of IQ, it suggests that you still uphold the arguments put forward by Jensen and yourself on the grounds of race and IQ. That argument can't be criticised because IQ is not a good measure?*
I think that criticisms of that sort are quite beside the point. They rest on a misunderstanding and the evidence doesn't bear those criticisms out.

• *You sound as if some criticisms are justified?*
Oh yes – and I have criticized it myself. I think we are working now on attempts to improve on Jensen's work. What we are trying to do now is to improve his analysis, which is very fundamental. What people correlate are test scores on, say, a hundred items. You can get two people who both score 50 but when you look at the answer sheet, you see they have answered questions very differently. The point is that we usually simply count the number of correct responses, but people differ in the amount of time they spend on a problem. Some will never leave a problem undone. Some will quite happily move on. The whole behaviour is entirely different and to regard their score as identical just because they

both got the same number right is wrong. And, particularly, because it can be shown that the kinds of error you make correlate with personality. I think it is very important to take each item as the thing to be analysed. There are other points, such as how long does it take to get to a solution. We have found that you can analyse scores on IQ tests into three independent components – first, speed of mental function, second, error-checking mechanism and third, persistence and continuance. I think it is very important to find in which of these three – it may be only one, it may be all three – there are racial differences or class differences; and how these differences are related to achievement. I think Jensen's model has to be criticized but at a serious professional level and not at the level that people write it in popular journals where they are often inaccurate and demonstrate nothing except that they don't know what they are talking about.

- *The body of Jensen's work holds, in your opinion?*
What I'm suggesting is that there is a pattern. Just as the concept of the atom was once thought to require an indivisible atom and, later, the atom was split, so with IQ. Spearman and Burt thought the general factor of intelligence was unsplittable but we have shown that IQ can be split into these three components. More possibly, later.

- *If IQ is so effective, would you not expect to find some physiological differences between high and low IQ scorers?*
Yes, and we have found some basis in evoked potential of the EEG in which we have shown there are marked differences between the latencies of those evoked potentials. Basically, the quicker the response, the higher the IQ. The greater the amplitude of the evoked potential, also, the higher the IQ. There are quite high correlations between IQ and evoked potentials, correlations of about 0.6. We have also done work on evoked potentials in twins. In identical twins, we have shown that evoked potential patterns are almost the same. In other words, they are highly heritable. All these lines of work go to show that IQ is still a very valuable concept which has by no means been disproved.

- *As far as race and IQ go, do you feel concerned that Jensen's work and your work may be used for political ends and that its conclusions ought to have been more cautiously put forward?*
In the first place, I think from the scientific point of view you cannot fault Jensen. I know him very well. He spent two years here. He picked up his interest in the intelligence debate here and he is really very knowledgeable and scholarly. I don't think you will find anything to criticize in his factual statements. I think you want to read the fine print. He does not assert that American blacks

are inferior in IQ. He sums up the evidence that it is quite likely to be so. It is put that way – and not that it has been definitely established, and I think I would go along with that. Suppose you take a black boy and a white boy of superior IQ, say 120. You then test their siblings. The IQ measures of the siblings will regress to the mean but the interesting thing is that the white siblings will regress to the white mean and the black siblings will regress to the black mean. You cannot account in environmental terms for any differences in IQ, as the high IQ black boy has the same environment as his siblings and the high IQ white boy has the same environment as his siblings so that differences in regression to the mean must be due to genetic differences between the two. Heredity segregates the genes of the parents and re-combines them so you expect to get wide variations between siblings, which you get. Jensen's results are quite in accord with genetic principles but not with environmental ones.

• *Do you regret now having become involved in the controversy about race?*
In one sense, I very much regret it because one doesn't like to be painted as a sort of devil. Furthermore, it's made it impossible to talk to students on anything. On the other hand, I feel it as a sort of duty. Society is setting aside large sums of money for universities and scientists and laboratories. It has a right to expect one thing from scientists and that is the truth. That is why they are there. If you say, 'Well, I know the truth but I won't tell because it may be to my disadvantage', you are really breaking that bargain that you have with people as a whole. I feel scientists have no right to do that. If I happen to know more than anyone else on an interesting subject – and this subject is both interesting and important – then I must say what I know and to hell with the consequences.

• *And do you feel you have been fairly treated?*
I know I haven't been. [He smiles.] There are so many things that happened that are clearly to a pattern. Most of the people who have written and complained are, unfortunately, those who know nothing about the subject. I have not had one biologist in this field, a geneticist or a psychologist with expertise, who has pointed out a single error. Those people who pretend to find these errors are journalists, if you'll forgive my saying so, and people in greatly different fields. It's very bad. Even some scientific journals, so called, have adopted a policy of hostility and suppression. The *New Scientist*, for instance, had a review of Jensen's book by Stephen Rose who wrote a stinking review, irrelevant and inaccurate. I wrote a brief letter pointing this out. Rose and other people replied, all in a hostile manner. I thought by the law of averages some letters should be on my side. Then, I got a letter from Eliot Slater, one of the elder statesmen in this field, who said he had written a letter to the *New Scientist* in my defence but that

this had not been published. Practically every geneticist I know is on my side though many are afraid to say so.

• *Do you feel psychologists have a duty, then, to do work that is useful to society?*
No. I don't think that one should ever prescribe for other people what they should do or shouldn't do. I think that many psychologists are interested in pure science and the best of luck to them. It's an important thing for people to do. I'm glad people are doing it. I have a kind of . . . I'm not sure what . . . a sense of duty to repay society in some degree for the leisure it gives one and the chance to pursue one's fancies and so I feel that some of the work I do should be useful, at least. It would go a little way to repay society, which was why I worked in behaviour therapy, though it didn't wildly fascinate me, but it was useful. I don't think everyone else should feel that way. It's just a personal feeling.

• *You seem to be very insistent on a scientific approach to psychology and I wondered if you had been impressed at all by any of the work like Rhine's ESP work and Gauquelin's on astrology that suggests there may be more to Man than scientists have traditionally allowed?*
I have looked at the studies Gauquelin has done and was very impressed in the sense that they indubitably show some relation. They were checked by the Belgian Academy of Sciences who were pretty hostile and came to the same conclusion. The results that showed the saturnine temperament indicates scientists are in agreement with what psychologists have said for a long time. I find it very difficult to make anything of this. On the other hand, it would be unscientific to reject it out of hand. Most people working in the field have found scientists are introverted, so possibly introverted people will show the same kind of horoscope. ESP I am even more impressed with – particularly recent work like that of Schmidt using decay of radioactive material and recording by computer right and wrong choices so that there is no possibility of error. I am also impressed with the work on animals.

My own interest is that I suggested years ago on theoretical grounds that you would expect extraverts to be better at this than introverts. This is precisely what happens. Extraverts show ESP and introverts show negative ESP. But, again, there is no theoretical framework into which one can fit these things and my feeling is that the people who work in it are so much obsessed by the need to prove there is such a thing, they don't care about the kind of investigation that a normal scientist or normal psychologist would do. Take a simple instance. They have never shown the reliability of an ESP score and that's the first thing one would do with a score on a normal psychological test. The distribution of ESP in a normal population, no one has ever bothered with. I think that that's a mistake. And, as long as people go on like that, simply trying to show there is such a thing, which will never convince those people who don't want to believe it, we won't get much farther.

• *Do you think it will be accepted in the end, as a sound body of knowledge, so that 40 years from now, it will seem strange it was ever excluded? Rhine has been doing the work for 40 years now and we still treat it as something a bit sensational.*

I should imagine it will be in due course. In a way, it's rather like Mendel. His work was not accepted because it didn't fit into any theoretical framework. Biologists and botanists weren't interested. It may be similar. After all, 40 years is not such an awfully long time. It took Newton 40 years to be accepted by the French physicists. In the purview of science, it's not all that long when you bear in mind how unlikely it is in terms of current forms of scientific thinking. If Schmidt is right and people are able to predict this radioactive decay, it throws out immediately Heisenberg's indeterminacy principle and all sorts of ideas physicists place great stock on, so naturally they wouldn't want to believe it.

• *How does it feel when some research that you have been doing works out well?*

You feel like the cat who got the cream. It's very difficult to describe. It's a general pervasive feeling of goodness. You feel very pleased with all things. I, at least, always feel somewhat astonished that something I predicted came off. I always feel it's so unlikely that, when it does, it deserves a celebration. Yes, you feel pleased with yourself, pleased with nature, pleased with the world. It's a feeling, perhaps, like you get when you listen to Brahms' Violin Concerto. You know this really is good and that life is worth living and so on.

• *What do you think of the new evidence that suggests maybe Burt did falsify some data?*

I suggested that there should be a small group set up by the British Psychological Society but they didn't do that. Did Burt invent some of his data? On a judicial basis, I think one would have to say not proven. Personally, I think he did. He was not an experimenter. I received his hostility because I told him his statistics were admirable but his data were lousy. He paid no attention to that kind of criticism. But the verdict is definitely not proven. A great injustice has been done to psychology because of him. There is a lot of data that shows the role of heredity in intelligence.

• *What do you make of the Sternberg theory of practical intelligence which suggests that IQ is a very limited way of defining intelligence?*

There are three ways of defining intelligence. Sternberg highlights practical intelligence. If you look at how people do in everyday life, that is determined by intelligence, personality, past history. If you go to MENSA, most of them are very bright but not very successful. To identify intelligence and worldly success strikes me as absurd. The second definition is psychometric and the third way of defining intelligence is biological. The work with the Hendricksons is coming to the fore.

• *What progress do you think will happen here?*
We are hoping to use a PET scan to show that glucose uptake is lower in intelligent people. The hypothesis is that if you're bright you need less energy to solve the same problem.

• *How has the work on personality developed?*
First, situationism – Michel's, you remember – well no one pays any heed to it now. Traits are accepted. There is a vast body of work on the relationship between traits and psychophysiological variables. There are perhaps 200 studies of my factors – arousal being fundamental to extraversion and of the various biological traits that underlie psychoticism. There is enormous difference between the work then and the work now in terms of sophistication. There is more understanding, for example, of where to place electrodes so that they won't be swamped by irrelevant brain activity.

• *You've also been involved in work on nutrition?*
We tested a group of perfectly average normal kids. This was a study that involved the nutritionist John Yudkin and the Nobel Laureate Linus Pauling. The nutrition of the kids was OK. But half were given some vitamins and mineral supplements. There was after three months an 11-point rise in IQ. After a year, the rise was still there. If you can improve the IQ of city kids this is important. I was absolutely thunderstruck. Lions Pauling, the great advocate of vitamin C, was disappointed that it was not vitamin C that worked best but rather a mix of vitamins and mineral supplements. Raising the IQ of the most needy would surely be a good thing.

• *In* Decline and Fall of the Freudian Empire *(1986), you maintain your hostility to psychoanalysis?*
At the time, most psychiatric professionals would have been pro Freudian. There was behaviour therapy. But psychoanalysis is still in the public eye even though it clearly is discredited among professionals. And interestingly, by their own admission, most psychoanalysts now admit their current ideas bear little

relationship to Freud's original notions. Psychologists usually are from literary rather than scientific backgrounds so they still find the notion of testing a theory rigorously a bit foreign and, often, theories are lauded far above their value and negative results are ignored. No one pays any attention to them.

• *What do you make of Paul Kline's views? He is after all a distinguished psychometrician and especially in his recent* Psychology Exposed, *he argues there is much merit in Freudian ideas.*
I think Kline is much too favourable. The studies on repression, for example, are less in favour of psychoanalysis. And I think some of the ideas in *Psychology Exposed* came because he was going through a bad patch. There is also another problem. Psychology is ahistorical. Take reminiscence – 50 years before the theory was discovered, Kraeplin produced the theory but no one recognizes it.

• *Where do you think the Gauquelin data is now?*
I'd like to talk about the work of Professor Irtl of Goettingen. He reanalysed the data Michel Gauquelin had analysed. He analysed the data in ways that Michel had not. He reconfirmed the data about the eminence of sportsmen and the Mars effect. What was most convincing was difference of the sexes. A true Mars effect was even stronger for women.

• *Irtl has taken this even further?*
Irtl has looked at sunspots. He consulted 20 textbooks to establish what he calls the creativity of an era, looking at achievements in the arts and science. It's been a very thorough process and has yielded intriguing results, which may be related to Gauquelin's ideas. Irtl put forward the thesis that was, revolutions occur when there are lots of sunspots. Irtl looked at the Renaissance, which is after all taken as a period of high creativity and found there was a minimum of sunspots. That is also true for other periods. What is more, he found that there is a transcultural effect. During periods of high creativity in Europe, you have the same being true in China and in Arabia. It is an effect that seems to transcend a particular culture. It needs collaboration between astronomers, physicists and psychologists to study this phenomenon.

The last time I left Eysenck, I marvelled at his energy given his age. I was sure he would keep on being involved in controversies and that he would remain slightly surprised by the fact that it upset people. He died in 1997. It's a sign of his lasting reputation that he is ranked as the 4th most important psychologist of the 20th century in the British Psychological Society survey.

Chapter 5: John Flavell

You would think that one of the fundamental problems of psychology always was to track how children grew up, to follow the "how do we get from there to here" question. Strangely however, for much of the 20th century, child psychology was not so fashionable. The famous humanist therapist Carl Rogers, for example, started out doing interesting studies on deprived children in upstate New York in 1929 and, then, ten years later, switched to clinical psychology.

Some 25 years later John Flavell took the opposite course. I was keen to interview him for at least two reasons. First, developmental psychology has been one of the most important areas of the subject in the last 20 years and an exciting one as it becomes clear either that earlier psychologists underestimated what young children could manage or, else, that we are seeing children change as the culture changes. Flavell has been at the centre of this work. Second, and more frivolous, his best-known book helped me get through my exams. Flavell's *The Developmental Psychology of Jean Piaget* remains the best heavyweight exposition of the ideas of the Swiss psychologist who was a pioneer of developmental psychology and still dominates the subject.

Much of the work of Jean Piaget (1896–1980) was based on observing his own children – though very often it was his wife Valentine Chatenay who kept tabs on what the babies did and jotted down the observations. The Piaget children, Jacqueline (born 1925), Lucienne (born 1927) and Laurent (born 1931) were psychological subjects from the moment they were born. The modern discipline of cognitive child development is based to a rather surprising extent on how these three Swiss children grew up in a very different culture a long, long time ago.

I met all three Piaget children at a conference in Lisbon in 1996 held to honour the centenary of their father's birth. Two were still living in Piaget's old house, the house they had lived in as children. I only raise the point because it highlights a methodological point. Some psychologists ask just how average and ordinary the Piaget children were. Should one base so much of a science on them?

Piaget argued that all children's minds always develop in four main stages. The sensory motor stage – roughly until the age of two, learning co-ordination is all-important here. The pre-operational stage – so called because the child could not perform the most basic logical tasks or operations, the stage of concrete operations – called 'concrete' because children now can reason as long as they perceive physically what they reason about. Concrete stands against abstract at the stage of formal operations – when the teenager becomes in theory a master of the logical universe. By operations Piaget always meant logical operations. In the final formal stage the child can master syllogisms and the theory of syllogisms and syllogisms squared as well as all the intricacies of logic and arguments. Much research suggests that most adults however never really master this last stage unless they are expert mathematicians, though Piaget, as Flavell jokes, certainly believed he had got there. And so had Einstein.

Piaget saw his ideas as rooted in the old culture of Europe. He disapproved of what he saw as the American "mania" for pushing children as he thought there was an intricate but largely natural pattern to the way children's minds develop. He often insisted there was not a "normal" age for a child to go into every stage but, inevitably, psychologists have tended to put typical ages against the stages.

As Flavell explains in the interview, he was never particularly close to Piaget. He had the idea of writing his own book on child psychology but he then discovered that there was nothing in English to introduce the ideas of an extremely important theorist – and a man who did not care to make his ideas too easy to understand.

Flavell had already been teaching psychology for nearly ten years when he decided to expound Piaget. It was not his first book either; that was a volume on the linked subject of role playing and perspective taking in children. That issue is that a key part of Piaget's theory; he claims that children cannot take the perspective of the other until they are about seven years old. Until then they are doomed to be egocentric. And by egocentric Piaget did not mean that they are only interested in themselves but that they literally cannot see things from someone else's point of view.

I went to see Flavell at Stanford University in San Francisco. The campus is stunning – a series of cloisters. Some of the front lawn is dominated by a brass version of Rodin's *Burghers of Calais*, ordinary men who sacrificed themselves to save their city. But Stanford is anything but ordinary. The psychology department at Stanford has a truly stellar faculty with Albert Bandura, Eleanor Maccoby, Robert Zajonc and Philip Zimbardo among its members. Flavell said it was that they did not just do good work but they got along rather well. Given my introductory remarks about the way psychologists often love power, that is some tribute.

Though he has just retired at the age of 75, Flavell still keeps his office. At one side of the room there are pictures of Piaget. There are also certificates of the many honours he has gathered including a certificate from the Université René Descartes in Paris. Piaget always looked a little austere except when he was photographed with his pipe. Flavell, on the other hand, reminded me of Great Uncle Bulgaria in the Wombles with a white beard and an air of amusement. I was not at all surprised when he explained how much he enjoyed working with little children.

Flavell gave me one of the most physically energetic interviews I have ever conducted. He often leapt up from his desk. Once, it was to pull out his Vita from a filing cabinet, a remarkable thing for a man in his seventies to do. Once, it was to extract a bell, which would play some part in the proceedings. Once it was to show me a children's book he loves about two hippos. One of the hippos has a bad hiccup. The scientific value of the book is that there is only one word used in all its pages. HICCUP.

The importance of Flavell's work is that he has been a prime mover in showing what young children can and cannot do. There is a preschool on the Stanford campus and the young children there have often been the subjects of Flavell's experiments. One has to wonder, of course, if these are not terribly clever children of terribly clever parents.

One of the criticisms that was made of Piaget is that he tended to underestimate what children could achieve at different stages of development. Since the 1970s partly inspired by Flavell, psychologists have revised their ideas. Flavell's work, together with that of Henry Wellman and Peter Bryant among others, has forced us to revise the ideas that young children are egocentric and have no conception of the mind. Though Flavell accepts that the data is "messy", as he puts it, children do have some very interesting competences from the age of three or four.

If children were egocentric, in theory, they should not have been able to grasp that other people had other ideas, other thoughts. This problem of how we know other minds is a key problem in philosophy. No man is an island but how do we know what is going on in the rest of the archipelago? How do we know that other people exist and how do we come to realise that they are almost certainly having thoughts of their own. We cannot be social animals unless we understand that other people think and feel and that these thoughts and feelings will be different from ours.

In the interview, Flavell explains how we have made advances in that field. He also reflects on why it may be that children are developing such psychological skills younger and links it to work by Flynn on IQ. Flynn has discovered that the average IQ has gotten about 10 points higher over the last century. As a result, psychologists keep pushing back the barriers of when children can master certain tasks.

To understand the interview, it is probably necessary to understand one technical detail. Flavell mentions research on the false belief tasks. These are a set of studies in which children are shown a box and a doll is hidden in the box. A stooge then walks in the room. The stooge has not seen the doll being hidden in the box. Till the age of four, children tend to say that the stooge believes that the doll is in the box even though there is no reason the stooge would think that as the stooge never sees the hiding of the doll. That is why this is called the false belief task. It's a sign of the fact that the child cannot yet adopt the perspective of another person. But five-year-olds routinely get the task right.

• *What was your background?*
My father was a civil engineer. We lived in a suburb of Boston and I went to Northeastern University. I commuted from home. I imagined that I would be a chemistry major but at university I discovered I had had a very bad teaching as a chemist, which was why I thought I was good at it. Then I was going to do pre-med but I did a psychology course and I quite liked that.

• *And after you finished your first degree?*
I was living in Boston and I was going to be a clinical psychologist and so I went to Clark University and I did their co-clinical course. My first job was as a clinical psychologist but by then my interests had switched to developmental. Henry Werner – who was a major character at Clark – it's to him and his group that I owe a lot because at the time development psychology was not well known and it wasn't very interesting. We did a bit of Piaget, which most people would not have done at the time so I found myself switching over.

• *And then you went where?*
My first job was at the University of Rochester and though I was hired in clinical psychology and taught clinical psychology, they needed someone to teach developmental psychology and I was the only person who had any and so . . . All my research was in developmental. But I even worked in Veterans Administration Hospital.

• *And how was that?*
It was awful, In the middle of nowhere, somewhere between Western Kansas and Colorado. We had dustbowls like they had in the '30s. I did a lot of testing and even some therapy with schizophrenics

• *But you weren't tempted to become a therapist?*
No.

• *What was the state of developmental psychology then?*
I'm not sure my recollection of history is entirely accurate. It's about the time that my book on Piaget came out . . . Hunt had just written a book on Piaget and so it seemed that cognitive and cognitive development were coming in the air – partly because of the cognitive revolution that was coming to the forefront. Bruner and Neisser were developing their ideas. But at that time developmental psychology was mainly child psychology with studies of child language and boring lists of the words children used and sentences. First you got simple, then complex, then compound and vocabulary. If you look at the old textbooks on child psychology of that period they're awful and it was also that nobody who was anybody was in it. There was Robert Sears' work but that was personality, but there was nobody apart from Piaget, who was not well known at the time.

• *I found your book on Piaget so clear and that's not easy because he is not easy and sometimes it is hard to be sure what he means.*
I couldn't agree more. My granddaughter is in senior high school and she was given or asked to do a book report on Piaget's *Psychology of Intelligence*. I re-read it and I said, 'no, no, stay away from that . . . it's so obscure'. And that's why it is so difficult to know if you've got Piaget right or not. [Not for the first time in our interview he laughed.]

• *How did Piaget react to your book?*
He wrote a preface, which was ambivalent. I think he was ambivalent but not wholly negative. But he certainly did not see things the way I did about his work. But he was not wholly negative because he welcomed the publicity the book would give him in America.

• *My question was more to do with whether he accepted as valid some of the criticisms you made?*
The book certainly has some critique of Piaget at the very end and I'm sure he didn't agree with that, which is not surprising. And you know the truth of the matter is that I am developmental psychologist, I'm not very gifted philosophically, I see things from the standpoint of developmentalist *à la Americaine*. And Piaget doesn't see his work in that way at all. He's an epistemologist, he comes out of a totally different cultural and intellectual tradition and he had the right, I suppose, to have his theory mean what he wants it to mean. What

I tried to do was to take what was useful . . . no . . . to translate it so that it would be useful to developmental psychologists and to give it a certain spin. I think for Piaget himself this was not the spin he would have liked the world to pick up.

• *There was a lot of experimental work trying to test Piaget's ideas after your book came out.*
I think that's true and I think I'll take the credit for it. I think the book did open up Piaget – his ideas, his work, the time was ripe, the cognitive revolution had prepared the ground. It was doing the right thing at the right time.

• *What was he like when you met him?*
There was a translation problem. I speak French but I am not terrific at it. He didn't speak English or almost never spoke it. I never spoke to him for long periods of time. I translated for him at one session at the University of Minnesota. I stood next to him at the urinal, my claim to fame. I didn't know him well personally, I was never a student of his. I went over to the summer school in 1967 but there were so many people around. I would never claim to have known him.

• *Piaget seems to be to have been – even if one should criticise him – one of those figures like Freud and Skinner who changed the way we see things.*
Yes I agree, he changed things.

• *How did your career develop?*
Now I am a professor at the Institute of Child Development at Minnesota, it is not a psychology department only and I spent 11 very happy years there.

• *Did you have a vision of the research you wanted to do?*
I wanted to finish the Piaget book. I had also begun to do some research on communication and perspective taking, the extent to which a child will adapt what they say to what the listener already knows – perspective taking in the service of communication.

• *What did you conclude about introspection and kids?*
In 1963 my family and I spent a year at the Sorbonne, which was where I was writing the book. On the basis of that and other things I was invited to Minnesota and I was beginning to do work on children's memory, their memory strategies and I was also starting to work on meta-memory and in visual stuff in perspective taking.

• *Like Piaget's three mountains tasks?*
Yes . . . but there are more examples but memory and perspective taking are the two things I'm doing in Minnesota. Then in 1976 I came here and I've been at Stanford 27 years. I've had a wonderful time here. Early during my time at Stanford I started work on theory of mind development and my principal contribution has been in looking at appearance–reality or kids' understanding of the appearance–reality distinction and a few other things.

• *Is your work on appearance–reality related to your early work on role-play?*
In a way it is linked to role-playing. Even in grad school I asked what does the child know about the other person's point of view and how do they use it in the service of communication. [This is one of the most physically energetic interviews of a psychologist I have ever done. Flavell now grabs some paper on his side of the desk and thrusts it forward.] I see it right way up and you see it upside down. To my eyes it looks like this but it also looks this to someone else's eyes. So I guess I've been doing what they call perspective taking for years for most of my career. Theory of mind – introspection – what are other people likely to be thinking, I put it all within perspective taking.

• *I talked to Henry Wellman about these kinds of issues . . .*
My most famous student!

• *He said that these days children were exposed to more complicated stimuli, to more TV and that they grew up younger. Would you agree with that?*
I wouldn't be surprised. Not at all. It may also be a more mentalistically inclined culture than when we were growing up. People talk to their children more about the mind, there is more stuff on television. Including voiceovers, which indicate the thoughts and feelings of the characters. There may be more storybook reading and children's storybooks are full of theory of mind stuff. Wellman has shown that consistently. It may be like the Flynn effect, which shows that IQ is going up all the time. It may be the influence of cultural inputs. I don't know the answer but kids get more education. I was six before I had seen anything like a school and now we have kids at school at 2, 3, 4. It's a different world.

• *What did you conclude about introspection and kids?*
Our own research shows that in the test we use that kids are very bad at this. I could give you one flashbulb example. Ok you're a five-year-old subject. Here's a bell . . . [Another manifestation of his physical energy: Flavell gets out an old-style school bell from the drawer in his desk. He leans forward and gazes

intensely at me.] I put it under the table. Just for a few seconds . . . [He takes the bell out, shows it to me, can't resist ringing in and again hides it below the table. I am supposed to be the child subject and I can't see it.] Just a few seconds again. I put it underneath the table. Are you thinking about anything?

• *I'm wondering if you're going to ring the bell again.*
Right. Kids are sitting right there where you are and when we ask that question and only about 35 per cent of them get it right at the age of five. Only 35 per cent say anything resembling like that. We would submit that we had forced their minds and their thoughts in that direction and if they don't report it you could say they did not have the thought that you just had. There may be a number of reasons for that but that's the kind of work we've been doing and it suggests that kids are not very attuned to mentation in themselves and other people.

• *So that suggests kids don't really understand what other people feel either?*
No, I don't think so. In the first place kids know more about feelings and desires than they do about thoughts and beliefs. 'How does Joe feel when something bad happens to him?' – kids are good at that aged even as young as two or three. It's not that they don't have awareness of that . . . But we if ask them to monitor the on-going here and now of mentation, that's not as good.

• *At what age does that change?*
It seems to change a lot between four and six. By early elementary school they are going to be a lot better at that, even better when they are eight or nine and fairly adult-like in their thinking.

• *So by introspection you don't mean reporting on feelings?*
I should somehow limit the term.

• *Is there a link with IQ or is it more of a, to use that word Piaget loved, stage?*
I think it's more of a stage, though I wouldn't be at all surprised if other things matter . . . some tasks are specially related to verbal intelligence. That's been shown a number of times. We've not done as much work looking at the correlates. We've just looked at what actually develops and when it develops rather than look at the correlates.

• *Have you at all considered the notion of whether some young children are specially good at introspection and other minds – that they might be what you might call baby Freuds and baby therapists?*

That's a very interesting idea. I've been working on a paper on . . . shall we call it extended development. And I suggest we should look not just at development at three or four but how about the later. It would be interesting to look at adult virtuosi in theory of mind who have great ability to introspect and to infer what is going on in other people's minds, to what makes great therapists. It's a long way from the little implicit intuition a young child has to experts in the theory of mind.

• *And then you looked at whether children understand inner speech?*
You'd expect logically that they'd know speech is usually overt, that it's out loud and that it's interpersonal. We wondered if they know some other genuinely not so well known or common aspects of speech – namely that it could be inner, could be philosophical non-external and non-social. We thought we'd give them a test of that. One of the ways we did that was to say imagine you are sitting here and there is another executive experimenter running the show and my job is to draw a picture of you. [Again Flavell acts out the part with relish. He picks up a sheet of paper and mimes drawing. As he draws he speaks but he is not speaking directly to me.]

'The eyes are here, the hair is so . . .' and the other experimenter says to the child 'right now John is talking'. And the child says 'yes', and we then ask, 'is he talking to anybody?' Then, there are follow-up questions like 'is he talking to you, is he talking to me?' And much to our surprise, we found that most three- to four-year-olds are very good at that because they seem to understand that speech was not talking to you. Three- to four-year-olds are good at that.

• *My question was about inner speech.*
Some of them aren't and some of them are. I'm not getting the right response . . . And that's probably what people are picking up on. They are telling you it's still messy. The other half is, do they know that speech can be overt but not communicative? But the second question is, do they know speech can be internal, that a person could be talking but it would not show? I'll give you the bottom line on that. They weren't as good at it but they were not half bad when they were three or four.

• *How did you achieve that?*
The experiment involved counting. The other experimenter says 'OK, now John is counting. How many coins are there? One, two three, you count those coins . . .' [Again Flavell acts out the situation with gusto, setting out coins on his table.] And then the experimenter says, 'Would you count them again John without moving your lips?'

- *So he is here at the side while you are doing this?*

Yes, he is here at the side when he says this. And the question is, 'is John speaking to himself?' and the answer is that 60 per cent of them were correctly able to say that I was speaking to myself.

- *Do you normally act a role in the experiments like this?*

No, no [he laughs]. This is literally the first time in 25 years apart from pilot studies that I am doing it. The children walk in the classroom in the company of this 23-year-old student experimenter and they see me. What a shock. I enjoy it so much. It is such fun asking these questions. Some of them really know what you're after. Some of the kids do not seem to believe that if you weren't making a noise you could be counting, but it looks as if we have some sort of competence there.

- *But you said it was contradictory?*

We did an earlier study, which we published in *Child Development* in which we found they were terrible at this and just exactly what is the difference between these two sets of tasks is still a mystery. I have no story to tell on that one.

- *Is one of the reasons that you find doing what you do enjoyable is that you find the mysteries engaging?*

Yes, I think so. I like doing studies with kids, which show what they can do and can't do. I'm a very simple-minded person when it comes down to it. I'm not trying to test out some kind of deep theoretical position, I don't have complex theories. I like to dig under the rock and find the developables, what competence do we have as older people that we didn't have before and that no one has discovered before. And what is the developmental course of getting that competence? Another one of the findings – one of my favourites – is that one of the strong intuitions you have in this culture is that as an adult, if you're awake, the mind is cranking away all the time, as William James's stream of consciousness has it. It may be low level, it may not be very articulate but the mind cranks. Young kids, we've discovered, are not very aware of that. In one experiment my wife Frankie and our collaborator Elly are in a classroom. And Frankie says to Elly, in front of the children, 'do you mind waiting over there – it's like waiting for the bus and the subway.' 'Right now?' 'Yes, right now, please.' And Frankie sits at the side and looks like this and we ask the kids, 'Elly is waiting right now. Is she having any thoughts or ideas or is her mind empty?'

We prepared the children by showing them stories with thought bubbles and telling them about thoughts. We did a lot of training and what we find is that 19 out of 20 adults say something is going on in the mind. With seven- to eight-year-old children it is about 80% but with four- to five-year-old children it is only 35 per cent and with three-year-olds it is down to 15%. Even when they have a choice because we give them a full and an empty thought bubble to choose from they pick the empty thought bubble. We've tried doing this a number of ways. But the young kids don't seem to be well aware and certainly not consistently aware that other people have some sort of mentation. If you show them someone like Rodin's *Thinker*, they'll say, 'well, it doesn't look like he's thinking, I don't know much about inner speech, I have no theory that says he ought to be thinking just now', while, on the other hand, older people pick up on introspection. They have the experience that the mind has this quality of pushing along all the time. If I had to pick what is my favourite discovery of the last ten years it would certainly be that one. So there is the excitement of something where I must have said to myself – that is something, which probably develops which no one has really looked at before.

• *Are you surprised by what you have discovered?*
Let me think. Yes and in both directions. I'm surprised that little kids do so well and then, when it comes to inner speech, do so badly. It really surprised us though we are getting used to it. They do well but they don't seem attuned to what is going on in the mind, which is why they are so bad at the bell task.

• *In my own PhD I found that what made even very little children laugh was more complicated than the literature often suggested and children use laughter to try to get away with naughty behaviour.*
You do see little kids of the age of three make attempts at deception, which suggests some awareness of that. One of the issues is how do you characterise what a kid has in terms of adult understanding. One test will show ability but another test will show no ability. That is one of the perennial problems in this area. You may be able to find what looks like an implicit understanding of belief aged one, two or three and yet kids that age will fail the false belief test. Turning this the other way you may be able to find some false belief situations that kids at eight or nine don't get or even adults so how do you characterise what kids have.

• *Well no one ever reached the full stage of formal development apart from Piaget.*
That's right and he's dead. It's the perennial problem, of assessment and diagnosis that we struggle with all the time.

• *But do you do a lot of observational work just looking at how children behave?*
No, not exactly. We never go into the preschool or any environment and simply spend time observing the kids in their natural habitat. We don't do

that, I almost never have. What we do is take this inner speech thing, we look at the previous literature and then we say let's try it this way and we do pilot studies and see if it works and we tinker. The tinkering sometimes can take a long time. Sometimes we think something is going to work and it does not work at all.

• *Can you give me an example of how you tinker?*
We've been doing two studies on inner speech and I read a page out loud. 'Well John would you read the page out loud?' And then the question is, 'is John reading story words?' Well, maybe kids of three or four who don't do well on this don't really know what it means to read, maybe they don't know what it means saying story words . . . it may be a misunderstanding or it may be that they don't understand print. This is one of my favourite books, *Hiccup*, the drawings of the two hippos are wonderful. The only word in the book is 'hiccup'. I say this word every time 'Hiccup. Hiccup.' I repeat the word, touching the word. Then the question is 'John would you mind reading this page without doing it out loud'. Kids did much better because it was much clearer.

• *Do you think there are still big differences between European and Anglo-American psychology in child development?*
No, I don't think very much. I think it is pretty universal now.

• *If you were to look forward in a crystal ball what areas of child psychology do you think will be important in 2025?*
Just extrapolating from what is in the picture now I think we will continue work on other minds.

Another thing is that people will be looking for the engines of change, how do all these developments happen. There will be more and more of that. I also think it likely that advances in neuropsychology will have a big impact. They will find ways of putting a three-year-old in MRIs [Magnetic Resonance Imaging which gives a picture of which areas of the brain are working at a particular time]. You can't do that now. At present the youngest you can do it is about eight or nine but that will change. If you can find ways of doing that you will be able to see some of the neurological goings on when kids are doing this or that. And just as adult psychology has been advanced by such studies that will happen with kids too.

I also think that there will be increasing work on cultural psychology, looking at differences between cultures and within cultures. And work with children who have special problems like learning disability. None of that is very surprising. The hottest topic in developmental psychology is infancy as people develop these clever, clever ways of probing into the infants' mind, of looking for early signs of understanding or intentionality of emotions.

• *Like the extraordinary ability of newborns to imitate the facial expressions of adults?*
Amazing, isn't it? And bizarre. Early on children detect regularities in speech. I don't have the deal but there is a new research, which shows when they are far too young to speak, they still detect the regularities. There's also been that pre-natal stuff on the pick up of speech and music.

• *Finally, does any of your work have implications in terms of schooling?*
The work on memory has been picked up by education. I was very surprised about a year ago to get given this award by the organisation of the teachers of foreign language but they found that useful. The theory of mind stuff has not been so much picked up by education even though it should be useful.

Chapter 6: Viktor Frankl

It's not often you interview a man Freud commissioned to write an article when they were both waiting for the traffic lights to change. Viktor Frankl had that experience and he still lives in the heart of Vienna's medical district. Its streets are narrow, quiet and a little dark. I push open the big heavy door of the block of flats where Frankl lives and find myself in a long, shabby hallway. My footsteps clang on the stone floor. The titles of Frankl's books like *Man's Search for Meaning* and *The Doctor and the Soul* suggest it will be a more sombre interview than most.

But Frankl isn't gloomy at all. He bubbles with energy and good humour. He is delighted to see me and leads me into his large light office. As I switch on my tape recorder, he smiles and switches his on too. This is not paranoia in case I misquote him but he does like to have his own record of an interview and adds, without a trace of embarrassment, that two American universities have asked him to record every interview he gives. For their archives – for posterity.

Frankl shows me photographs of him and his wife rock climbing. "Not bad still doing that at 70," he smiles. And he does not mind presenting himself as a man the media are after. The phone rings. A Swiss television station wants to book him to appear on a programme and he's impressed by the way they have coaxed him. He almost seems to embody the motto that a full life is a fulfilled life.

Frankl was one of the first psychiatrists to treat patients as responsible human beings rather than superior soft machines that had a screw loose. Freud expected that one day scientists would be able to pin a biochemical cause to every individual act; scientific progress would be the end of free will. It never turned out to be so simple. From the start, Frankl had patients who wanted something more than to be debugged of their hang-ups. The snag, he found, was that getting rid of their complexes did not suddenly make sense of their lives.

The psychological "discovery" of the First World War was that soldiers suffered from shell shock. After the horrors of the Second World War and the Holocaust, there was no such "discovery". But Frankl learned that it was not enough to cure patients. They had what could be called "spiritual needs". Frankl doesn't shy away from that and, in the interview Frankl talks about ways in which his work resembles that of Abraham Maslow, the founder of humanistic therapy who stressed that every person strives to actualize themselves, to have "peak experiences".

Frankl's answer to the great why are we here question is *logotherapy*, an approach that recognizes the fundamental need for meaning in a person's life. In the 21st century it has become a successful branch of therapy and Frankl's books sell enormously well even though some are 50 years old.

But in some cultures metaphysics remain louche, a hobby for French and German intellectuals who can't really think logically. Bandy words such as the meaning of life around and the decent British don will suspect you of being pretentious and self-serious. I was surprised to find that Frankl laughed a lot and was, even, able to tell the odd joke about himself. Not quite the same as telling jokes against himself but a step in that direction.

Frankl sees a desperate need for meaning all over the world and does not dismiss it as childish or as simply a stage that a person outgrows once he, or she, knows better. This stress on meaning has made a number of enemies for Frankl. They don't just snipe at the metaphysics but at the man; they comment he can be a little vain, for example. After speaking with him, I dined with some Freudians who rebuked me for having interviewed "their enemy". I was told a number of malicious anecdotes. It was familiar territory since I have written about power battles between psychologists but this was astonishingly personal.

It is not clear why some Freudians are so hostile to Frankl. He was never formally a Freudian analyst but a doctor. In becoming that he fulfilled an ambition of his father. Frankl senior, however, could not afford to study at university and ended up a civil servant in the Ministry of Social Work. "My father did more than encourage me to become a doctor, he wanted me to fulfill his dream", Frankl told me.

Frankl's parents were liberal Jews. No one made him go to the synagogue but he developed a feeling for the spiritual and he insists that is different from the religious. You can believe in ultimate meanings without believing in any ritual available at a synagogue or church. At 15, the would-be doctor discovered psychoanalysis. Today no one becomes a therapist in their teens but curiously in the anything goes Vienna after the First World War, some very precocious analysts did flourish. These Mozarts of the mind included Wilhelm Reich, who Freud sent patients to when Reich was just in his early 20s, and a little later Frankl. Both were treating people when they were in their early 20s.

But, according to Frankl, one of his key moments of inspiration came younger. He describes a vision he had when he was only 14. It was a vision of Nirvana and it made him very receptive to Freud's famous book *Beyond the*

Pleasure Principle. Freud argued that all living things seek both pleasure and the release from tension that can only come with death. When we are a feast for the worms, we are finally hassle free. Is it surprising that we should all tend toward the tranquility of the inorganic state?

Frankl began to send Freud articles that he thought might interest the great man. They did interest him. The two began to correspond, Freud was meticulous, as we shall learn in the interview. Frankl says, Freud's courtesy to him – he knew in the Vienna village that Frankl was only a schoolboy – touched Frankl. Once, Frankl enclosed a short essay with some ideas about the origins of gestures like nodding and shaking the head. Freud suggested it be published. So at the age of 18 Frankl made his entrance into the literature in the *International Journal of Psychoanalysis.*

Freud suggested then that Frankl visit Paul Federn, then the secretary of the Psychoanalytic Society, to discuss when Frankl should start his training analysis. But Federn said the teenager should first get his medical degree and Frankl accepted this advice. It meant he never did have a training analysis and never formally became a Freudian. He thought, he told me, that might be why he found it so "easy to be disloyal" to Freud when he became disenchanted. The reasons for disenchantment were simple. Frankl felt that Freud exaggerated the sex and denied the rich spiritual side of humanity. Sex could not cause everything.

Curiously, though, Frankl only met Freud once – later and by accident – a meeting he describes with much affection in the interview. He is less affectionate about Freud's once disciple Alfred Adler who founded the individual school of psychoanalysis. What sex was for Freud, power was for Adler. It seemed too dogmatic to explain everything in terms of power, Frankl told me. He was eventually "excommunicated" from Adler's group and Freud's rival refused to have coffee in the same café. So by the age of 22, Frankl felt no need to cling to any particular psychological school.

While studying medicine, Frankl helped set up a number of youth counselling centres in different parts of Austria, Germany, Czechoslovakia and Hungary. Their main aim was to help young people who felt suicidal and to, literally, talk them into living. It was his first practical therapy.

The holocaust provided Frankl with the motivation he needed to refine his ideas. Although Frankl was working toward this position when he was in his 20s, it was after he was sent to Auschwitz that he decided he had to get it out into the world if he survived the camp. He believes the technique may even have saved his life. After the Germans took over Vienna in 1938, Franks explains, "I was called to the Gestapo offices and this officer examined me. But soon it seemed all camouflage. What he really wanted to squeeze out of me was whether and where there were still psychoanalysts and psychotherapists in Vienna. The Gestapo man asked how such people would treat agoraphobia; he said he had a friend who suffered from agoraphobia. I realized, of course, that he was the person who suffered from agoraphobia and that he wanted to be treated. It was an instance of pure technique in therapy, because there could be no encounter between me and him. So, finally, I told him that if there were psychotherapists working in Vienna and if his friend went to see them, this would probably be what they would do". And Frankl told the Gestapo man how paradoxical intention would treat "his friend". The purely technical treatment may have succeeded, and it may help explain why Frankl and his family were not deported to their first concentration camp until 1942. Frankl, his first wife and his parents were deported to the concentration camp at Terezin in Czechoslovakia. His father died there.

In 1944, Frankl was deported to Auschwitz and, from Auschwitz to Dachau, "When I entered Auschwitz, I had hidden in the lining of my coat the full-length manuscript of what later became my first book, *The Doctor and the Soul*." Auschwitz did not inspire a new therapy but it did teach him, Frankl insists, he believes that meanings can be found in extreme and terrifying situations. "Those people who felt they had a reason, a goal, to survive were most likely to survive. They did not give up and die as did one inmate Frankl knew. This man dreamed that the war would end for him on March 30, 1945. At first, he was optimistic; then, as March dragged on, he began to despair. There seemed no end of the war in sight, on March 29th, he became delirious; on March 30th he lost consciousness; on March 31st, he died. As in North Korean and Japanese prisoner-of-war camps, Frankl says. "those who were most oriented toward a meaning to fulfil in the future tended to survive."

After the war, Frankl rebuilt his practice and became a very successful therapist. He did sometimes try to collaborate with other kinds of therapy – like behaviour therapy.

Early in his career, Frankl also became aware that many patients had learned to live very well with phobias and compulsions. "Again and again, I became aware of what in modern behaviouristic language one would call the coping mechanisms that allowed patients to deal with anxieties and obsessions." During this period, Frankl hit on and developed his first original therapeutic technique – paradoxical intention.

"The essence of paradoxical intention is to get the patient to do or to wish to happen exactly what it is that he fears to do." Frankl was amused by one case, that of a young surgeon would always tremble when a superior entered the operating theatre. Frankl told him that the next time a superior came in, the young surgeon had to try to tremble as hard as he could to show what a good trembler he was. It quite took the wind out of the phobias, Frankl recalls, smiling. Frankl admits that he stumbled onto the technique out of intuition and impatience, rather than by research. It was also a reaction against psychoanalysis and what he calls their "excessive attention to their inner life. I felt the impulse to help man to break out of all this inner turmoil, the introspections and retrospectives that were increasing their problems. And this paradoxical intention seemed to be a way." Don't flex the complex too much. Frankl explains that in more detail in the interview and waxes lyrical about the link with the human ability to be detached, to laugh, and especially to laugh at oneself.

No good therapist is short on impressive cases of his own and Frankl is no exception, but like most humanist therapists, he can point to only modest scientific proof that his system works. The only experimental study of logotherapy was one carried out in 1972 by W. Solyem and colleagues at the University of Montreal. They used paradoxical intention on patients who had had obsessive-compulsive disorders for between 14 and 25 years and reported a 50 per cent drop in compulsive thoughts for the group who were treated with paradoxical intention applied. Since obsessions are notoriously hard to treat, these are encouraging figures but there has been little research since then because of all too traditional suspicions between scientists and therapists.

For Frankl, people's ability to see themselves in this detached ironic way goes with humanity's other unique gift – the capacity for self-transcendence. And that does have links to Abraham Maslow and his idea. People can find a meaning because they are capable of self-transcendence. "Self-transcendence means that human existence is directed to something or someone other than itself. Being human is to reach out for a meaning to fulfil. For example, in loving a person or serving a cause, we become ourselves in the best sense of the word. I maintain there is a motivation to find meaning." Humanity has a will-to-meaning.

Unlike every other psychologist I interviewed, Frankl stresses the value of suffering. Suffering can be creative. Once, an old physician came to him, extremely depressed after the death of his wife. Theirs had been a very happy marriage. Frankl said he had said: "tell me, what would have happened if you had died first and your wife had survived you?" "That would have been terrible", he said. "How my wife would have suffered." "Well you see", I answered, "your wife has been spared that, and it was you who spared her, though of course you must now pay by surviving and mourning her."

This new perspective did not make the physician glow with happiness, but it did give him a feeling that there was some point, some meaning, to his suffering. And, as a result, he could handle it much better.

Frankl believes that we need to develop our capacity for finding meanings.

One of the reasons for his popularity is precisely that he pays attention to the fact that we hanker after meaning to make sense of our lives. He doesn't see it as a weakness or an immaturity, as Freud and the behaviourists did. It is typical of the paradoxes of Frankl's position that this hankering after the religious does not make him antiscientific, "Frankly, I must admit that logotherapy has been developed on purely intuitive grounds by me, which is a personal strength, perhaps, but a scientific weakness," he admits. But he is glad empirical psychologists and psychiatrists bother to look experimentally at his ideas. Apart from the Montreal therapy study, James C. Crumbaugh and Leonard T. Maholick devised a Purpose in Life test (known as PIL) and tried it out on 1151 subjects. They concluded that there was evidence of a neurosis caused by a lack of meaning in one's life.

"Logotherapy," Frankl claims, "has made a contribution by opening up the human dimension which shows that resources can be drawn on once people are aware that man is not just a mechanism, a being that seeks satisfaction of drives, instincts and needs. Beyond what can be explained in sub-human terms, there is specifically human motivation. Man can suffer deliberately for a cause. This is what eludes you if you restrict on *a priori* bias your research to, say, animals. This does not mean that man ceases to be a biochemical entity, but he is more than that. The noetic (the specifically human) dimension encompasses the psychic and somatic one."

Don't dismiss Freud, Pavlov or Watson but logotherapy is the more inclusive – and perhaps more relevant, Frankl suggests, "because the collective neurosis today seems to be that people feel they are suffering empty and meaningless lives. And, in that sense, not in the sense of possessing some universal truth logotherapy does appeal to the predicament of today's man." As he says that, Frankl positively radiates confidence.

As we finished our talk, Frankl showed me around the room in the flat that he has made his own personal archive. He takes an almost naive pleasure in the room. It has copies of almost everything he has written, of lectures he has given; of tapes he has made. Frankl has certainly carved out for himself a distinct place as one of the first psychiatrists to see the value of exploring both the spiritual and the humorous side of humanity. The contradiction fits him. He cares both about spirit and science, about meaning and measurement – and he enjoys a joke.

• *How did you come to be psychiatrist?*
Since the age of three, I wanted to be a doctor. But it was only when I was 35 or so that I thought I should become a psychiatrist. You see, my interests were always divided between medicine and psychiatry, in particular, on the one hand and philosophy on the other. More and more I saw psychiatry as the field that

would allow me to combine my interests (and, hopefully, my talents). The way I have approached problems in psychiatry might show that.

• *Where did you study?*
I studied in Vienna as a schoolboy. Then when I was about 15, I discovered there was something called psychoanalysis. I took university extension courses offered by Hitschmann who was one of the first generation of disciples of Freud. I also went to lectures given by Paul Schilder who spoke every Saturday evening for two hours in the University Hospital. The head of the psychiatric department was Waggner Jauregg, so you can see from this that it is a myth that he suppressed psychoanalysis. Schilder was his first assistant at the time and had full liberty to preach psychoanalysis. For several years I spent each Saturday evening at the hospital. Schilder was the first man to apply psychoanalysis to the psychoses. We also developed psychiatric system.

• *Did any books influence you particularly at that time?*
I read a lot of Freud. What impressed me most deeply was *Beyond the Pleasure Principle* because there was some metaphysical, metapsychological material in it. In the meantime I had developed certain ideas about what I proudly thought to be a basic cosmic tendency. When I was 14, I was on deck of a steamer on the Danube, I looked at the stars and I arrived at the vision that Nirvana is entropy seen from within. In entropy, energy dissipates. There are no differences between things. And because differences do appear, there is absolute unity and equality but nothing is there. At the end of the world there is perfect lack of tension. I saw Nirvana as being this lack of tension seen from within. I found in *Beyond the Pleasure Principle* the basic tendency of life is to seek the form of death the tranquility of the inorganic state. Then I started to correspond with Freud. Did you know that?

• *What was he like as a correspondent?*
He answered each single letter if only in the form of a postcard within eight hours. Once I enclosed an essay I had typed with some ideas about the origins of mimic gestures like nodding and shaking the head. Freud replied that he had kept it and would forward it with my permission to the editor of the International Journal of Psychoanalysis. It was published in 1924.

• *Did you ever meet Freud?*
Once, much later, I saw an old man with a black stick with a silver handle beating the pavement and murmuring to himself, it seemed. I don't believe he was talking to himself but the pains in the jaw might give that impression. He

had a worn out coat and a worn hat but I recognised him from the photographs. I decided to follow him and see if he turned into Berggasse [the street where Freud lived]. He did turn and I decided to introduce myself. I remember now that there was very little traffic and he was in the middle of the street when I asked him if I had the honour of addressing Professor Freud. He said, 'Yes, I'm Freud'. 'My name is Viktor Frankl.' And he reacted at once by remembering my address: 'Czerningasse number 6, apartment 25, isn't it?' It was exactly that!

• *So you never met Freud while you corresponded with him?*
No, but he knew I was a very young schoolboy. He still found it worthwhile to answer each letter. Towards the end of the correspondence he invited me to visit Federn to discuss the question of when I should undergo my training analysis. I went to see Federn. He said I should first finish my medical studies because the training analysis might interfere too much with them. When I was a doctor, then I could begin.

• *So who was your training analyst?*
I had none. This was in 1924/25. Soon after that I became involved with the Adlerians. Incidentally, the correspondence with Freud was confiscated by the Gestapo when I was deported in 1942.

• *Why did you part company with the Freudians?*
When there is a war. We had no idea what Leibniz's pre-established harmony meant. From that moment on, Adler never spoke to me. When I approached the tables where the Adlerians sat at the Cafe Siller – the Freudians had a different cafe – Adler left. He never answered letters. I felt very hurt. I loved him and I admired him. I knew his weaknesses but I loved him. Then he let me know I should leave the Adlerian Society. I said I saw no reason to do so. I was invited to resign several times in the next months. Then, finally, he decreed I was no longer a member. He excommunicated me. It was embarrassing for me. But, in another way, it may have been beneficial for I no longer had to consider problems of loyalty.

• *What did you do then?*
I pursued my medical studies. I became involved in founding some youth counselling centres that aimed to prevent suicide. And I was allowed to treat patients at the Psychiatric University Hospital in my own right as a psychotherapist. There I learned to forget what I had learned from the great teachers, Adler and Freud. I learned to listen to my patients. Again and again, I became aware of what in modern behaviouristic language one would call the coping mechanism

that allowed patients to deal with anxieties and obsessions. It was during this period I discovered the technique of paradoxical intention.

• *How does paradoxical intention function?*
I remember once asking a patient how it was that he had gotten rid of his anxiety. And he said: 'I simply followed what you suggested.' And I said what did I suggest, for I had learned to remember what my patients said but I was prone to forgetting my own words. And he said: 'You said, doctor, that when the anxiety mounted up in me, when I became afraid that I would have a heart attack and collapse in the street, I should go out and tell myself OK, let's try to collapse as often as possible – yesterday I died from collapsing, today let's try to die five times.'

Let me give you an example of a very anxious young woman. From past experience I knew that asking her to relax would only increase her tension. Instead I responded with just the opposite. 'Linda, I want you to act as nervously as you can.' 'OK' she said 'being nervous is easy for me.' She started by clenching her fists together and shaking her hands as though they were trembling. 'That's good' I said 'but try to be more nervous.' The humour of the situation became obvious to her and she said, 'I really was nervous but I can't be any longer. It's odd but the more I try to be tense, the less I'm able to be.' The essence of paradoxical intention is to 'get the patient to do, or wish to happen, exactly what he fears.' This is the definition of paradoxical intention.

• *Were you aware of what you were doing when you began to make these very paradoxical suggestions?*
No, no.

• *So how did the discovery come about then?*
I have often asked myself that. In a way I felt it was better to have an end to the horror than to have a horror without end – constant, repetitive anxieties. You see, for a change, let it collapse. I also sometimes had to deal with patients who had been through psychoanalysis and who had been induced to focus attention on their inner life, on the past, on their pathology – then I felt the impulse to tear out of all this inner turmoil, all this excessive introspection and retrospection that was still increasing their problem and desperate situation, and this seemed to be a way.

• *What I find interesting about this technique is that it seems to be one of the few to use humour and irony. You seem to be saying that, in the end, everyone can look at himself or herself in a fairly detached way.*

You have hit the core of the matter. As in behaviour therapy, the principle is that what is at the root of phobias is the avoidance of fear-arousing situations. You have to approach them as directly as possible. Intuitively, I hit upon this around 1929. The fact that the technique does mobilize the uniquely human sense of humour and irony has now been recognized by behaviour therapists. Isaac Marks at the Maudsley had colleagues take groups of agoraphobics to Trafalgar Square for instance. But the psychiatrists went along not as leaders but only as observers. The psychiatrists saw that a pattern began to develop. The agoraphobics began to cope by teasing each other, by exaggerating their fears and laughing at them. In other words, people spontaneously re-invented the coping mechanisms underlying paradoxical intention. There have also been studies in Montreal carried out by a group that has never sought to contact me – which gives their studies more strength. In one study, they took patients who had symptoms of equal severity and got one patient to treat one with means of self-administered paradoxical intention. It was very successful.

• *You are obviously a humorous man. Do you think you hit on this technique because of your own personality?*
There is no doubt. I am used to saying that the psychotherapy you choose depends on two factors – the individual case you have at hand and the unique characteristics of the therapist. In other words, not every technique can be applied with equal success or hope of success in every case. And not every therapist can use every technique. I have found that some therapists are now using paradoxical intention with much more success than I myself. Also, many people who read my work especially in the USA use it on themselves. In *Man's Search for Meaning* I had two to five pages devoted to paradoxical intention and people try it on themselves. It's unbelievable the success they sometimes they have. If I didn't have letters from them thanking me for it, I wouldn't believe it.

• *Why do you think it works? Does using our sense of humour or of irony reflect something that is particularly human?*
I spoke of logotherapy entering the noetic dimension – the dimension of specifically human phenomena. There are two ways this manifests itself – self-transcendence and self-detachment. Self-transcendence means human existence is directed to something, or someone, other than itself. Being human is to reach out for a meaning to fulfil which may be achieved by having another human being to love. In serving a cause or loving a person we really become ourselves. We actualise our human potential at its best. I maintain that there is a motivation to find meaning. Or, as I am used to saying: man has to have a 'Will to Meaning.' There is also the capacity for self-detachment. This is mobilised in

humour. Self-detachment can be heroic or ironic. Then someone is tortured by the Gestapo and everything looks as if he could give the names of his collaborators and he doesn't – this is the defiance that the human spirit is capable of: the noetic in man can detach itself from the psychophysical situation. But you can also get this self-detachment in an ironic way. It is human specifically to cause. No animal can laugh, least of all can it laugh at itself. And – again to take up self-transcendence – no animal can pose the question 'what is the meaning of my life?'

Self-detachment and self-transcendence must be put to therapeutic uses. But you cannot do this if you are a reductionist. As long as you say man's reaching out for meaning is nothing but a reaction formation or a defence mechanism, you cannot mobilise these capacities. You cannot do it if you say that it will only lead to symptom substitution even though the evidence shows this is not true. Freud once said in a review of a hypnosis by Auguste Forel something like reverence before a great genius is OK but our reverence before the facts should be greater. That is why we have to be open-minded as to recognising the human phenomena, and not give away therapeutic assets because of our preconceived ideas of what man is.

- *Could you explain the idea you have of meanings a bit more fully?*

Meanings must be found in unique life situations. I am not talking of universal or ultimate meaning for example of how a person faces the fact that he is dying of cancer. I grasped when I was 16 that one may find meaning either in a creative way: in experiencing something that is good or true or beautiful, or someone as a unique person which means loving him. There is a third way. If your situation is unchangeable then you can find meaning by the way that you live through it, by the way you bear witness to the uniquely human potential at its best which is: to turn a tragedy into a human achievement. Thus the resources for meaning are inexhaustible. But we need to develop that intuitive sense which allows us to smell out the meaning hidden and dormant in each single life situation. This is very important today. Education should see as one of its main tasks training people to be sensitive to the potential for meaning which has a lot to do with Gestalt perceptions. The way that people do confront some situations is admirable. As someone who is close to despair about man, I find this silent greatness of many people is very impressive.

- *Could you give me some instances of existential neurosis, of people suffering from a lack of meaning or of what you call a 'noogenic' neurosis?*

For example, I had a student in San Diego who reported that he was suffering a lot of anxiety. He was employed as a psychologist by two psychologists. Finally, they suggested he go into analysis with someone else. He did so and he deteriorated. After the first lecture of my course he wrote to me that suddenly he became aware that he was suffering from noogenic neurosis. He had surpassed all the criticisms he had about psychoanalysis. He never spoke or ventured to speak out. After a few weeks he understood his neurosis and he did speak out. He was immediately better. Imagine – a psychoanalyst could not even have seen what the problem was. Another case I came across was of a doctor who was suffering doubts about his life. He thought his life was meaningless. Instead of helping the doctor face his existential problems, the behaviour therapist he went to suggested 'thought stopping'. Every time he felt one of these existential doubts, he was to stop thinking of that and attend to something else. He was to deliberately forget that and think of something else. In both these cases, the treatment was detrimental because it would feed, instead of treating, the noogenic neurosis. In general, you may assume, about 20 per cent of neuroses are noogenic. The therapist has to understand the existential problem facing his patient and help him overcome it by directing him towards a purpose and meaning in life. And this can help in overcoming the other 80 percent of neuroses too.

• *Had you reached this position when you were deported to Auschwitz or did the importance of meaning become clear to you there?*
Many publishers seem to think I came out of Auschwitz with a brand new form of psychotherapy. The silly title given by my publishers to one of my books, *From Death Camp to Existentialism*, shows this. This is not the case. When I entered Auschwitz I had hidden in the lining of my coat the full length manuscript of what later became my first book carrying, in English, the stupid title *The Doctor and the Soul.* (The word 'Seelsorge' as included in the German title, is ambiguous as it could mean caring for the soul or the psyche.) Anyway, I had the manuscript with me and this already was a systematic presentation of logotherapy.

• *What effect on your work did the time in the concentration camp have then?*
It served as a field in which to validate my teaching. What is more crucial than anything in affecting the chance of survival in such extreme circumstances is the orientation a person has to his future. Is there a goal, a meaning waiting in the future for you and to be fulfilled exclusively by you? This was later tested and confirmed by psychiatrists who had experience of Japanese, North Korean and North Vietnamese Prisoner of War camps. In San Diego, I had a panel discussion with three officers who had been the longest-serving prisoners in North Korea, where they had been up to about seven years. They testified to

the basic experiences: those survived best who had a strongly developed will to meaning.

• *But in terms of Jewish history was it not true that the mood often was to be resigned, to argue that God had brought the pogrom on in a way? Were not many prisoners resigned?*

Those who were were the bravest. In the USA I have taken issue with Hannah Arendt and others who blame the Jews for not attacking the SS. There was hardly the possibility. First when those groups of 1000 people at a time marched to the gas chambers and the kapos encouraged them to attack the SS saying they were really going to the gas chambers. Some laughed at it. Second, they were powerless. An attack would have been unrealistic and irresponsible. You know that when one or two German soldiers were shot by Jews in Amsterdam, a thousand times more Jews were deported to the gas chambers. The revenge that would have been taken would have been a thousand times worse. There would be a terrible price to pay so it is unrealistic and, even more, immoral, to preach that. Even in Israel, I think, the younger generation has accepted this view.

• *You say that the bravest were those who were resigned. In terms of your psychology, was this because they understood the situation and so, could transcend it?*

They understood the situation. I have always argued there are three ways to meaning. One is creative, one is experiential, one is attitudinal. You can achieve meaning by creating a work or doing a deed. You can achieve meaning by experiencing something good and true and be useful in nature or culture or, indeed, by experiencing someone in his personhood which means loving. And thirdly, by your attitude. Even if you are caught as a helpless victim in hopeless situations you may transcend that situation and turn a tragedy into a triumph on the human level by the attitude you adopt and bear it with. As long as you have a chance of altering that situation that makes you suffer, you must try to alter it actively. Only when you cannot change it may you submit and try inwardly to overcome it by your heroism. When you are confronted with an incurable disease, an inoperable cancer then the question is how should you shoulder it in a worthy way? But if the cancer can be removed, you must undergo surgery, of course. An advertisement in an American newspaper makes the distinction quite clear. 'Calmly Beat Without Ado/That Which Fate Impose on You/But to Bedbugs Don't Resign/Turn for Help to Rosenstein.' There is no way in which suffering from bedbugs can be ennobling because it is unnecessary suffering.

Once those 1000 people – including my mother by the way – had been cramped in the gas chambers and they saw the canisters of cyclone B gas thrown into the crowd of naked people, then they saw there was no help. Then they began to preach the Shema Israel and surrendered themselves to what God had bestowed on them – the Communists singing the Marseillaise, the Christians saying the Our Father, the Jews saying Kaddish upon each other.

• *And for you was that realising as much as they could – turning a tragedy into a triumph?*
Fortunately, I was spared watching this ever. I've seen our own neighbours deported and marching out with prayers and devotion and surrender. I'm sure that often a mother, in that minute in the gas chambers turned her eyes to heaven just for a couple of seconds and thought 'I'm going to die, maybe my death should serve as a sacrifice so that my son could live.' What else can you demand of a simple humble mother in such a situation? But by last having this in mind, she would manifest her deepest humanity. This is what was left to her. But, in its way, this can be as great as the heroic deed of a soldier or poet or scientist because who tells us what is the criterion of greatness. Something that might last one second in the mind of an ordinary man in the street might be as great as the 'greatest deed'.

• *In your work, you say that in these very extreme conditions, some people behaved like saints and some people like swine . . . What do you feel about those who failed, who behaved like swine?*
I personally would have forgiven them. I have forgiven some I know. There is a Christian doctrine, the *mysterium inequitatis*, which says, I believe, that if everything about a human being can be explained, you are robbing a person of his humanity. There must be at least in some instances, the possibility of a decision to behave this way or that way. That is why, though personally I would be prone to forgive and to understand, I would not allow psychologists to explain everything away as a result of such understanding. You must leave the possibility of deciding, say to behave as a swine or as a saint. Only then can you admire people. Only then can you be impressed by someone's humanity. If it is just the result of conditioning or innate patterns of behaviour then there is nothing to praise and nothing to blame. I want to retain the right to be impressed.

• *But, surely, you're hemmed in by certain patterns. Your own personal history – which is both what you do and what happens to you – is bound to determine you though, perhaps, not totally.*
As a psychiatrist I know man is determined in many ways – psychologically, sociologically, biologically, but he is ultimately free to take a stand towards his conditions. I wrote *Man's Search for Meaning* only to show that even in the

extreme conditions of a concentration camp which left only a very narrow space to human freedom, there was still the possibility of behaving this way or that. You could still decide how to confront the situation.

• *Isn't there a danger that you are merely retelling the teachings of the Stoics – whatever life imposes, you must accept with dignity?*
In a way you are right. But it's more than that. The Stoic just says maintain your tranquility. I could as well prescribe a tranquilizer. I have nothing against tranquilizers – I was the first to develop one on the Continent – but stoicism would just amount to tranquilizing people. Be quiet, relax, take it easy, be stoical. I am saying not that you should ignore but that you should stick by your tension. Through your suffering and delving into your suffering, you can make the best of it. You have to suffer fully to be able to actualize yourself by transcending it. That was why I did not blind myself in the concentration camp. I faced what I saw. I went to the utmost of disgust, of empathy, of co-suffering. I looked into it and placed this demand on myself – not to let my attention be distracted and to overcome it.

• *In much of logotherapy you speak a lot about religion – what is the relationship between the two?*
In some of my books I speak of religious issues as a person. But I am also responsible for logotherapy and I have to see to it that it is available to every patient – including atheists. Logotherapy is a technique, the application of a secular scientific approach. We see in religion a human phenomenon we have to take into account. We have to consider the fact that so many people have become or remained religious. We deal with religion in logotherapy in the most general sense – that is believing in an ultimate meaning or super meaning which is beyond the capacity of our intellect to grasp. When we say a man has a strong will to meaning it means that he is motivated to find and fulfil a meaning in each life situation. But there is also an overall meaning – and here we no longer refer to individual life situations – about life in general. This ultimate meaning may also be the target of motivation. I could speak therefore of a will to ultimate meaning and by that mean being religious in the widest sense of the word. That is not my contention but that of Einstein and of other writers. Logotherapy is particularly concerned with religion because it is a form of will to meaning and there are people who are content except with such ultimate meanings

• *Do you need to have any grasp of what ultimate meaning might be?*
You cannot understand ultimate meaning. You can only believe in its existence and its counterpart, an ultimate Being which human beings have called God.

There are people who see this ultimate meaning through symbols and who carry out their devotion to it in the form of rituals.

• *From the psychological point of view does it matter if that sort of ultimate meaning is a complete delusion?*
I cannot issue any judgement. But I have most recently returned to an idea I developed when I was 14. In this, I defined God as the partner of our most intimate soliloquy. When you speak to yourself in utmost solitude and utmost sincerity, then, in a way, it is a prayer. You address yourself in honesty, whether you are speaking to yourself or to God is a matter that you have to decide. It may be an honest monologue. Honesty gives us an operational definition of God, I think I may be justified in saying. If you say that this partner of your most intimate soliloquy is what has been called God, it may be an ultimate being or your superego or your authentic self or your true self or your real self. But it doesn't matter. One may say that this partner in your soliloquy may operationally be called God.

• *Do you think that there is a great deal of mock suffering since people in the rich West sometimes seem to feel they ought to suffer. The easy target is well-off Americans who camp on the analyst's couch . . .*
Those people are focusing on superficial suffering which is not worthy of spending 50 minutes a day five weeks a day. They try to escape confronting real suffering by that because the human condition is a tragic one but they centre on the trivial. They don't even suffer but they have a complex. The language shows it is not authentic and not deep. To suffer is not pathological anyway. In fact if you are incapable of suffering that is a sign of sickness.

• *Your work has often been compared to that of Maslow. How do you differ?*
For me self-actualisation is not enough. Maslow offered things I could not offer and I'm offering things Maslow did not touch. He was always claiming me for humanistic psychology. I had no objection. But I believe self actualization is neither the primary intention nor the final destination for man. It cannot be made a target of striving. It would then become an illusion. Similarly pleasure cannot be made an aim. The more you aim for pleasure, the more you miss it. Ninety-five per cent of sexual pathology in my view derives from that fact. Self actualization is a by product of self-transcendence. Maslow in his latest work subscribed to my criticism and was good enough to invite me to contribute a paper to his Journal of Humanistic Psychology on which he commented. He went so far as to declare that the will to meaning is man's primary motivational force. I liked him very much. He was always very generous.

• *But you're critical of some aspects of humanistic therapy?*
Yes, I refer to encounter groups, marathon encounter groups and nude encounter groups.

• *Not to mention marathon nude encounter groups?*
My criticism is that encounter groups indulge in self-expression and ignore self-transcendence. When there is a speaker and a listener there is also a third thing – what they are speaking about. This is what is missing in these groups. People are just expressing themselves, venting their anger and emotions as an end in themselves rather than expressing themselves in a dialogue. It is a mutual mono-logue. What is needed are groups in which people are not just encouraged to vent but also to help themselves and others find specific meanings in their lives. It's rather pathological to free all emotions. Any neurologist will tell you that. The brain is involved in inhibition as well as releasing inhibitions.

• *But we do need meanings?*
Meanings are inexhaustible. We need to develop our intuitive sense that allows us to smell out meanings hidden and dormant in life situations. This is very important today. I am not talking about ultimate meaning. I grasped when I was 16 that I may one day find meaning either in a creative way – in work or doing a deed in an experiential way. In the way one experiences something or someone as good or true or beautiful. There is also a third way. If your situation is unchangeable, if you are suffering from an incurable disease then you can find meaning by the way you live through it.

Chapter 7: Daniel Kahneman

New Jersey in the late summer of 2002. At 9.15 a.m. the phone in the house of Daniel Kahneman, Professor of Psychology at Princeton, rings.

> "Someone with a very distinct Swedish accent called, and he read me a citation – actually, I was a bit excited, I suppose I didn't really hear it. And then he said . . . I will give you the chair of the committee, who happens to be someone I know, and so we verified that this was for real and not a particularly nasty crank call."

At the not particularly advanced age of 68, Daniel Kahneman learned he had won the Nobel prize for Economics. It was the only Nobel he could possibly be nominated for, as there is no Nobel Prize for psychology. In a review of his achievements *The Psychologist* claimed he was only the fifth psychologist to win, citing Pavlov, Roger Sperry (who did the work on split brains), Hubel and Wiesel (who did the work on visual cortex) and Herbert Simon as the only previous champions who did psychology. One should add Tinbergen and Lorenz to that list as their research was on animal – and to some extent – human behaviour. All these laureates won the prize for medicine or physiology until in 1979 Herbert Simon won the Economics prize.

At least the Royal Swedish Academy of Sciences had the grace to mention psychology as it said Kahneman won "for having integrated insights from psychological research into economic science, especially concerning human judgment and decision-making under uncertainty." His work, said the Nobel citation, had "laid the foundations of a new field of research by discovering how human judgment may take shortcuts that systematically depart from basic principles of probability."

Much of Kahneman's most important research was carried out with Amos Tversky. Kahneman was scrupulous in remembering his long-time collaborator, telling the Swedish press that "The work for which I'm honoured is work I did collaboratively with a close friend and a very famous psychologist, Amos Tversky, who died in 1996. Certainly we would have received this together, and that's one of the things that this means to me today. There is that shadow over the joy I feel." They were close. When preparing for this interview, I found a note Kahneman had posted on the Internet at the time Tversky was very ill. Kahneman circulated friends asking them to write for news rather than ring Tverksy's house. The endless well-meant phone calls only added to the pressure the family was under.

Kahneman is very open about that collaboration. "Amos and I shared the wonder of together owning a goose that could lay golden eggs – a joint mind that was better than our separate minds," he wrote in the autobiography he prepared after winning the Nobel Prize. The statistical record confirms that their joint work was superior, or at least more influential, than the work they did individually (Laibson and Zeckhauser, 2000). Amos Tversky and Kahneman published eight journal articles during what he calls "our peak years". Five had been cited more than a thousand times by the end of 2002. Of their 200 separate works, only Tversky's theory of similarity (Tversky, 1977) and Kahneman's book on attention (Kahneman, 1973) did better.

An early referee spotted the "special style of our collaborative work" and that led to the rejections of their first theoretical paper (on representativeness), by *Psychological Review*. The eminent referee pointed out that he was familiar with the separate lines of work that Tversky and Kahneman had been pursuing, and considered both quite respectable. However, he added the unusual remark that "we seemed to bring out the worst in each other, and certainly should not collaborate." A major irony, Kahneman laughed.

In 30 years of reporting psychology I have sometimes wondered what the pioneers of the art and science might make of how specialised it has become. At the start of his career in Israel, Kahneman had to be very practical and try to predict which soldiers would turn out to be good leaders on the battlefield. He obviously remembers this period with affection. He came to the States in 1958 but did not yet feel he was a truly grown up psychologist. He was just 24 at the time. It took him about seven more years and a lot of research on vision – especially on the relationship between pupil size and memory and pupil size and the complexity of certain mental tasks – before he felt grown up.

Forty years on, Kahneman is working on more obviously relevant problems to the well being of the species – though one of them does have a definite Woody Allen aspect. One of the topics Kahneman has been studying is whether Californians in hot tubs are really happier than New Yorkers. Kahneman has made the discovery that people in hot tubs in California are not actually happier than people in hot tubs in Manhattan but people in Manhattan think the California soakers have a higher happiness quotient.

But, of course, Kahneman would not have won the Nobel Prize if he had confined himself to the East Coast West Coast hot tub dilemma.

Kahneman was born in Tel Aviv in 1934 when the British ruled Palestine as it then was. His father then had a job in France and Kahneman survived as a Jew in Nazi-occupied France for five years. He describes in the interview what that was like and the effect it had on him. He started his career at the Hebrew University and soon found himself as a psychologist in the Israeli army where he specialised in trying to assess soldiers and their skills. He soon got into trouble because he was challenging the assumptions the military used.

Kahneman is now Professor of Psychology at Princeton University's Woodrow Wilson School of Public and International Affairs, which reflects how his work has become very much about real social, financial and political decisions.

You can't really understand Kahneman's work without a sense of classical economic theory. According to Paul Ormerod in his *Butterfly Economics*, economists have been fixated for over 250 years on the theory of the rational man or woman. This assumes that it is normal to be rational about money and risk so that Mr and Mrs Average are actually calculating machines, carrying a little actuarial device in their head that allows them to analyse the risks and rewards not just of investments but of every economical situation perfectly. The problem with classical economic theory however is that few classical economists got out of their armchair and observed how people behaved. John Kenneth Galbraith wrote a book about the Wall Street crash, which looked at how people got sucked into market bubbles – but apart from the madness of speculative bubbles, human beings were rational about risk.

By the late 1960s Kahneman came to believe that the so-called rational model of economics did not deal with psychological reality. How individuals analyse risk is distorted by what he calls cognitive illusions as well as the individual psychology of risk takers. We are not that good at calculating a reasonable interpretation of probabilities. As Piaget might have put it, most of us do not reach the stage of "formal operations". Kahneman was surprised – the only moment of our surprise when we talked – when I told him of a study that found that only 1 per cent of people ever reach the stage of formal operations. "People manage quite well without it," he said.

The tracing of our systematic departure from the rational has been a constant theme of Kahneman's work. For example, in some situations we become unwilling to risk anything because the fear of losing is greater than the possible joy of winning. In other situations, people grossly over-estimate the likelihood of success.

Risk has become a hot topic in the social sciences because it affects so many areas of life including medicine and, of course, the risk of terrorist attacks. Insurers assess the risks of floods and thefts, doctors have to help patients assess the risk of certain operations, and investors try to assess financial. Will shares in "Smell Sweet Perfumes" rise or fall? Kahneman has examined what influences the way we perceive risks.

Some human beings adore risks – there is research that shows extroverts like them more – while others will do anything to avoid risks. And it is not just a matter of personality. The person who will take a punt on some risky new stock may well refuse to take the slightest physical risk. As a young man I worked for a famous film producer Alexandre Salkind who made the Superman films. He was willing to take huge financial gambles but refused to step on a plane because that was too risky. When he was told that the statistics showed far more pictures crash than planes, he replied that far more planes with him in it crashed.

To understand risks Kahneman and Tversky worked on many nooks and crannies of the subject. He has examined aversion to loss, distortion by hind-sight, lack of statistical awareness, framing of choices, previous memories, and worries about the future. How we frame questions is one that pollsters know all about. In the interview, he discusses that at length.

One of his real achievements has been to provide a framework which makes it possible to handle the complexity of consciousness when dealing with risks and our susceptibility to cognitive illusions. Say you are a trader for Investment Bank Alpha. Your performance review is coming up and you know that you have not met your quotas. You should have made 15 per cent profit in the last year in your trades and you have only made 13.8 per cent. You get a tip that Stock A will rise by 20 per cent over the week because they are negotiating a huge contract to sell their oil exploration technology to Azerbaijan. You whoop with delight and that makes you weigh rather poorly the risks of this investment. You forget possible negatives such as the fact that there often are positive rumours that turn out to be worth nothing. You look for confirming evidence rather than critical evidence. So you make the trade and you lose the bank a packet as well as your job. You have neglected also to take into consideration the fact that you had rather more than your usual dash of cocaine the night before because your girlfriend had just told you she was going off with someone else. The question is how do you measure many of the variables involved? And in other areas of human behaviour they become only more complex. Kahneman has extended his analysis of risk well beyond questions of finance and game theory. He has looked at consumer behaviour, at how we deal with medical risks and, which is hardly surprising if you have both American and Israeli citizenship, at issues of conflict resolution. In the interview he reflects that he was recently in Israel and struck by how irrational and hawkish both sides were. He saw little hope of educating them.

The failure to understand probabilities, Kahneman argues, is perhaps most marked at the upper and lower ends of the scale. For example, we are unable to meaningfully assess the difference between 1 per cent and 5 per cent probability, or between 90 per cent and 95 per cent probability. We usually weigh low probabilities too high and high probabilities too low relative to certainty. We tend to categorise some factors in "either/or" terms (say, that vaccination is either "safe" or "dangerous"), without incorporating any numerical likelihood in the choice.

As his work has become more relevant, it is not surprising that Kahneman has turned his attention to the risks of medicine. Traditionally research into what risks patients would accept asked patients to assign odds, to gamble in effect on what they imagined might be the benefit of an outcome of treatment they haven't yet experienced. Patients find it hard to work out the value of a hypothetical treatment outcome, but they understand the familiar.

Instead of focusing on *outcomes*, Kahneman and Tversky shifted the focus to measuring *change* – the gains and losses each individual experiences. These are personal and in order to quantify them you have to devise new scales to tap into people's own reality.

One conclusion is that patients can be like gamblers. In life-and-death situations, survival overrides all other factors but when the issues are less critical, people are sometimes more frightened of what they might lose than interested in what they might gain. So patients will accept high risks with low probabilities of success (say, in radical head-and-neck surgery for cancer) when the payoff from success is high but they may quibble if they might have to leave home to get treatment for more minor conditions.

But much of it does depend on the words in which choices are put. Kahneman and Tversky were the first to show that the way questions were "framed" affected the answers patients gave – and one presumes what they were really feeling. Imagine a situation in which it is explained that a particular medical procedure carries a 30 per cent risk of death, a 40 per cent probability of cure so that your life is better and 30 per cent likelihood that you will not get better or worse but that you have will gone through considerable pain or discomfort.

If patients are asked questions that are phrased so that it is a matter of Operation X "saving lives" then people are more likely to accept such medical risks. But if patients are asked questions that reflect the same probabilities of death or cure but the questions are phrased around "lives lost" then they are likely to be more risk-averse. Knowledge does not inoculate. Doctors who should know better are just as likely as patients to have their perceptions of risk affected by how the questions were framed.

Reviewing Kahneman's work when he won the Nobel Prize, the Australian *Journal of Medicine* admitted that, "in our discussions with patients, we often use vaguely quantitative terms, such as 'frequent', 'likely', 'common', 'rare' and 'possible'. These approximations honestly reflect the real world of partial knowledge within which decisions are made. If clinicians don't use, and don't know, the predictive probabilities that shape their therapeutic decisions for each patient, attempts to weigh significant numerical variables against one another to reach a decision may be no more than pseudo-accuracy.

"We need to develop a little 'science of the individual' that can weigh all the human and medical factors at play, together with a calculus for clinical judgement that guides the parties to a decision most likely to optimise the chosen outcomes."

A Nobel Prize may be waiting for the clinical researcher who cuts a sound and workable path through these complexities of the real world! Kahneman tried to revive the magic of his collaboration with Tversky in 1996 when his friend only had a few months to live. "We decided to edit a joint book on decision-making that would cover some of the progress that had been made since we had started working together on the topic more than 20 years before. We planned an ambitious preface as a joint project, but I think we both knew from the beginning that we would not be granted enough time to complete it. The preface I wrote alone was probably my most painful writing experience."

- *What was your background?*

My parents were Lithuanian Jews, who had immigrated to France in the early 1920s and had done quite well. My father was the chief of research in a large chemical factory. But although my parents loved most things French and had some French friends, their roots in France were shallow, and they never felt completely secure. Of course, whatever vestiges of security they'd had were lost when the Germans swept into France in 1940. What was probably the first graph I ever drew, in 1941, showed my family's fortunes as a function of time – and around 1940 the curve crossed into the negative domain.

I will never know if my vocation as a psychologist was a result of my early exposure to interesting gossip, or whether my interest in gossip was an indication of a budding vocation. Like many other Jews, I suppose, I grew up in a world that consisted exclusively of people and words, and most of the words were about people. Nature barely existed, and I never learned to identify flowers or to appreciate animals. But the people my mother liked to talk about with my father were her friends and they were fascinating in their complexity. Some people were better than others, but the best were far from perfect and no one was simply bad. Most of her stories were touched by irony, and they all had two sides or more.

In one experience I remember vividly. It must have been late 1941 or early 1942. Jews were required to wear the Star of David and to obey a 6 p.m. curfew. I had gone to play with a Christian friend and had stayed too late. I turned my brown sweater inside out to walk the few blocks home. As I was walking down an empty street, I saw a German soldier approaching. He was wearing the black uniform that I had been told to fear more than others – the one worn by specially recruited SS soldiers. As I came closer to him, trying to walk fast, I noticed that he was looking at me intently. Then he beckoned me over, picked me up, and hugged me. I was terrified that he would notice the star inside my sweater. He was speaking to me with great emotion, in German. When he put me down, he opened his wallet, showed me a picture of a boy, and gave me some money. I went home more certain than ever that my mother was right: people were endlessly complicated and interesting.

My father was picked up in the first large-scale sweep for Jews, and was interned for six weeks in Drancy, which had been set up as a way station to the extermination camps. He was released through the intervention of his firm, which was directed (a fact I learned only from an article I read a few years ago) by the financial mainstay of the Fascist anti-Semitic movement in France in the 1930s. The story of my father's release, which I never fully understood, also involved a beautiful woman and a German general who loved her. Soon afterward, we escaped to Vichy France, and stayed on the Riviera in relative safety, until the Germans arrived and we escaped again, to the centre of France. My father died of inadequately treated diabetes, in 1944, just six weeks before the D-day he had been waiting for so desperately. Soon my mother, my sister, and I were free, and beginning to hope for the permits that would allow us to join the rest of our family in Palestine.

• *Were you good at school?*
I had grown up intellectually precocious and physically inept. The ineptitude must have been quite remarkable, because during my last term in a French lycée, in 1946, my eighth-grade physical education teacher blocked my inclusion in the Tableau d'Honneur – the Honour Roll – on the grounds that even his extreme tolerance had limits. I must also have been quite a pompous child. I had a notebook of essays, with a title that still makes me blush: 'What I write of what I think'. The first essay, written before I turned eleven, was a discussion of faith. It approvingly quoted Pascal's saying 'Faith is God made perceptible to the heart' ('How right this is!'), then went on to point out that this genuine spiritual experience was probably rare and unreliable, and that cathedrals and organ music had been created to generate a more reliable ersatz.

• *And then you moved to Palestine?*
At age 17, I had some decisions to make about my military service. I applied to a unit that would allow me to defer my service until I had completed my first degree; this entailed spending the summers in officer-training school, and part of my military service using my professional skills. By that time I had decided, with some difficulty, that I would be a psychologist. The questions that interested me in my teens were philosophical – the meaning of life, the existence of God, and the reasons not to misbehave. But I was discovering that I was more interested in what made people believe in God than I was in whether God existed, and I was more curious about the origins of people's peculiar convictions about right and wrong than I was about ethics. When I went for vocational guidance, psychology emerged as the top recommendation, with economics not too far behind. I started out in technical fields because I wanted the experience. I call that being a short order cook before I became a chef.

• *How did your education proceed?*
I got my first degree from the Hebrew University in Jerusalem, in two years, with a major in psychology and a minor in mathematics. I was mediocre in maths, especially in comparison with some of the people I was studying with – several of whom went on to become world-class mathematicians. But psychology was wonderful. As a first-year student, I encountered the writings of the social psychologist Kurt Lewin and was deeply influenced by his maps of the life space, in which motivation was represented as a forcefield acting on the individual from the outside, pushing and pulling in various directions. Fifty years later, I still draw on Lewin's analysis of how to induce changes in behaviour for my introductory lecture to graduate students at the Woodrow Wilson School of Public Affairs at Princeton. I was also fascinated by my early exposures to neuropsychology. There were the weekly lectures of our revered teacher Yeshayahu Leibowitz – I once went to one of his lectures with a fever of 41 degrees Celsius; they were simply not to be missed. And there was a visit by the German neurosurgeon Kurt Goldstein, who claimed that large wounds to the brain eliminated the capacity for abstraction and turned people into concrete thinkers. Furthermore, and most exciting, as Goldstein described them, the boundaries that separated abstract from concrete were not the ones that philosophers would have set. We now know that there was little substance to Goldstein's assertions, but at the time the idea of basing conceptual distinctions on neurological observations was so thrilling that I seriously considered switching to medicine in order to study neurology. The Chief of Neurosurgery at the Hadassah Hospital, who was a neighbour, wisely talked me out of that plan by pointing out that the study of medicine was too demanding to be undertaken as a means to any goal other than practice.

• *You must have done military service?*
In 1954, I was drafted as a second lieutenant, and after an eventful year as a platoon leader I was transferred to the psychology branch of the Israel Defense Forces. There, one of my occasional duties was to participate in the assessment of candidates for officer training. We used methods that had been developed by the British Army in the Second World War. One test involved a leaderless group challenge, in which eight candidates, with all insignia of rank removed and only numbers to identify them, were asked to lift a telephone pole from the ground and then led to an obstacle, such as a 2.5-meter wall, where they were told to get to the other side of the wall without the pole touching either the ground or the wall, and without any of them touching the wall. If one of these things happened, they had to declare it and start again. Two of us would watch the exercise, which often took half an hour or more. We were looking for manifestations of the candidates' characters, and we saw plenty: true leaders, loyal followers, empty boasters, wimps – there were all kinds. Under the stress of the event, we felt, the soldiers' true nature would reveal itself, and we would be able to tell who would be a good leader and who would not. But the trouble was that, in fact, we could not tell. Every month or so we had a 'statistics day,' during which we would get feedback from the officer-training school, indicating the accuracy of our ratings of candidates' potential. The story was always the same: our ability to predict performance at the school was negligible. I was so impressed by the complete lack of connection between the statistical information and the compelling experience of insight that I coined a term for it: 'the illusion of validity.' Almost 20 years later, this term made it into the technical literature (Kahneman and Tversky, 1973). It was the first cognitive illusion I discovered. Closely related to the illusion of validity was another feature of our discussions about the candidates we observed: our willingness to make extreme predictions about their future performance on the basis of a small sample of behaviour. In fact, the issue of willingness did not arise, because we did not really distinguish predictions from observations. The soldier who took over when the group was in trouble and led the team over the wall was a leader at that moment, and if we asked ourselves how he would perform in officer training, or on the battlefield, the best bet was simply that he would be as good a leader then as he was now. Any other prediction seemed inconsistent with the evidence. As I understood clearly only when I taught statistics some years later, the idea that predictions should be less extreme than the information on which they are based is deeply counterintuitive.

The theme of intuitive prediction came up again, when I was given the major assignment for my service in the Unit: to develop a method for interviewing all combat-unit recruits, in order to screen the unfit and help allocate soldiers to specific duties. An interviewing system was already in place, administered by a small cadre of interviewers, mostly young women, themselves recent graduates from good high schools, who had been selected for their outstanding performance in psychometric tests and for their interest in psychology. The interviewers were instructed to form a general impression of a recruit and then to provide some global ratings of how well the recruit was expected to perform in a combat unit. Here again, the statistics of validity were dismal. The interviewers' ratings did not predict with substantial accuracy any of the criteria in which we were interested.

My assignment involved two tasks: first, to figure out whether there were personality dimensions that mattered more in some combat jobs than in others, and then to develop interviewing guidelines that would identify those dimensions. I visited units of infantry, artillery, armour, and others, and collected global evaluations of the performance of the soldiers in each unit, as well as ratings on several personality dimensions. It was a hopeless task, but I didn't realise that then. Instead, spending weeks and months on complex analyses using a manual Monroe calculator with a rather iffy handle, I invented a statistical technique for the analysis of multi-attribute data, which I used to produce a complex description of the psychological requirements of the various units. I was capitalising on chance, but the technique had enough charm for one of my graduate-school teachers, the eminent personnel psychologist Edwin Ghiselli, to write it up in what became my first published article. This was the beginning of a lifelong interest in the statistics of prediction and description.

I had devised personality profiles for a criterion measure, and now I needed to propose a predictive interview. The year was 1955, just after the publication of *Clinical versus statistical prediction* (Meehl, 1954), Paul Meehl's classic book in which he showed that clinical prediction was consistently inferior to actuarial prediction. Someone must have given me the book to read, and it certainly had a big effect on me. I developed a structured interview schedule with a set of questions about various aspects of civilian life, which the interviewers were to use to generate ratings about six different aspects of personality (including, I remember, such things as 'masculine pride' and 'sense of obligation'). Soon I had a near-mutiny on my hands. The cadre of interviewers, who had taken pride in the exercise of their clinical skills, felt that they were being reduced to unthinking robots, and my confident declarations – 'Just make sure that you are reliable, and leave validity to me' – did not satisfy them. So I gave in. I told them that after completing 'my' six ratings as instructed, they were free to exercise their clinical judgment by generating a global evaluation of the recruit's potential in any way they pleased. A few months later, we obtained our first validity data, using ratings of the recruits' performance as a criterion. Validity was much higher than it had been. My recollection is that we achieved correlations of close to .30, in contrast to about .10 with the previous methods. The most instructive finding was that the interviewers' global evaluation, produced at the end of a structured interview, was by far the most predictive of all the ratings they made. Trying to be reliable had made them valid. The puzzles with which I struggled at that time were the seed of the paper on the psychology of intuitive prediction that Amos Tversky and I published much later.

• *Was Freud an influence on your work?*
No.

• *But you were influenced by one leading psychoanalytic thinker?*
In the summer of 1958, my wife and I drove across the United States to spend a few months at the Austen Riggs Clinic in Stockbridge, Massachusetts, where I studied with the well-known psychoanalytic theorist David Rapaport, who had befriended me on a visit to Jerusalem a few years earlier. Rapaport believed psychoanalysis contained the elements of a valid theory of memory and thought. The core ideas of that theory, he argued, were laid out in the seventh chapter of Freud's *Interpretation of Dreams*, which sketches a model of mental energy. With the other young people in Rapaport's circle, I studied that chapter like a Talmudic text, and tried to derive from it experimental predictions about short-term memory. This was a wonderful experience, and I would have gone back if Rapaport had not died suddenly later that year. I had enormous respect for his fierce mind. Fifteen years later, I published a book entitled *Attention and Effort*, which contained a theory of attention as a limited resource. I realised only while writing the acknowledgements for the book that I had revisited the terrain to which Rapaport had first led me.

• *But you left the States still feeling not fully trained?*
I had learned a lot in Berkeley, but I felt that I had not been adequately trained to do research. I therefore decided that in order to acquire the basic skills I would need to have a proper laboratory and do regular science – I needed to be a solid short-order cook before I could aspire to become a chef. So I set up a vision lab, and over the next few years I turned out competent work on energy integration in visual acuity. At the same time, I was trying to develop a research programme to study affiliative motivation in children, using an approach that I called a 'psychology of single questions.' My model for this kind of psychology was research reported by Walter Mischel (1961a, 1961b) in which he devised two questions that he posed to samples of children in Caribbean islands: 'You can have this (small) lollipop today, or this (large) lollipop tomorrow,' and 'Now

let's pretend that there is a magic man . . . who could change you into anything that you would want to be, what you would want to be?' The answer to the latter question was scored 1, if it referred to a profession or to an achievement-related trait, otherwise 0. The responses to these lovely questions turned out to be plausibly correlated with numerous characteristics of the child and the child's background. I found this inspiring. Mischel had succeeded in creating a link between an important psychological concept and a simple operation to measure it. There was (and still is) almost nothing like it in psychology, where concepts are commonly associated with procedures that can be described only by long lists or by convoluted paragraphs of prose.

I had the most satisfying Eureka experience of my career while attempting to teach flight instructors that praise is more effective than punishment for promoting skill-learning. When I had finished my enthusiastic speech, one of the most seasoned instructors in the audience raised his hand and made his own short speech, which began by conceding that positive reinforcement might be good for the birds, but went on to deny that it was optimal for flight cadets. He said, 'On many occasions I have praised flight cadets for clean execution of some aerobatic manoeuvre, and in general when they try it again, they do worse. On the other hand, I have often screamed at cadets for bad execution, and in general they do better the next time. So please don't tell us that reinforcement works and punishment does not, because the opposite is the case.' This was a joyous moment, in which I understood an important truth about the world: because we tend to reward others when they do well and punish them when they do badly, and because there is regression to the mean, it is part of the human condition that we are statistically punished for rewarding others and rewarded for punishing them. I immediately arranged a demonstration in which each participant tossed two coins at a target behind his back, without any feedback. We measured the distances from the target and could see that those who had done best the first time had mostly deteriorated on their second try, and vice versa. But I knew that this demonstration would not undo the effects of life-long exposure to a perverse contingency.

• *As well as the results of your research, the way you collaborated with Amos Tverksy is obviously rather interesting?*
From 1968 to 1969, I taught a graduate seminar on the applications of psychology to real-world problems. In what turned out to be a life-changing event, I asked my younger colleague Amos Tversky to tell the class about what was going on in his field of judgment and decision-making. Amos told us about the work of his former mentor, Ward Edwards, whose lab was using a research paradigm in which the subject is shown two book bags filled with poker chips. The

bags are said to differ in their composition (e.g., 70:30 or 30:70 white/red). One of them is randomly chosen, and the participant is given an opportunity to sample successively from it, and required to indicate after each trial the probability that it came from the predominantly red bag. Edwards had concluded from the results that people are 'conservative Bayesians': they almost always adjust their confidence interval in the proper direction, but rarely far enough. A lively discussion developed around Amos's talk. I learned recently that one of Amos's friends met him that day and heard about our conversation, which Amos described as having severely shaken his faith in the neo-Bayesian idea. I do remember that Amos and I decided to meet for lunch to discuss our hunches about the manner in which probabilities are 'really' judged. There we exchanged personal accounts of our own recurrent errors of judgement in this domain, and decided to study the statistical intuitions of experts.

I spent the summer of 1969 doing research at the Applied Psychological Research Unit in Cambridge, England. Amos stopped there for a few days on his way to the United States. I had drafted a questionnaire on intuitions about sampling variability and statistical power, which was based largely on my personal experiences of incorrect research planning and unsuccessful replications. Amos went off and administered the questionnaire to participants at a meeting of the Mathematical Psychology Association, and a few weeks later we met in Jerusalem to look at the results and write a paper.

The experience was magical. I had enjoyed collaborative work before, but this was something different. Amos was often described by people who knew him as the smartest person they knew. He was also very funny, with an endless supply of jokes appropriate to every nuance of a situation. In his presence, I became funny as well, and the result was that we could spend hours of solid work in continuous mirth. The paper we wrote was deliberately humorous – we described a prevalent belief in the 'law of small numbers,' according to which the law of large numbers extends to small numbers as well. Although we never wrote another humorous paper, we continued to find amusement in our work – I have probably shared more than half of the laughs of my life with Amos.

• *How did the collaboration affect you?*
Amos's work was always characterized by confidence and by a crisp elegance, and it was a joy to find those characteristics now attached to my ideas as well. As we were writing our first paper, I was conscious of how much better it was than the more hesitant piece I would have written by myself. I don't know exactly what it was that Amos found to like in our collaboration – we were not in the habit of trading compliments – but clearly he was also having a good time. We were a team, and we remained in that mode for well over a decade. The Nobel

Prize was awarded for work that we produced during that period of intense collaboration.

At the beginning of our collaboration, we quickly established a rhythm that we maintained during all our years together. Amos was a night person, and I was a morning person. This made it natural for us to meet for lunch and a long afternoon together, and still have time to do our separate things. We spent hours each day, just talking. When Amos's first son Oren, then 15 months old, was told that his father was at work, he volunteered the comment 'Aba talk Danny.' (In Hebrew Aba means father.) We were not only working, of course – we talked of everything under the sun, and got to know each other's mind almost as well as our own. We could (and often did) finish each other's sentences and complete the joke that the other had wanted to tell, but somehow we also kept surprising each other.

We did almost all the work on our joint projects while physically together, including the drafting of questionnaires and papers. And we avoided any explicit division of labour. Our principle was to discuss every disagreement until it had been resolved to mutual satisfaction, and we had tie-breaking rules for only two topics: whether or not an item should be included in the list of references (Amos had the casting vote), and who should resolve any issue of English grammar (my dominion). We did not initially have a concept of a senior author. We tossed a coin to determine the order of authorship of our first paper, and alternated from then on until the pattern of our collaboration changed in the 1980s.

One consequence of this mode of work was that all our ideas were jointly owned. Our interactions were so frequent and so intense that there was never much point in distinguishing between the discussions that primed an idea, the act of uttering it, and the subsequent elaboration of it. I believe that many scholars have had the experience of discovering that they had expressed (sometimes even published) an idea long before they really understood its significance. It takes time to appreciate and develop a new thought. Some of the greatest joys of our collaboration – and probably much of its success – came from our ability to elaborate each other's nascent thoughts: if I expressed a half-formed idea, I knew that Amos would be there to understand it, probably more clearly than I did, and that if it had merit he would see it. Like most people, I am somewhat cautious about exposing tentative thoughts to others – I must first make sure that they are not idiotic. In the best years of the collaboration, this caution was completely absent. The mutual trust and the complete lack of defensiveness that we achieved were particularly remarkable because both of us – Amos even more than I – were known to be severe critics. Our magic worked only when we were by ourselves. We soon learned that joint collaboration with any third party should be avoided, because we became competitive in a threesome.

• *You then had a year that you described as the most productive of your life?*
From 1971 to 1972, Amos and I were at the Oregon Research Institute (ORI) in Eugene, a year that was by far the most productive of my life. We did a considerable amount of research and writing on the availability heuristic, on the psychology of prediction, and on the phenomena of anchoring and overconfidence – thereby fully earning the label 'dynamic duo' that our colleagues attached to us. Working evenings and nights, I also completely rewrote my book on *Attention and Effort*, which went to the publisher that year, and remains my most significant independent contribution to psychology.

Some time after our return from Eugene, Amos and I settled down to review what we had learned about three heuristics of judgement (representativeness, availability, and anchoring) and about a list of a dozen biases associated with these heuristics. Our enjoyment of the process gave us unlimited patience, and we wrote as if the precise choice of every word were a matter of great moment.

We published the article in *Science* because we thought that the prevalence of systematic biases in intuitive assessments and predictions could possibly be of interest to scholars outside psychology. This interest, however, could not be taken for granted, as I learned in an encounter with a well-known American philosopher at a party in Jerusalem. Mutual friends had encouraged us to talk about the research that Amos and I were doing, but almost as soon as I began my story he turned away, saying, 'I am not really interested in the psychology of stupidity.'

The *Science* article turned out to be a rarity: an empirical psychological article that some philosophers and a few economists could and did take seriously. I attribute the unusual attention at least as much to the medium as to the message. Amos and I had continued to practice the psychology of single questions, and the *Science* article incorporated questions that were cited verbatim in the text. These questions, I believe, personally engaged the readers and convinced them that we were concerned not with the stupidity of Joe Public but with a much more interesting issue: the susceptibility to erroneous intuitions of intelligent, sophisticated, and perceptive individuals such as themselves. Whatever the reason, the article soon became a standard reference as an attack on the rational-agent model, and it spawned a large literature in cognitive science, philosophy, and psychology. We had not anticipated that outcome.

The conclusions that readers drew were often too strong, mostly because existential quantifiers, as they are prone to do, disappeared in the transmission. Whereas we had shown that some, not all judgements about uncertain events are mediated by heuristics, which sometimes, not always produce predictable biases, we were often read as having claimed that people cannot think straight.

• *I have argued that psychology does involve a great deal of attack and riposte. Your ideas were attacked?*

The interpretation of our work as a broad attack on human rationality – rather than as a critique of the rational-agent model – attracted much opposition, some quite harsh and dismissive. Numerous experiments were conducted over the years, to show that cognitive illusions could 'be made to disappear' and that heuristics had been invented to explain 'biases that do not exist'. After participating in a few published skirmishes in the early 80s, Amos and I adopted a policy of not criticizing the critiques of our work, although we eventually felt compelled to make an exception in Kahneman and Tversky, 1996.

Frederick and I recently reviewed the experimental literature, and concluded that the empirical controversy about the reality of cognitive illusions dissolves when viewed in the perspective of a dual-process model. The essence of such a model is that judgements can be produced in two ways (and in various mixtures of the two): a rapid, associative, automatic, and effortless intuitive process (sometimes called System 1), and a slower, rule-governed, deliberate and effortful process (System 2). System 2 'knows' some of the rules that intuitive reasoning is prone to violate, and sometimes intervenes to correct or replace erroneous intuitive judgments. Thus, errors of intuition occur when two conditions are satisfied: System 1 generates the error and System 2 fails to correct. In this view, the experiments in which cognitive illusions were 'made to disappear' did so by facilitating the corrective operations of System 2. They tell us little about the intuitive judgments that are suppressed.

What happened, I suppose, is that because the 1974 paper was influential it altered the context in which it was read in subsequent years. Its being misunderstood was a direct consequence of its being taken seriously. I wonder how often this occurs.

• *You are sometimes taken as not having that much faith in human rationality?*

Amos and I always dismissed the criticism that our focus on biases reflected a generally pessimistic view of the human mind. We argued that this criticism confuses the medium of bias research with a message about rationality. This confusion was indeed common.

There is no denying, however, that the name of our method and approach created a strong association between heuristics and biases, and thereby contributed to giving heuristics a bad name, which we did not intend.

• *What did you learn from the controversy about heuristics and biases?*

Like most protagonists in debates, I have few memories of having changed my mind under adversarial pressure, but I have certainly learned more than I know.

For example, I am now quick to reject any description of our work as demonstrating human irrationality. When the occasion arises, I carefully explain that research on heuristics and biases only refutes an unrealistic conception of rationality. Was I always so careful? Probably not. In my current view, the study of judgement biases requires attention to the interplay between intuitive and reflective thinking, which sometimes allows biased judgements and sometimes overrides or corrects them. Was this always as clear to me as it is now? Probably not. Finally, I am now very impressed by the observation I mentioned earlier, that the most highly skilled cognitive performances are intuitive, and that many complex judgements share the speed, confidence and accuracy of routine perception. This observation is not new to me, but did it always loom as large in my views as it now does? Almost certainly not.

As my obvious struggle with this topic reveals, I thoroughly dislike controversies where it is clear that no minds will be changed. I feel diminished by losing my objectivity when in point-scoring mode, and downright humiliated when I get angry. Indeed, my phobia for professional anger is such that I have allowed myself for many years the luxury of refusing to referee papers that might arouse that emotion: if the tone is snide, or the review of the facts more tendentious than normal, I return the paper back to the editor without commenting on it. I consider myself fortunate not to have had too many of the nasty experiences of professional quarrels, and am grateful for the occasional encounters with open minds across lines of sharp debate.

• *Do you think the work you have done has affected economics?*
Although behavioural economics has enjoyed much more rapid progress and gained more respectability in economics than appeared possible 15 years ago, it is still a minority approach and its influence on most fields of economics is negligible. Many economists believe that it is a passing fad, and some hope that it will be. The future may prove them right. But many bright young economists are now betting their careers on the expectation that the current trend will last. And such expectations have a way of being self-fulfilling.

• *What have been the latest topics of research for you?*
For the past 15 years, the main focus of my research interests has been the study of various aspects of experienced utility, including some errors that people make in forecasting their future tastes and in remembering and evaluating the quality of their past experiences. In some of our experiments people make wrong choices between experiences, because they are systematically wrong about their 'affective forecasts' and even about their affective memories.

The concept of utility in which I am interested was the one that Bentham and

Edgeworth had in mind. However, experienced utility largely disappeared from economic discourse in the 20th century, in favour of a notion that I call decision utility, which is inferred from choices and used to explain choices. The distinction could be of little relevance for fully rational agents, who presumably maximise experienced utility as well as decision utility. But if rationality cannot be assumed, the quality of consequences becomes worth measuring and the maximisation of experienced utility becomes a testable proposition. Indeed, my colleagues and I have carried out experiments in which this proposition was falsified. These experiments exploit a simple rule that governs the assignment of remembered utility to past episodes in which an agent is passively exposed to a pleasant or unpleasant experience, such as watching a horrible film or an amusing one or undergoing a colonoscopy. Remembered utility turns out to be determined largely by the peak intensity of the pleasure or discomfort experienced during the episode, and by the intensity of pleasure or discomfort when the episode ended. The duration of the episode has almost no effect on its remembered utility. An episode of 60 seconds during which one hand is immersed in painfully cold water will leave a more aversive memory than a longer episode, in which the same 60 seconds are followed by another 30 seconds during which the temperature rises slightly. Although the extra 30 seconds are painful, they provide an improved end. When experimental participants are exposed to the two episodes, then given a choice of which to repeat, most choose the longer one. Our evidence contradicts the standard rational model, which does not distinguish between experienced utility and decision utility.

• *You have tried to develop a new way of working with people you disagree with?* One line of work that I hope may become influential is the development of a procedure of *adversarial collaboration,* which I have championed as a substitute for the format of critique-reply-rejoinder in which debates are currently conducted in the social sciences. I have been appalled by the absurdly adversarial nature of these exchanges, in which hardly anyone ever admits an error or acknowledges learning anything from the other. Adversarial collaboration involves a good-faith effort to conduct debates by carrying out joint research – in some cases there may be a need for an agreed arbiter to lead the project and collect the data. Adversarial collaborations will usually lead to an unusual type of joint publication, in which disagreements are laid out as part of a jointly authored paper. I have had three adversarial collaborations. In another case I did not succeed in convincing two colleagues that we should engage in an adversarial collaboration, but we jointly developed another procedure that is also more constructive than the reply-rejoinder format. They wrote a critique of one of my lines of work, but instead of following up with the usual exchange of unpleasant comments we decided to write a joint piece, which started by a statement of what we did agree on, then went on to a series of short debates about issues on which we disagreed. I hope that more efficient procedures for the conduct of controversies will be part of my legacy.

• *Does your work have any implications in helping people negotiate more sanely?*
Well, in principle, yes . . . I was in Israel recently, however, giving a lecture on t he implications of psychology for negotiations in the conflict. My conclusion was that most of the biases make people more irrational. But then again, you know, I don't expect that to penetrate the consciousness of negotiators.

• *Is part of the reason for our inability to deal with the kind of probabilities you study that this is a skill we didn't need as a survival skill?*
You know, that's a very big statement, inability to deal with probability. We are equipped in many ways to deal with a probabilistic world. I mean, we respond to frequencies, to relative frequencies of events. Our expectations are attuned to the frequencies we encounter in the world. What people are not good at, are particularly not good at, are word problems . . . they are more abstract problems. And indeed we were not equipped to do that. There has not been much evolutionary pressure to deal with that kind of problem in the logical fashion that is expected of a rational agent in the modern theory.

• *I was always struck when I studied Piaget by studies which showed only one percent of people – and most are mathematicians – ever become competent in his fourth stage of development – formal logical operations*
I didn't know that statistic, but you can do very well without being competent in formal operations. I mean you can, you know, live your life without ever becoming very competent in formal operations. Most of life is carried out intuitively and successfully. But there are systematic errors – which are not corrected. And they are not corrected because the feedback is remote. I mean, in situations where there are good opportunities to learn what the optimal procedure is, people learn that, but we have identified errors where the feedback loop is not closed very quickly so that people don't have an opportunity to learn.

• *What are the educational implications of your work?*
I think people ought to be taught about their psychology and systematic biases and ways to argue and so on in high school. I'm convinced that it would be quite useful to do so but I don't think it would solve the problem. It would elevate the quality of debate and the quality of the conditions people work in but I don't think it would change human nature very profoundly.

Chapter 8: R.D. Laing

Ronnie Laing was a psychiatrist who became a cultural guru. He came to reject the label of psychiatrist since he saw the profession as oppressive. Given his later history, it is ironic that Laing was willing to section patients when he first started to 'shrink'. A biography of Laing by one of his sons, Adrian, is a sad and brave book; it confirms both Laing's enormous influence in the 1960s and 1970s and his decline.

Laing was born in Glasgow in 1927. He went to grammar school and then to Glasgow University. He graduated as a doctor in 1951. Till 1953, he worked as a psychiatrist in the British Army. He joined the Glasgow Royal Mental Hospital and also worked at the Department of Psychological Medicine at Glasgow University. In 1957, he moved to London. From 1957 to 1961 Laing was at the Tavistock Clinic where he started to develop some of his radical ideas. In 1962, he became a director of the Langham Clinic.

Laing started to make a name for himself just as the then Minister of Health, Enoch Powell, argued that it was high time to run down the great Victorian asylums. Powell was then something of a progressive thinker – it was nine years before he made his deplorable "I see the Tiber foaming with blood" anti-immigration – speech. He argued many psychiatric patients ought to live in the community.

After 1965, Laing gradually abandoned the role of a scientific medical investigator. He preferred to be a poet with a political edge. The most poetic – and in some ways the most controversial – of his enterprises was Kingsley Hall in London's East End. Fabulous tales reached the outside world of strange goings-on. Patients ran wild. Their psychiatrists ran wild with them. Walls were smeared with shit. Local residents complained. The hostel closed.

By 1968, Laing had acquired the status of superstar, the sage, the mage, but also the elusive folk hero. I was asked by the *Times Educational Supplement* to see if I could get an interview with him. They doubted it was possible. I had suggested the same to Granada Television who had assured me that they had been trying for six months to persuade Laing to appear on a programme about Kingsley Hall. The literary editor of the *Times Educational Supplement* knew, however, a man called Zeal. Zeal, good name, was a disciple of the great man. He might even have his phone number.

I rang Zeal. Would he help get an interview with Laing? Zeal hesitated: he was not sure Laing would approve as he didn't want sensational press comment. Zeal promised, though, to see what he could do, as the *Times Educational Supplement* could hardly be considered frivolous. After a few days, Zeal telephoned again with a number. He could not say whether or not Laing would grant the interview but if I were to ring, I would be listened to.

I rang. A very efficient medical secretary told me I could have an interview if I came to an address in Wimpole Street. The time was fixed. It would have all been too easy if I had not lost the address. Why? Fear of being received by the sage and mage? How many people fall ill before they are to be received at Buckingham Palace?

I was at a terrible loss. I did not dare ring Zeal up again so I decided to look in the phone directory. We had all assumed the guru's number was ex-directory. There, however, it stared me in the face: R.D. Laing. The elaborate rigmarole had been unnecessary. Laing, the great critic of mystification, had become so mystified himself I had thought it impossible to reach him except by the most tortuous means. You do not expect to come easily into the presence of a Master.

This story shows the hype and halo that surrounded Laing. Later, it went even further. The gossip on the psychological grapevine buzzed with tales of patients who had gone 'mad' when Laing refused to see them any more. Some said the guru had himself gone on a voyage into the dark regions of the soul, and no one knew if he would voyage back.

One has to disentangle Laing's work, his studies and his theories, from the image that has been projected.. No contemporary psychologist had the kind of following Laing enjoyed. When he addressed a meeting of the Philadelphia Association in 1972, the large hall at Friends' House was packed out. Disappointed queues waited outside.

In the interview Laing showed how aware he was of the misrepresentation of his views. He especially resented the implication that he was a guiding light in the extreme left, that his psychological insights somehow supported revolution.

The first time I interviewed Laing was in that formal medical setting in Wimpole Street. He sat facing me. He chain-smoked Gauloises. I took this as a sign that he looked on the interview as a lecture. He ran quickly, efficiently, through his views. The hour came to an end. I was dispatched to make way for a patient.

The second time I interviewed him (in 1974) he was working from a dark-green room in Belsize Park. The room was lined with books. A.J. Ayer jostled with Indian mystics on his table. He said he spent a great deal of his time here, working with his ideas and with people that he saw. He liked to work in the midst of his family. He stressed the point to emphasize how wrong it was to see him as part of the anti-family lobby. It was David Cooper who wrote *Death of the Family* (1972). The fact that he and David Cooper had once written a book on Sartre together did not mean he agreed with all that David Cooper said. But the press had seized on him, on Cooper and, to some extent, on Thomas Szasz, the American anti-psychiatrist, as critics of contemporary psychiatry and jumbled all their views together.

Just as Laing carefully dissociated himself from some of David Cooper's views, Szasz was always critical of Laing. Szasz always argued that psychiatrists both in America and in the UK are used to repress people and to deny them legal rights. Szasz gathered evidence that the authorities used psychiatrists as spies and that families used psychiatrists to get relatives committed to grab their assets. The 1990s American craze for putting children on medication proves how right Szasz was, and is. All this, Szasz insisted in the 1960s, Laing failed to attribute with enough zeal – that tag again – to psychiatrists. Differences among the 'antipsychiatry' school may seem academic now in the 21st century when the main issues are the crisis in community care and whether we should detain people who may become violent. But in the 1960s and 70s these differences felt passionately important. They remain key in assessing Laing's position.

Laing's work saw a logical development through a number of books. His first book with Cooper, *Reason and Violence* (1964) outlined some ideas of Sartre's philosophy. Then, in *The Divided Self* (1960), Laing tried to make us, the readers, understand what was going on in the mind of a person diagnosed as schizophrenic. At this point, Laing did not hold the view later attributed to him – that no one is mad. Rather, he wanted to show that the actions of the mad, are not so incomprehensible. With imaginative sympathy, you could perceive the method behind the madness.

In *The Divided Self*, Laing gave the following account (p. 29). He began by citing Kraeplin:

"The patient sits with his eyes shut, and pays no attention to his surroundings. He does not look up even when he is spoken to but he answers beginning in a low voice, and gradually screaming louder and louder. When asked where he is, he says, 'You want to know that too? I tell you who is being measured and is measured and shall be measured. I know all that and could tell you but do not want to.' When asked his name, he screams 'What is your name?' What does he shut? He shuts his eyes. What does he hear? He does not understand; he understands not. How? Who? Where? When? What does he mean? When I tell him to look he does not look properly. You there, just look! What is it? What is the matter? Attend: he attends not. I say, what is it then? Why do you give me no answer? Are you getting impudent again? How can you be so impudent?"

In his book, Laing elaborated this example at some length. He also quoted Kraeplin's notes on a young girl patient whom he used to demonstrate some of his ideas in the lecture theatre to the awed students. Kraeplin showed his class that, if he tried to stop her moving about, she would resist very strongly.

If he put himself in front of her, his arms outstretched as a barrier, she would duck under them.

If he tried to take a piece of bread which she held clutched in her hands, she would not let him take it.

If he took a firm grip of her body, her usually rigid and impassive expression would change and she would start "deplorable weeping", as Kraeplin put it.

If he pricked her forehead with a needle, she hardly reacted. To any questions the eminent doctor put to her, she would only reply: "O dear God, O dear Mother, O dear Mother."

Laing's point was simple: Can you blame her? Can you blame the first patient? If Kraeplin tried to do in the street what he was doing to them in a hospital, he would soon be in jail. The patients are not acting like lunatics: they are resisting. They are using the few means they have left to resist. In *The Divided Self*, Laing gave a detailed analysis of the conversation of the patient in the extract quoted. Laing argued the patient is carrying on a dialogue between his own parodied version of Kraeplin and his own "defiant rebelling self".

When the parody Kraeplin asks him where he is, the patient snaps back, "You want to know that too. I tell you who is being measured and is measured and shall be measured. I know all that and could tell you but I do not want to." This is quite sensible when you see it, not as raving, but as defiance backed up by irony. The patient mimics the outrage of the psychiatrist who snaps, "Are you getting impudent again? How can you be so impudent?"

This interrogation was in public, in front of a lecture-hall of students, Laing pointed out. Instead of getting help, the patient was being used as a device to illustrate Kraeplin's definitions of various mental diseases. What is more reasonable than for the patient to react in the kind of way that Kraeplin labels mad? It is, Laing argued, a question of perspective. Our usual perspective has been to see such behaviour as a confirmation of insanity. There is, however, a different interpretation. The patient's experience of Kraeplin is of a man who has power over him and is using that power to torment him. Laing asks: "What is he 'about' in speaking and acting in this way. He is objecting to being measured and tested. He wants to be heard" (p. 31).

In his book on Laing, Friedenberg (1973) complained these passages have been, perhaps, used too much. The way Laing analysed them, however, gives a valuable clue to why he was so persuasive, not only to the psychiatric fringe but to a number of professional colleagues. Laing showed how one could make sense of behaviour that seemed unintelligible and, therefore, mad. He used many case histories to illustrate the relationship between the way in which a person went 'mad' and the social or family situation he had found himself in. For example, James, a young chemist, felt he could not become a person. He lacked a self. Other people mattered and had substance but he, he said, was "only a cork floating on an ocean". He used two manoeuvres to preserve what Laing called his 'ontological security'. First, he appeared to comply with what other people said or required of him. That was his outer self. His inner self, however, turned the person he was complying with into an object. In his own eyes, he was destroying the other person as a person. He maintained a paradoxical relationship with his wife. On the one hand, he saw himself as a parasite, ineffectual beside her; on the other hand, he referred to her as "It". Laing said that she had become an "It" to James. He would say things like "It started to laugh" and he would then, with almost clinical precision, explain how she had been conditioned like a robot to laugh. Laing's use of these case histories was impressive.

While he was writing his next book, *Sanity, Madness and the Family* (with A. Esterson, 1963), Laing was also involved with David Cooper in a series of experiments that set out to show their kind of family therapy worked as well as, if not better than, the drug treatments for schizophrenia. The results of these experiments were reported in detail at the end of Cooper's book, *Psychiatry and Anti-Psychiatry* (1967). Laing struck an interesting and paradoxical attitude to this quite traditional scientific approach. He used it to refute the idea that he was not a scientist but he did not bother to elaborate in any detail on the experimental work. One of the alterations he made when I sent him the text of the interview to check dealt with this question.

Sanity, Madness and the Family was also scientific. Laing and Esterson studied 12 cases of schizophrenia. They interviewed the patients and the families at length and analysed their replies to show that a person was diagnosed as schizophrenic because of what was happening in his or her family nexus. The 'madness' was a means of coping with an impossible situation. It wasn't crazy. Rather it was the only strategy, the only way out of intolerable contradictions.

In *Sanity, Madness and the Family* the authors blistered the way we label schizophrenics. Laing and Esterson argued that there were no generally agreed objective criteria for the diagnosis of schizophrenia. They claimed there was no consistency in pre-psychotic personality, course, duration and outcome of the disease. No post-mortem anatomical findings had been discovered. Schizophrenia, Laing and Esterson argued, was being treated and studied as if it were a well-established disease. In fact, however, none of the proper medical criteria that define a disease could be applied to "schizophrenia". It was a myth.

In this argument, Laing drew a good deal on *The myth of mental illness*, Szasz (1960). Szasz contented himself with a radical critique of psychiatry as muddled, and psychiatrists as exploitative. They were more jailers than healers. The shrink was an all too willing instrument of social control. Schizophrenia had no agreed symptoms, no agreed diagnosis, no recognized form of treatment. Szasz did not create a new kind of therapy, though. He remained a fairly orthodox Freudian. He wanted to show up the confusion of modern psychiatry in order to curb its power. Much of his best writing is legal rather than strictly medical. The United States gives great power to its psychiatrists. Szasz was never hailed as a guru as Laing was, though he has been an eloquent critic since 1960.

There was a more positive side to Laing, however. He also warned we are all so alienated that none of us can ever realize our authentic possibilities. The sane are certainly mad: it is also just possible that some of the "mad" are sane. At the beginning of *The Politics of Experience* (1967), Laing accused: "We are all murderers and prostitutes – no matter to what culture, class, society, nation one belongs, no matter how normal, moral or mature one takes himself to be." A few paragraphs later, he mourned: "We are bemused and crazed creatures, strangers to our true selves, to one another, and to the spiritual and material world – mad, even from an ideal standpoint we can glimpse but not adopt."

Scientists do not mourn or accuse. They observe, they dissect and, if the facts turn out conclusive, they conclude. They are not supposed to make the kinds of value judgments Laing made.

Laing's reputation for being more of a prophet and, even, poet than a scientist rests upon two books – *Interpersonal Perception* (1966) and *Knots* (1972). *Knots* is set out as a series of poems. They describe what Laing wants us to recognise as universal human situations. These are the tangles we get ourselves into; they are typical meshes; they enmesh us. It is worth quoting some of these "knots":

"They are playing a game. They are playing at not playing a game. If I show them I see they are,
I shall break the rules and they will punish me.
I must play their game, of not seeing I see the game."

and:

"There must be something the matter with him because he would not be acting as he does unless there was
therefore he is acting as he is because there is something the matter with him.
He does not think there is anything the matter with him because
one of the things that is the matter with him
is that he does not think that there is anything the matter with him."

It is a poem, of course. It also happens to be, however, a very formal state-ment of observations. These are axioms of human behaviour. To be satisfactory, it would be necessary to give some idea of the circumstances that force people into such "knots". But my point here is only that the gap between Laing, the once scientist, and Laing, the alleged poet, is not perhaps so very great. It is pos-sible to imagine PhD students using *Knots* to devise hypotheses to test. Laing offered them, of course, as something already true. He saw it happen. We will recognize it as being within our experience. It is true. It does not need statistics to enshrine it as fact. It is an experiential fact. Many psychologists object vio-lently to such assumptions. They reject not only Laing's assumptions but also the possibility that these "knots" might be true and are, therefore, worth testing.

Most psychologists gave up on Laing and Laing gave up on conventional sci-entific method, so it was easy for each side to accuse the other. But the interview should, once and for all, dismiss the idea that he was anti-science in the mid-1970s. But Laing did not regard the way that human behaviour was being studied as being particularly scientific. It ignored how we experience people, things and situations. It focused on behaviour rather than feelings. It left out what is most essential about being human.

In the late 1970s and 1980s, Laing's work went along a path which seemed esoteric and bizarre. He wrote a book which looked at birth and involved some material which described his own attempts to re-experience his birth. Many conventional psychiatrists were always acutely critical of Laing and some of these felt they eventually got revenge. Antony Clare in a devastating edition of *In the Psychiatrist's Chair* got Laing to admit his alcoholism. The General Medical Council withdrew Laing's licence to practise medicine. Some of his obituaries suggested that he really didn't deserve his once-towering reputation.

Laing was, however, an important figure both in psychiatry, psychology and contemporary culture. His ideas had considerable cultural impact, though often they were less than wholly original. Well before Freud, Strindberg's play *The Father*, written in 1887, deals with all the familiarly Laingian themes. A family "drives" a man "mad" and, a nice Victorian touch, the Captain's old nurse who really loves him is the one who tricks and coaxes him into his straitjacket. The notion that it is the family nexus which leads to insanity is old. Hamlet and King Lear are only the most famous examples of a persistent theme in literature, a theme that 19th-century psychiatry largely managed to ignore.

Nevertheless, Laing saw what so many before him had ignored. It is telling that after his death, the Institute of Contemporary Arts devoted a programme to his influence on novels, poems and the cinema. The Royal College of Psychi-atrists did nothing even though Laing had undoubtedly been read and studied more for the last 25 years than any other "shrink" and even though many of the issues he grappled with are at the heart of contemporary dilemmas.

It has to be said that no one now disputes that schizophrenia is a real illness, however. The World Health Organization's painstaking study of diagnostic criteria round the world has led to agreement across cultures. Most psychiatrists now agree that first-rank symptoms include hearing voices in the head. An interesting debate has developed, however, about whether the voices are always mad or, sometimes, oddly, helpful, a way of releasing tensions.

Laing also influenced the legal framework within which patients are treated, which has changed in the UK at least. The 1983 Mental Health Act in Britain enshrined many advances which owed a great deal to Laing's ideas. He was not the author of the reforms and he played only a small part in fighting for them, yet the work of MIND, the pressure group for psychiatric patients, was deeply influenced by his ideas and the respect for patients as persons that he demanded.

I would have also liked to have been able to put to Laing some of the dilemmas of community care. Far more patients than ever before are out of hospital but is that really doing them good? When Laing advocated, following in the footsteps of Enoch Powell, that far fewer patients should be kept in locked wards, he did not foresee that they would be sleeping rough in doorways, railway stations and under the arches of bridges.

Yet, the long-term impact of Laing's ideas has been as much in psychiatry as in the general culture. When he first started to practise psychiatry, patients were seen as medically ill and treated in isolation. It was normal practice to treat the 'patient' without talking much to their family. He, or she, was ill just like someone with measles was ill. Today, few psychiatrists ignore the role of the family so stubbornly. One reason is practical. Fewer and fewer patients spend long periods in hospital. To make community care work requires, where possible, involving the family.

Laing died before it became clear what a failure community care had become. The problems of community care involve at least three factors. Without proper resources, the community doesn't offer any care at all. Second, it looks as if there are some patients who really cannot cope with life outside the asylum for prolonged periods. Third, there is a very small group of patients who clearly are at risk, and much more likely to be at risk, if they don't get proper supervision in the community. It would have been interesting to put these issues to Laing.

In many ways Laing reminds me of Wilhelm Reich, once Freud's assistant and a man whose ideas on sexual liberation had a profound influence. Yet Reich's last years were rather tragic and with his weird theories of UFOs, he put himself beyond the scientific pale. Yet the strangeness of the work Laing did from 1980 on should not make us forget how much he did contribute. The interview that follows has been reproduced from the first edition.

• *Why did you become a psychiatrist?*
It's a difficult question to answer if one is trying to ferret out one's most radical motivations. I became interested in psychiatry via an interest in how people feel and how people see things and how people act in the light of their different ways of seeing things. And I suppose I became aware of these issues quite early in my childhood. I grew up with a very lively sense of the problematic, as you might call it, of human relationships. So it was a perfectly natural extension of my own untutored interest to get into the domain of the special study of interpersonal relationships. However, when I got into psychiatry a bit, I discovered that that was only a very small part of psychiatric theory and practice. And that psychiatry as it was practiced seemed not the unequivocally most advantageous position from which to study how people go on with each other because a great deal of psychiatric theory is, in a way, discounting the relevance of those very matters.

I came to psychiatry from that route and, also, from the scientific route. In my medical student days, I was particularly interested in embryology and what is now called neuroscience. My first job as a doctor was as an internist in a neurology and neurosurgery unit. I was very interested in those changes of consciousness, those changes of mind, those changes in function and conduct which are related to known organic disorders of the nervous system. Then, again, in the present state of our knowledge, most of the people seen as patients by psychiatrists, when they are examined and tested, are found not to have anything organic the matter with them. These were the problems in that domain of psychiatry that I came to be drawn to.

• *What were the major influences on you? Sartre, presumably?*
I went to a grammar school during the Second World War. There, I came across Sophocles and the Greek tragedians. I read them before I read any modern interpretations of these myths and stories. So I actually read Oedipus in Greek before I came across Oedipus in Freud. I would say that Greek drama was one of my most profound influences. Then, when I was 15 or 16, I became interested in finding out what other people had left as records in the written form from the European tradition. I worked my way alphabetically through the shelves of my local public library. And there, at the age of 16 or 17, I came across the complete translated works of Nietzsche. And in chronological order, or rather in alphabetical order, I came across Kierkegaard first and then Nietzsche. These were the major influences that were backed up by Marx and Freud.

Of my nearest contemporaries, Kafka, Sartre and Camus were the main influences. And, in terms of philosophical position, Heidegger, Husserl and Merleau-Ponty. Sartre, I think, has never been quite the superordinate influence on my intellectual development that some people take him to be because I did a joint book, *Reason and Violence*, with David Cooper, on some of his untranslated stuff. The main reason for doing that was that it was untranslated. If it had been translated, there would have been no reason. It was a piece of intellectual carpentry to translate a long, involved, complex text which was important for our theoretical background so that English-speaking people could have some idea of what that particular aspect of that background was. But Sartre doesn't stand out to me. He's one of a few major influences but nothing like the major one.

• *Among psychiatrists, was Freud the main influence?*
I was influenced by Freud more than by any other psychiatrist or anyone else in psychiatry. I was also very influenced by Jung. The influence of Jung has been less explicit and has been less because of the ideological implications of some of his formulations in the direction of racism. Also, Jung's reputation, particularly at the time when my influences were being formed, was considerably tarnished by the allegation, whether it be justified or not, that he was sympathetic to the Nazi movement at the beginning and by the implication of anti-Semitism. That was reported and you could see it might be a factor. So I've always been a bit wary of Jung in that respect though, at the same time, there is an enormous amount of stuff that Jung went over which still waits to be picked up more generally.

• *Were you in any way reacting against a religious upbringing in becoming a psychiatrist?*
I'm not quite sure what you mean by rebelling.

• *Professor David McClelland has suggested that people who become interested in psychology and psychiatry often seem to be reacting against rigid moral ideas. They may even have toyed with becoming ministers. Is that true of you in any way?*
Not especially – no.

• *How did the ideas that it was social rather than biological causes that were involved in 'schizophrenia' develop?*
When I was in Glasgow, having come out of the British Army in 1955 or so, I worked for 18 months in a mental hospital. I spent most of my time during the

day in the most refractory, so-called refractory ward of the female division of the hospital. This was a ward of about 60 women who, before the days of tranquillizers, were supposed to be stark raving mad, Bedlam. It was the snake-pit scene. These were women who had no dresses, who queued up every morning to have a different dress put on them by whatever nurse was on duty. All these women had been in hospital more than six years, and they were the chronics of the place. Most of them, in fact, had only a very tenuous relationship with the outside world. Many of them weren't visited by anyone. Some of them, no one knew who they were.

I made an arrangement for 12 of these women whom I selected on the basis that they were most withdrawn, they were the ones that the nurses interacted with least, they were the ones who interacted with people least and, according to a questionnaire I put out to the nurses, they were the ones the nurses felt most hopeless about. So these were the 12 most hopeless chronic women in the hospital. I tried to make more radical changes than turned out to be possible in the end. But what I did arrange was for these 12 to be with two nurses five days a week from nine to five. The nurses were seconded from other duties and didn't have any ward duties during that time. Well, in the course of it developing, a number of things went on. There were major changes in the hospital. There were ructions all over the place. But these 12 people were able to have the nurses and have the room. And, in under a year, all these 12 people had left the hospital. They had all been given up as completely hopeless and none had been out of hospital for a minimum of six years. Most of them had been in for up to 12 years. All were women between 35 and 50.

I left the hospital at the end of that year. Within a year, all 12 were back again. That impressed me. Increasing lobotomy, using lobotomies, using shock treatment seemed beside the point. But increasing the dose, if you like, of a little human personal relationships made far more total change in the whole situation. The other things were beside the point. But it seemed to me that these women had gone out of the hospital and back to the different versions of the same circumstances from which they had come into hospital in the first place. So the study of people in a hospital was completely missing the point. You really had to study people, not in a mental hospital as psychiatrists had done in all their studies of mental patients, but in the ordinary circumstances of their life. It seemed like trying to understand the behaviour of dolphins by studying them in dolphinaria or aquaria instead of in the ocean. If dolphins ever got hold of a human being, put him in a cage in the ocean and got him to do tricks and if, suppose, that guy happened to be Einstein, what would happen? If our brothers and sisters the dolphins who seem to be as intelligent as we are, if not more so, set up Einstein in a human zoo, in a humanarium, I wonder what they could learn about human intelligence by getting Einstein to do tricks and trying to get him to speak dolphin language.

It's ridiculous to try and have any understanding if you are studying people who are herded 60 to a ward, and who have been allowed to rot away for years and years and years. If one wants to seriously get any understanding of that situation, then surely one should look at the circumstances in which people live their lives in order to get there in the first place.

It would be as ridiculous as if you had an institution from which doctors never went out. Someone turns up with a black eye. So, doctors examine his eyes and there is damage to the blood vessels and around the eyes and the blood is leaking out, and they say that this is due to some congenital defect of the blood vessels of the eye. If no one had ever gone out of that institution, gone out into the world, they would never, it would seem, know that black eyes were due to the impact of a fist which is a punch. But unless you look at it, you can never tell. But it seems to me that this is quite a mild comparison with what psychiatrists are actually involved in.

After that mental hospital, I decided I wanted to know about what you might call the ecology of mind in its natural habitat. I didn't want to study it under these artificial conditions, and when I looked to see what had been written and what had been investigated in that respect, I found there was practically nothing. All that existed was a few research teams in North America who had started looking into it a few years before and that was only just beginning. Before that, there was nothing.

• *Would you say that there is any predisposition, any biological predisposition, to schizophrenia?*
I can't talk about schizophrenia in that sense, in the same way that Levi-Strauss refuses to speak about totemism. The history of medicine is full of non-existent illnesses and conditions. The history of medical treatment is, too. Now that we look back on it, I don't think any contemporary doctor would like to be treated by one of his colleagues by the methods employed a hundred years ago. I mean you'd be appalled. If you do a little timeswitch, how would you like to be treated for what we now know to be anaemia by blood-letting or how would you like to be treated for epilepsy by castration or for masturbation by castration. These were standard forms of treatment in 19th-century psychiatry and medicine. I'll lay a bet that a hundred years from now, doctors will cringe with horror at the thought of being treated by our methods that are so arrogantly purveyed when they're just scratching in the dark. It's like trying anything. Instead of an electric shock it is much simpler just to give people a cosh, a knock on the head and call it 'cosh therapy'. Electric shock is just an electrical way of producing concussion.

When the brains of rats that have been given electric shock are compared with the brains of rats that have been hit on the head, the brain lesions are indistinguishable. It seems a way of producing an electrical concussion. It's a very simple-minded idea. Someone is worried about something, he is terribly distracted and agonized, so you hit him on the head and that helps him.

• *In* The Politics of Experience, *you said that in a hundred cases that had been diagnosed as schizophrenic and which you, Cooper and Esterson had studied, there wasn't one where the so-called 'schizophrenia' wasn't, in fact, a strategy for living in an unliveable situation? Why did you not present these findings in a formal, one might say acceptably scientific, way?*
Well, I have done so. The book *Sanity, Madness and the Family* is a study, a research report of an anthropological kind of a number of families. I also published with them in either the *Lancet* or the *British Medical Journal* a report in detail of our family therapy and compared the statistics we had with what statistics we could obtain from Medical Research Council sources.

• *So the idea that you oppose a scientific presentation of your work is a misguided one?*
The Politics of Experience is a book that comes out of a number of lectures I was giving, to professional audiences for the most part, in the years before it was published. Friedenberg in his book on me never even mentions my actual scientific writing or the presentations to learned societies where, in a more technical way, I present the material that in a non-technical, non jargon, in some sense a programmatic manner, I put out in *The Politics of Experience.* That is not meant to be a scientific report in the manner of science. There, I'm putting out things from the background of the work in a way that I hope isn't misleading. Technically, you have to follow up the references. There are references given.

• *Yes. You were going to say something just then, I didn't mean to cut you off.*
For the kinds of reasons you talked about, an interview like this is a valid thing to do, to get at influences, at clarifications. There is a lot of unclarity about my published work.

• *What made you write* The Divided Self?
As I said at the beginning of *The Divided Self,* I thought that a lot of the ways in which people carry on that many people find completely incomprehensible are not, in fact, nearly as incomprehensible or not as incomprehensible as they appear to be. It was an attempt to give an indication of a way of seeing people in terms of which comprehensibility could come to light. It also suggested that

if you looked at people in what you might call an uncomprehending way then no comprehensibility could possibly arise so one needn't be surprised that it doesn't. But it doesn't mean to say because you can't find something that it's not where you're looking for it or that it doesn't exist.

• *In that book, you described the false-self system, a sort of outward face for public viewing many so-called schizophrenics used. Do you think many normal, quite undisturbed people also use this because they are alienated?*
Yes, I would say that's true. If I'm to believe what many people actually tell me, yes, but this isn't a matter where I speak from any particular position of competency. I think that anyone living in our society cannot help being aware that a great deal of one's social interplay uses a sort of mask, a sort of persona, a sort of front or a sort of set of social stereotypes of actions and expressions which are not intended and not designed to be expressions of anything particularly personal. And we all know the extent to which that mask grows into some people, grows into their faces so they can't take it off. We are, as it were, stuck with it. As far as that goes, far more people are stuck with it than are aware of it and a lot of people are aware of it and find it very painful because they can't disencumber themselves of it once it's sort of grown in.

• *In* The Divided Self, *too, you called for an authentic science of persons. Would that investigate how you could rid yourself of that mask?*
Oh yes. The practice of what is called therapy has a great deal to do with the possibility of being able to discard that mask. People cling to it more out of fear than anything else. It's a mask which is like a castle inside which one can defend oneself from the attacks of what are felt to be other people as one's enemies and, at the same time, it's a prison from which one can't get out. That is the double ambiguity about it. The possibility of being able to function efficiently and competently in our society without actually being a prisoner is something that quite a few people that I meet regard as a rather remote possibility for them. And a lot of people feel so frightened at the prospect of doing without it that the idea seems horrendous to them.

• *How does one get over that fear?*
How does one get over any fear? It's very nice if one can discover that what one was afraid of doesn't exist. If you, as I think many people do, grow up in a childhood in which there's violent pressure and plenty to fear and when you have grown up you haven't incorporated and internalized the person, and you don't carry it around with you continually, then there is some prospect, one can realize with a sigh of relief, that, as far as external circumstances go, one is no longer in

prison, in quite the same way at least. It's all very well to say ideologically that our whole society is a prison but there's more breathing space in some sections of it than in others. I don't agree with what might be stated as a possible extreme position – that all possibility of actual open spontaneous behaviour between people is now lost. I think that still happens and still goes on in completely ordinary, unsung, undeclared ways all over the place all the time. It goes on. But it's another world to millions of people.

• *One position linked to this that you have been seen to hold is that it is society which is ill and the 'schizophrenic' who is sane. Is that a proper statement of your view?*

I never said that society was ill. I don't see how one can talk about a society being ill. One could say I was ill if I had the flu. But to talk about society being ill is all right if one is using it *en passant*, as a metaphor, or even as an extended metaphor, as long as one never forgets that it is a metaphor and an analogy. One can compare society, say, to a sick animal. I wouldn't want to say it's anything more than a comparison and I feel that it's a comparison that is made so often now, it's become so trite, that you might as well not make it.

I never said that everyone diagnosed as schizophrenic was sane. It's a ridiculous statement to make to say that all people diagnosed as psychotic are sane. That's as stupid as any other fantastic generalization. What I did say was that all sorts of people get diagnosed as psychotic. Really, all sorts of people do get diagnosed as psychotic. And, sometimes, when people are diagnosed as being mad or psychotic or what not, they are indeed in a state such that they might seem shattered, scattered, bewildered, unable to function, unable to act, unable to move, unable to think, unable to perform the most basic functions. So if we say that is someone who for reasons that we don't immediately know doesn't seem to want to, or to be able to, talk or move or perform many basic functions, someone in whom life is suspended, it's impossible to avoid the conclusion, just looking at the person and not at his social situation, that he or she is definitely in a very disturbed, disordered state – whatever may have brought them to this pass. However, psychiatrists do often diagnose plenty of people as psychotics who don't seem to me to have anything intrinsically the matter with them. In that case, the diagnosis comes to be like the positioning of someone on a social chessboard. Let's say the knight is in a particular position and, the next move, he may be taken. There's nothing wrong with the knight as a piece. Pick up the knight or any of the pieces that have been taken. There's nothing wrong with any of them. It's their positions in relation to the game that determines whether they should be captured. It's that position that determines whether one should be socially helpless. And it falls to other people to decree what should happen to them. That's a position of political weakness. It seems to me that in that kind of small-scale political situation, they lose all power. In our society, zero power, that position belongs not to the convicted criminal but to the committed mental patient because the person who gets put in that position is stripped of everything. They are even stripped of the right to decide if parts of their brain are going to be removed. Almost anything can be done to them, whether they like it or not. And the position is that one is at the mercy of those representatives of society that society has appointed to be in complete control of one's life under those circumstances. I feel that power is at the moment in the west and in Russia completely unmoderated. It can be used all the way to destroy someone totally.

• *If someone had an organic brain condition, would you feel differently about the control over him? Is there a distinction between the medical and the political points in your argument?*
If I'm knocked down in the street and I'm rendered unconscious and I'm bleeding from internal injuries, then I am completely at the mercy of how other people are going to act towards me. In those circumstances, I've got no objection at all to other people acting according to the arrangements our society makes under those circumstances. I hope they will do their best for me.

But my own view of how far a doctor can go to give someone help is probably a minority view. For instance, if I'm dying of cancer, I feel it is absolutely abhorrent, as is common medical practice, that the patient isn't told he's dying. Everyone else might know but not him. If I'm dying, I want to be the first person to know. I also feel that it is my absolute right to die in my own way as long as I'm not imposing unfairly on other people. I have a perfect right to die in my own house. If I happen not to want what the doctors say is the best thing for me, if I have cancer and I don't want an operation, I don't feel there should be any question. I'm entitled to refuse treatment, to refuse to go into hospital, I'm entitled to die in my own bed or wherever else I want to. I also feel quite entitled to kill myself, as far as the law of the land is concerned. Whether it's against the law of mankind is another matter. But I don't feel the state has the right to interfere with what's going on inside my body, in health or in sickness. What chemicals I have inside my body, all that, seems to me to be my own business and no one else's. And that goes for everybody else.

• *In legal theory, people do have all those rights. Do you think they are denied in practice?*
Oh yes, not for everyone. But it's daily, undramatic routine for hundreds of thousands of people in our western industrial-technological-medical system for them to be denied those rights.

• *In* The Politics of Experience, *you wrote that therapy was extending itself and that a therapist needed to be able to combine great authority with an ability to improvise.*
All sorts of things go on within the general scope of therapy and psychiatry. There are some psychiatrists who see therapy in those terms, but I would say that the majority of psychiatrists aren't interested in therapy of this order.

• *What are psychiatrists interested in then?*
They're interested in the chemical control of mental states and behaviour. They're interested in exploring ways in which the different forms of what I'd call mental illness or psychopathology can be classified. And they're interested in the way that different syndromes within that classification can be defined clinically and medically. They're also interested in the way they can be treated by medical means. They're interested in pursuing and developing that line of country. In what I've written and what I've practised, I've found, for me anyway, that that is an extended metaphor for seeing these things which is counter-productive for me. And I've given some of the reasons.

• *It seems to me that people have a gut reaction to what you say, it's an emotional thing, yes or no. It's not analysed. Has that been your experience?*
It seems to be, yes.

• *Why do you think that is?*
Why do *you* think that is?

• *I think because it's rather threatening and especially so to conventional psychiatrists who, if one follows you, should be out of their jobs and out of their expertise. Don't you think it is matter of your work being threatening?*
In a way, yes, and in a way, no. For instance, when I was on the *Dick Cavett Show* in America, they also had on Rollo May and Nathan Klein, who is a director of one of the major drug research programmes. The question of primal screaming came up and I said, I was in a way being naive, that I wondered what all the fuss was about. The great thing that Janov had managed to do, in a very American style, was to somehow make it respectable, if you've got enough money, to scream. Not just allowable but respectable. Anyone who had $3000 could yell and scream and groan and writhe and sob and agonize. Even without any particular guidance, I'm sure that someone would feel better for it at the end of three weeks. What's wrong with that? Isn't it obvious to anyone with any common sense that you would feel better if you had had the chance to do that. But Nathan Klein said, and he looks like a perfectly healthy guy: 'Well, your

patients go to see you to help them to do things that my patients come to me to stop them doing because they don't want to do them.' Tranquillizers are quick, cheap and effective. I think there will always be a majority of people who, in our present civilization, don't want to have any truck with the sort of thing I spend my time doing. They don't want anything to do with it. So I don't feel psychiatrists need feel threatened by it. All I say is, if they let me and my crowd live, we're not going to stop them doing what they're doing except in some of the worst excesses. And I'm certainly entitled to say that something is ethically wrong and, also, a lot of it is sheer stupidity and very bad science, very bad medicine.

• *If I felt depressed and went to a doctor who gave me a tranquillizer and that made me happy and I felt happy to be made happy like that, would you see anything wrong with that?*
Not if that's what you're asking for. I'm thankful for Alka-Seltzer, for aspirin, for coffee and, at different times, for amytal and benzedrine and amphetamine. If I find that for all my meditation, for all my insight, that I get into some sort of downer that a cup of coffee will raise me from – fine. The same thing if I take a tranquillizer.

• *But you don't want them rammed down your throat?*
No, I don't want them rammed down my throat or into my bloodstream or into my mind if I don't want them and haven't asked for them. I also want some measure of honesty as to what I'm getting. These drugs are commodities, they're manufactured. A great deal of money goes into researching them. Between themselves you will find that chemical manufacturers are aware that these drugs are very imprecise blunt instruments. They know there are serious side-effects. But, partly because they are imbued with the sheer sweetness of the technology of getting it sharper and better – and, in a way, I sympathize with it because if you're going to have something, let's pick it off quickly – and partly because they need a lot of money to do the research in these things, in advanced molecular chemistry, they want to sell the stuff to people. Psychiatrists are not chemists, are not pharmacologists. A lot of the people who give these drugs are family doctors who just give, more or less, what is sent through the post. An occasional article might reverberate if it comes out in the major medical journals but the vast amount of stuff that comes out makes it practically impossible for anyone, unless they are very close up to a research field, to know just what is going on. If, for instance, someone's pushing it a bit. Conning is going on all the time. So that, within the scientific club at that level, trust is really established only through personal contact. So this guy is really honest, he really wants to find

out, he's not using the most complex problems of science just to advance his own firm.

• *You have been represented, and this perhaps follows from what you have said, as holding a very left-wing revolutionary position politically. Is this right?*
Never ever. I'm not anything like that politically and I have never indicated at any time that I was. In the collection that came out of the Roundhouse in 1967, the paper that I delivered was entitled 'The Obvious' and, in that company, I made it quite clear in the last two paragraphs what my position was, which was one of extreme scepticism of all sides of the question. At the same time, I wasn't going to shut up if I felt like speaking out on social anomalies and injustices that come my way.

At that time, people like me were aware that the US launched a mass air effort in Vietnam and Cambodia. A year ago, the then US Secretary of Defence said he was unaware of it. I don't know who to believe or what to believe. It's very difficult to tell. I was talking in an atmosphere like that and I still am. The stuff that's going on today is even more . . . zanier.

• *Have you continued to work with family therapy on the lines suggested in* Sanity, Madness and the Family?
Yes. It's almost ten years since that book was being researched and written. I've been working with families and continued to be involved with different sorts of family systems and social systems. I've had a chance to travel a bit and had experience of families in different parts of the world, Indian families, Singhalese families and New Zealand families.

• *Is the family nexus particularly pernicious in the west or did you find much the same sorts of things going on in India?*
Well, this is one of the things I'd be glad to correct. I don't, and some people seem to confuse me with David Cooper and his attitude towards the family particularly as expressed in *The Death of the Family*, condemn the family. His spirit, that spirit, isn't my spirit about the family. You're interviewing me right now in the midst of my family. I enjoy living in a family. I think the family is the best thing that still exists biologically as a natural thing. I wouldn't like to see it disrupted by state control or interfered with, as could very easily happen if you adopted the slogans of the '60s psycho-politico anti-psychiatry anti-family left and used that an excuse to take over. Parents will soon have to have a licence to be allowed to have a child. I have someone who comes to see me who goes along to a psychiatric facility because she's distressed, emotionally disturbed. The first thing they do is to test her. They test her and they find that she's very

emotionally disturbed and one of the things that she's disturbed about is the possibility of having a child, whether she's a suitable case for maternity. So, they say, OH NO, NEVER, on no account, never have a child! That just needs a bit more touch on the switch and she'll have to have special permission to have a child. Unless she passes her psychological aptitude test, she won't be one of those who is allowed to have a child. The family is, I think, potentially a great thing, potentially a place where adults can play and be with children and the child can be with some people who are still a bit more human than a lot of those they will run into later. If the kids and the adults who make up a family get it off together well, then it's absolutely great.

My attack on the family is aimed at the way I felt many children are subjected to gross forms of violence and violation of their rights, to humiliation at the hands of adults who don't know what they're doing, and are so arrogant in their ignorance, they're not likely to get the point. Nevertheless, every generation is a new generation. There's no reason basically why these disturbed children of these even more disturbed adults can't remain children with their children and move out from there.

• *Do you think people can be very different, more human with their own children then?*
Yes.

• *Another position you have appeared to hold is that to become more whole, more complete, one needs some form of religious experience, not God in capital letters. You describe one voyage of a so-called schizophrenic not as an episode of madness but as something spiritual. Is the need for the religious something you hold?*
There seem to be spontaneous happenings in the lives of some people, at least they seem to be spontaneous, where these people become engrossed in some sort of inner psychic state. While in that, they sometimes become completely incompetent socially, unable to carry on and function. I've seen enough of what used to be, and still is called in psychiatric practice, a schizophrenic episode or a schizophrenic form episode or a schizoaffective-reactive state or what might be an acute episode in a progressive schizophrenic process of hebephrenic deterioration or, if you prefer, what not. From my clinical experience, I have come to believe that for many people, if they are not interfered with when they go into that sort of thing, they seem to come out of it again. Sometimes like Jesse Watkins did, in ten days, or sometimes longer. Now in the household environment asylums that we have in London, the successors of Kingsley Hall, this sort of thing happens and goes on. That is the sort of concentrated experience every other week they have in these set-ups. By the person who is going through it, it's

often said to be spiritual whatever they mean by spiritual. There's a feeling of profundity very often and a sense of realizing all sorts of things that hadn't been realized before, sometimes in such dazzling profusion that the whole thing is impossible to decipher. People who from their point of view are in the midst of that might well appear to others to be incoherent and disorientated. In a way, they are incoherent and disorientated.

What has all the fuss been about? I think it's a matter of impatience and regimentation and the mechanization of man, of having no other timesense than clock time. Whatever is going on is not given any credit for having any method in this apparent madness. There's no sense in it and there's no real readiness to listen to a few people like me when they say that if you don't do this, this will pass because they don't want to know that.

These experiences are, in a way, the flash, the razzle-dazzle. It's compared to acid. It's made into an ideological position. It's a question of 'Is that a flash of different states of mind?' and I'm speaking here of the best of it, for the worst of it is absolute hell and no one would ever want to live in the states of mind some people can get into. But my point is that if you look at what psychiatrists do to what seem to me to be pretty normal people, it beggars description what they do when someone is out of their mind. It's like an isometric situation when what is being done is the absolute opposite of what ought to be done, of what clinical tradition and medical sagacity in the western tradition dictate should be done.

• *But do you think that one must go through some such spiritual experience to become better, become ennobled?*
No.

• *You have been represented as holding that.*
I have never ever said that.

• *What happened to Kingsley Hall? Did it come to a natural end or was it forced to end?*
A group calling ourselves the Philadelphia Association was formed in 1964. That group still exists with some different people. I'm still the chairman. We continued to operate in London. Our aim as a group was to develop work in this field along our lines. One of the main things was having households where this sort of thing could be allowed to happen. Kingsley Hall was the largest such place. We had it for five years from 1965 to 1970. We leased the building for five years in 1965 from Muriel Lester and the trustees of the building. They gave us the building for five years and we had it for five years. Now, we have a cluster of buildings in Bayswater and Archway. The work is going on.

- *Do you do much therapy there yourself?*

I'm around but I spend most of my time in this room. I sort of stay here and see people here. I go around to the places. I may go and spend an evening there tonight. But I go around once a week apart from what may happen *ad hoc.*

- *One of the things that I'm trying to see is what different psychologists and psychiatrists think Man is if 'What is Man?' isn't too vast a question. Do you think we are limited by our physical-chemical make-up?*

That depends what you mean by one's total chemical make-up and that depends on what you mean by 'limited by'. Are we limited by those objects of our sight, taste, smell and body perception that we can measure or not? Chemistry belongs to that domain. If we're talking about what we think is the main thing that is being studied when we look at ourselves, or what is apparently ourselves, in the manner of science then we get a certain picture of things. If you want to weigh this book, it can be measured absolutely precisely. But if you ask me if I feel it as heavy or if you give me the book and ask 'How heavy does it feel to you?', it might feel different depending on the temperature of the room or how my body feels. My body may feel heavier or lighter. But, at the moment, it's impossible to weigh that feeling of heaviness. You can weigh a book but you can't weigh the feeling of the weight of that book. Now that goes for everything else. You can describe in detail the objects in this room that I see and you see but we cannot find a scientific way, at the moment, of getting at the seeing. I'm talking about a really hard natural science way of the most impeccable genuine order, the type of science that astronomy, physics, chemistry is, where any scientist who meets another scientist recognizes him as such right away. I think that that is the sort of science, if we're talking about how I feel, not what can be picked up from my EEG, not what can be picked up from my heart as a pump or from any instrument that measures to compare and contrast. Even if you can pick up when I have a feeling, even if you can pick up when I'm dreaming, even if you can put an electrode into my brain and make me dream what is put there by a microcomputer that might set up certain patterns of colour in my cerebral cortex or temporal lobe that could induce me to see a colour or a different shape, it's still not my feeling or dream. We know that very slight changes in enzymes at the molecular level affect it. But, even then, I don't see that if you looked at my brain and my nerves, how you could ever infer this whole world that I see is coming out of there. Suppose you could probe my brain. Now, the eyes aren't like a photographic plate that I can take out so that I can examine the plate. The whole world is the photographic plate. The chemistry is absolutely there all the way and the whole world is there. As William James made clear, you need only the slightest touch of nitrous oxide, laughing gas, in the way of an acid trip or mescalin or anything can take you far out, through centre point, through the total void and back again in a few seconds. So the whole thing seems to be chemical but it's still the whole thing which isn't chemistry.

It seems to me at the moment to be absolutely mysterious. It seems absurd to say that all it is is the stuff that is in here. [He points to his head.] Yet, in some mysterious way, the slightest changes in here affect what we see out there. If we didn't dream, neuroscientists couldn't take stuff off the brain, couldn't take EEG measures in different stages of sleep to correlate them with dream states. But when we dream, it isn't someone looking down a microscope though we might dream of someone looking down a microscope. We might say that we dream our molecules. The whole thing might be an auto-perception of our brain by our brain. But then, what's our brain? A brain itself is an object of perception. Therefore, it can be classified as all the objects it itself sees are. All the stuff we see is inferred from what is going into the brain. If the brain is itself an object of perception, it's occurring after all the events it has inferred. You can't say the brain is inferring it because the brain has yet to exist. The brain can't see itself, according to the brain, till distal stimuli enter the eyes, go through total trans-formations in electric wave impulses at the retina, go to optic chiasm, go through two sets of synapses and to the optic cortex. Then, if the rest of the body and its chemistry and its hormones are all right, we suppose we see the visual world. In that case the visual world in occurring after all that and all I have just said is an inference from what is, we are inferring, occurring after. Is the visual brain a part of the set of visual objects? So how can the visual brain which is one of the set of visual objects be used, since it is one of the members of the set that is up for explanation? So, we don't seem to have managed to explain it that way.

There are different intellectual paradoxes too. There's all that science can't begin to get. It's like throwing a net over the surface of the ocean and trying to drag out the ocean.

• *Do you think science will arrive some day at a fairly total explanation of these mysteries in the end?*
No, science is looking in one direction only. Science can only see what it sees down the microscope.

• *But it can't reintegrate that up the microscope?*
A scientist can – and without stopping being a scientist. But he can't have science as a superordinate central position from which he is integrated as a full man. He will have to accept that science is one of the enterprises of the human spirit which is subsumed within that enterprise.

• *From what you have said, it would seem that you approve the classical scientific tradition and aren't opposed to it as one might think?*

It's not possible to answer that in a few words without being misleading because you have to discuss what is really classical science. I'm here concerned with classical biological science. It's a question of the exact knowledge of biological systems. I think that the way we go about studying biological systems is, unfortunately or not, a consequence of a prior attitude to biological systems which is pre-scientific in the mind of the scientist. Until the scientist studies biological systems he isn't a biological scientist yet. And the way he studies biological systems is not determined scientifically. It can't be. He hasn't yet started to be a scientist. He's got to take a gamble. I think that some of the best credited biological science, Galvani, Volta, Sir Charles Sherrington, is a monumental mistake. Monumental. But my main critique of it, if I ever get it systematized, will have to be made on scientific as well as ethical grounds.

• *And this pre-scientific attitude leads to bias in scientists?*

That goes for all of us. That's where my ground is: that pre-scientific ground that infuses the scientific is my ground, my special subject of study. I can't say object of study.

When you look back at a set of interviews and it is now impossible to go back again to ask the nagging question that you somehow forgot at the time, you feel sad. I would have liked to have been able to ask Laing if he felt he had lost his way and if he regretted that. For all we know, though psychiatry doesn't know how to make such a frivolous point, he may have enjoyed losing his way.

Five years after Laing's death, his son Adrian published the first biography of the guru. Adrian Laing catalogued a very flawed father who felt unable to seek help when he knew he was depressed, drinking too much and aggressive. Adrian Laing said pointedly that his relationship with his father "improved greatly after his death". The book is brave but not the definitive biography that Laing deserves (Laing 1994), especially given the growing concern about the use of medication, the fact that new drugs seem to make some patients homicidal and suicidal and the appalling estimate that one American child in seven is on some form of tranquiliser.

Chapter 9: Herbert Simon

Very few psychologists have ever won a Nobel Prize. The four most recent winners who have done significant work in psychology – Konrad Lorenz, Niko Tinbergen, Daniel Kahneman and Herbert Simon – were not really psychologists. Simon, in fact, got his Nobel laureate for work in economics. He wrote that many people thought his victory a fluke and countered that he was the fifth most-cited economist during the period 1945–78.

I went to see him, however, because of his work in psychology. Simon was one of the pioneers of artificial intelligence. It was the chess-playing program that he designed with Allen Newell in 1957 that brought him recognition among psychologists. The program could hold its own with a grand master. Simon always believed that the day would come when a computer would find it easy to beat the best chess players in the world. Since then we have had the failure of Gary Kasparov to beat IBM's chess computer and before that the chess press was surprised by the fact that a new program defeated Judith Polgar, the 17-year-old Hungarian chess prodigy. One up to computers!

For Simon chess playing was, always, a means to an end. He believed from the early 1950s that computers could shed light on how people think. His ideas were enormously influential in paving the way for the revival of cognitive psychology.

I went to see Simon at Carnegie Mellon a rather old university in Pittsburgh. He was 77 and frail when I interviewed him but he was very lively and laughed often. He talked, with relish, of not falling for the statistical hype some doctoral students tried to palm off on him. As an economist, he could out-stat the best of them. His room suggested frantic activity. All the desks and tables overflowed with papers.

Simon had published an autobiography. Like Skinner's *Particulars of My Life*, it is surprisingly personal in places. Simon sketched in rather moving details about his childhood and his marriage – and especially one temptation he had to run off with a younger woman – a temptation he resisted.

Simon was born in 1916 in Milwaukee, Wisconsin. His father's family was Jewish. Various German laws restricting the occupation of Jews meant that they grew vines and produced wine but Simon's father had managed to get trained as an engineer and had come to America in 1903. Simon's mother was German too, part Jewish and part Lutheran. Till he was in his teens he was much closer to his mother but then he began to feel closer to his father. Young Simon was clever at school, clever enough to be bitterly disappointed when he did not do well in final exams. Eventually, though, he got a scholarship to go to the University of Chicago.

The world in which Simon grew up was sheltered. The boy did not realize that during the Great Depression his father had nearly been sacked by the company he had worked for for 30 years. Simon was all for turning the scholarship down on the grounds that he didn't need it. It came as a shock to discover how vital it was. His autobiography records the debt to his father. "My values are hard to distinguish from my father's values as he expressed and lived them while I was growing up."

His father's engineering skills influenced the young Simon, though not immediately. At the University of Chicago, Simon's main interests were economics and politics. After he finished his graduate studies, he worked for the International City Managers Association. This association was trying to introduce scientific principles into local government – a worthy but unlikely ideal. When he was only 22, Simon wrote the major part of a volume called *The Technique of Municipal Administration* while he was working for the Association.

It was at this time that Simon began to hear of the technology which was to determine so much of his contribution to psychology – the computer. In 1938 computers didn't quite exist but there were rumours that IBM International Business Machines were working on some kind of device that could save massive amounts of work by performing all kinds of calculations.

Simon married at the age of 25. Then at the age of 26, he went to work at Berkeley. He had become known in economics as an expert on measuring public services and seeing whether they were providing value for money. He became Director of the Bureau of Administrative Studies and, during this period in California, he got his doctorate from the University of Chicago. It was also while he was out in California that Simon collaborated with the Los Angeles office of IBM. At the same time he became involved with some radical intellectuals, later he was amazed to discover under The Freedom of Information Act the extent to which he had been kept under surveillance by the FBI.

The war, of course, gave computer technology a huge boost. In 1945 Simon met one of the pioneers of computing, John von Neumann. Through him Simon became aware of modern digital computers and their potential. Simon also told me that he read Edmund Berkeley's book *Giant Brains*, which gave a good account of the new machines. Simon stressed that at the time everyone imagined that the most important use of the computer would be as a number cruncher. No one dreamed that it would be to offer a model that could represent human intelligence symbolically.

In 1952 the idea that computers might provide a program that in some way paralleled human intelligence came to Simon. He published a short sketch of a program that might play chess. In 1946, a Dutch psychologist called Adriaan de Groot had published a book on chess players' thinking. The years from 1952 to 1958 were obviously crucial in developing this idea. Simon joined forces with Allen Newell to work on the chess-playing programme. The idea of artificial intelligence was born then though the phrase was not used till later. As Simon outlined in his autobiography these were strong egos, strong clashes and touching reconciliations throughout the birth of AI.

Simon did not believe in some mechanistic utopia. He was convinced that artificial intelligence had to draw from psychology and psychology from artificial intelligence. The relationship between the two is still the subject of vigorous debate between those who argue for what is called soft AI and those who argue for hard AI. The hard AI position is that fairly soon we will be able to design computers and programs that mimic, and outstrip, us. Human brains, machines that think for themselves and have creativity and even personality – like the well-loved androids like Data in *Star Trek: The Next Generation*. The soft AI position is that computer modelling of intelligence is useful and provides insights into brain organization but doesn't actually replace human agency.

Outside sci-fi epics like Kubrick's *2001: a Space Odyssey*, computers have no will. Some material in the interview suggests Simon vacillated between the two. He clearly thought it vital for students to observe human behaviour and extract real data from walking, talking, living subjects. Yet, he was slightly irritated by neuro-psychologists who haven't yet told us a single definite thing about just how memory is stored or what the engram is. (The engram was supposed to be the fundamental unit of storage.) Equally, Simon told me it was true that no one had guessed how hard it would be to create machines that could do the simple things none-too-intelligent humans manage naturally, like seeing and tracking movement. But he was proud of the fact that he had been involved with robots that could see and manoeuvre well enough to drive down the highway without human help. Unfortunately, there's no way of insuring a non-human driver yet, so the machine could not actually travel solo on the highway. But its track record, as it were, is good enough to stifle critics.

When Simon and Newell produced their chess-playing program, they sent a copy to Bertrand Russell, who replied that he was delighted that *Principia Mathemtatica* could now be done by schoolboys and said that "I am quite willing to believe that everything in deductive logic can be done by machines better". Later, they sent Russell more information and the radical earl replied that: "I quite appreciate your reasons for thinking that the facts should be concealed from schoolboys." In a paper in 1958 that they gave to the American Psychological Association, Simon and Newell argued they were not inventing yet another new school of psychology, but rather that they were building on traditional models of thinking put forward both by associationists and Gestalt theory. It's certainly true that most computer models of thinking remain highly associative though, to some critics they don't seem to be able to cope with how individual associations can be.

In 1960, this new and exciting work led to what could have become a major row. Three well-known psychologists – George Miller, Eugene Galanter and Karl Pribram – wrote a book called *Plans and the Structure of Behaviour.* Plans was, of course, another way of saying programs. Simon and Newell were upset. As Miller put it: "Newell and Simon felt we had stolen their ideas and not gotten them right." Miller is on record as saying that there was a row one minute with Simon shouting at him and then that the next minute they could be drinking. He added, "You just don't back off with Herb Simon – otherwise he'll bully the hell out of you."

Miller amended some of the scholarship in the book and he pointed out that some of the ideas they elaborated had actually been around in psychology for a long time. I mention the row because the resolution was unlike those of many theoretical rows. The two men who had been friends made it up. In his autobiography, Simon quoted Miller at some length so that the reader could get Miller's side of the story.

The chess-playing program was, of course, intriguing. Ever since science fiction started to boom in the late 19th century, human beings have been fascinated by the idea that machines could do what we do. It led to considerable recognition for Simon. In 1969, he was given the Distinguished Scientific Contribution Award by the American Psychological Association. There was a gratifying number of honorary degrees. But the best was yet to come. On 16 October 1978 at 6 a.m. in the morning, fully dressed and rather nervous, Simon waited for a call he had been half told to expect – the call that told him he had won the Nobel Prize for economics.

The Nobel Prize changed some things for Simon but not his fundamental concerns. He continued to be interested in computer models which he believed offered the royal road to human thinking. He didn't see this as something that should frighten people off. As early as 1940, he told executives that, when he was lecturing them on the latest business technology, that IBM'S new machines wouldn't make them obsolete and he continued to believe this,

Despite being in his late seventies when I saw him, Simon was determined to force on with new work and not hark back to the past, though he was more aware than most of the history of psychology (for he grew up during some of its most turbulent battles and he had some acid things to say about Skinner's ideas). He said he was determined to carry on working, especially in visual and other kinds of imagery. He remained a very contemporary psychologist until his death in 2001.

• *Can I begin by asking you – you seem to take a view that people have a lot of fear about artificial intelligence and the analogy with the computer. Can you explain how that's affected the way your work's been received and what you try to do to get away from that?*
Well. I think it's affected the way my work is received by the fact that many people put a very low prior probability on the proposition that computers can think or do anything which would be relevant to thinking. And so the evidence on the other side of the coin has to be very massive and convincing evidence to change people's opinions. And the notion that the process going on in our computer simulations of thinking has any close resemblance to human thinking is still very much a minority notion – maybe even more in computer science than probably in psychology. Psychology people are fairly willing to talk about the computer metaphor. And of course, that isn't what I'm talking about.

• *Why is that?*
I've always supposed that this is related to the fact that the notion of machines thinking again challenges human uniqueness. We've seen previous challenges of human uniqueness receive fairly strong responses. So here thinking is a sort of – if you want to look at it that way – last rampart of human uniqueness.

• *And do you think that eventually your kind of computer simulations will be able to deal not just, if you like, with problem solving and conscious thinking, but with unconscious thinking or do you think that's a dream . . . ?*
No, they already do deal with a good deal of unconscious thinking, because if you look at the models that we have constructed, including models of problem solving, they don't particularly draw a boundary between what's going on in the conscious mind and what's going on in the unconscious. For example, take the program called EPAM, which is an attempt to model a whole wide range of perceptual and memory processes. A large part of the processes in EPAM are the steps that lead up to recognition of a familiar object. Well, they're not accessible to consciousness. So there's no implication in the models we do that what we are modelling is particular to the conscious aspect of the action. If we were only

doing that then of course the models wouldn't work, because problem-solving models do solve problems and if unconscious processes are implicated in solving problems, 'they'd better be in the model or it's going to have a huge and glaring gap in it. –'

• *What kind of relationship do you have with neuropsychologists? Do you expect the models to clearly identify neurological corridors?*
Yes. Our hypothesis from the beginning has been that you understand complex systems by studying them in levels. Protons and neutrons are made up of quarks but in organic chemistry you certainly don't go down to quarks. So there are these levels. There are bodies of theory about these levels and the structure of the scientific disciplines has a lot to do with the nature of those levels. Some disciplines define a particular level and other disciplines are specifically aimed at reduction. So, in human thinking there is a neurological level – nobody wants to argue with that – but also there is a symbolic level which is realized, implemented by neurological structures. Well unfortunately, the bridges between the two are very shaky, they're almost non-existent. To some extent we know a little bit about localization of certain behaviours, with studies of brain damage, using new techniques that are just coming in now but neurologists I regret haven't told us yet what the engram is. They haven't even told us in what form – chemical. electromagnetic or what – a memory is held. They can tell us what memories you can damage if you smash part of the brain but that isn't quite the answer to the question. Forty years ago or whenever, Hebb (a very distinguished psychologist in Canada) had proposed some things called cell assemblies which were his engrams. I'm perfectly prepared to believe when somebody gives me some nice physiological evidence, that if it turns out to be true, I'm prepared to believe that the symbols that we talk about and that we model, are something like that. And I'll be delighted when we begin to build that bridge but I think it's going to have to be a bridge in two layers, each of which has got to be fairly well developed. I don't know of any other complex systems that take very minute primitive parts and suddenly build them up into complex structures without intervening layers and molecules and below that we have DNA components. They build up into molecules. They build up into cells, the cells are made up of little organelles. Everywhere there's this evidence of layering.

• *When I talked to Skinner, as far as he was concerned what went on inside the organism was of no interest.*
Yeah, I've always thought that an extraordinary position because if you think of it in the following way. Suppose you had a device that happens to have a storage system in it. Now there are two ways you can think of such a system. You can

say: 'MY which is behaviour is a function of X1, X2, X3, X4', which is the whole history of everything that ever happened to it. Or you can say; 'You can do that in astronomy too', or you can say: 'Y the behaviour is a function of what's happening to it right now and the stored result of everything that happened to it in the past'. That's what we do in astronomy because we talk of the state of the system, the present positions and momentums of the bodies and that sums up their history for the rest of it. Forget the history. That turns out to be true for any system with any complexity, or any dependence on their history. That turns out to be a far more parsimonious way of stating laws of their behaviour. And so I think it's kind of suicidal for psychology to try to stay outside the head. They've got these terribly complex theories. As a guess, having theories of behaviour which the present state of the organism plus what's presently impinging on it determine what's going to happen next. So we're just imitating what people do all the time with differential equations, except you use computer programs which are difference equations.

• *One of the things that you say in your autobiography is that creativity is always the last refuge of those who hate the computer.*
Did I say scoundrels? I should have. You know the old proverb about patriotism?

• *Oh, in England it's the legal profession. But keep on talking about bounded rationality. Do you think there are any kinds of creativity that this kind of modelling might not be able to cope with?*
I don't think so but of course, that's an empirical question. I may have very decisive evidence in my lifetime. I don't see any reason, I don't know of any evidence that I've seen about the way creativity works but there are exceptions.

• *One of the other things that struck me . . .*
I should just add a word to that. One of the reasons why in our research on creativity over the last decade or so, we've done a lot with historical instances, is that we don't want to fall into the trap that some creativity researchers fall into of studying events which other people might not agree are creative. If you can make some progress in explaining how Einstein did what he did, at least you can't deny that that's studying creativity.

• *When you first got into the cognitive field, was it very hard to persuade psychologists to have any interest in cognitive, mental processes?*
No, you had to work at it a little bit. There always was a parallel strain of psychology, The world was fairly full of behaviourists, but it was also full of middle-western functionalists who were much less orthodox and less theoretically fixed

in the way that they thought. But I do say that first of all our early publications were not in psychological journals. But around 1958 there were stirrings. George Miller was already very open to these ideas. Carl Holland was very open to these ideas they were moving in this direction themselves and those two in particular assisted us in getting access to the profession. So it really is the summer of 1958. I was participating in a conference in Colorado where Giber and Wertheimer were speaking. I already had some standing as a social psychologist so they couldn't quite shut the door on me. I was already inside. And they were kind of interested to hear this weird stuff about computer programs so I had no trouble in getting some interest.

• *So it wasn't that you met with outright hostility because you were . . .*
Not with monolithic hostility. Hostility's too strong, We met with enormous scepticism. It goes back to an earlier question I didn't answer. What did we do about the abolition of scepticism? The basic principle the whole time was the old anarchist principle – propaganda of the deed – not propaganda of the word. But models don't make speeches.

• *You obviously are quite a political person.*
These are political times. Yes I am.

• *Do you think that's affected the way you've done any of the psychology, or are they very compartmentalized things?*
I don't see the connection but maybe other people can observe it where I wouldn't.

• *Can you also talk a bit about the work that you're doing now on mental imagery?*
Yes. It grew out of a lot of things, but it grew out of maybe two things primarily. The first is that one of the next steps we have to deal with in modelling the whole person, as it were is to find out where representations come from. How do people get the problem representations they have? You get it all of a sudden after much frustration if you get it at all. But when one thinks about representation and representation change, of course one thinks about visual imagery or external diagrams as being one form of representation that people actually and allegedly use in a wide range of thinking. So we'd better understand them. And in the last five or ten years there's been a long-term interest, it's warmed up, it's gotten on the agenda and I've been working at it. It's a very tough area because it's not easy to design tasks which in an objective and demonstrable way give interpretable cues about the internal representation. The mind's eye is a very

private little thing up there. We can see what people draw on paper and we can see what information they can take from drawings on paper. That's great and useful but then you've got to connect that up with what's going on up here in the imagery. And so that's been kind of the focus of the work. Two things are going on mostly at the moment. One doctoral student just finishing, she is looking at how people understand Einstein's 1905 paper on the special relativity. Why that paper other than that it attracts attention when you mention it? Because in the first seven pages of the paper, there's almost no mathematics and what mathematics there is should be trivial to a high school student. The whole argument is developed by Einstein asking the reader to form a mental picture, of light bouncing back and forth off a mirror . . . And then he writes down a simple equation. which looks like one of those equations you wrote in high school – about a river when you saw problems about river boats going up and down and how long it took them to go down and up the river. I'm sure you remember such problems. Or aeroplanes which had two wings in modern times. It used to be river boats when I was a boy. Anyway, the equations happen to be identical with those equations. Interpretations are a little different. Einstein writes the equation and you're supposed to see that that's the right equation because of the mental picture you've formed about this, The question remains. How do people understand that? What convinces them that this is the right equation? So we've been studying that. And then another doctoral student will be examined two days from today. She has finished her thesis on the area of economics – again on how people reason about supply and demand. If you give them some verbal information then you give them a numerical table of the supply and demand with different prices, you give another group the graph, you give another group the equations describing the lines on the graph. What do they do with all of this? So the trick is to make up tasks, cognitive tasks, and to first of all see whether you can demonstrate that giving information in different forms leads to different behaviours, different abilities to infer information. Then follows the more difficult task of trying to determine from that what their visual imagery is, and what they are able to do with the visual imageries.

• *And where is that getting you?*
Well it's got two students through doctorates. It's hard to say in a word where that's getting us. We're gradually piling up evidence about what people can and can't image in the mind's eye, for example. We find, even when we're dealing with things that involve change through time, like the river boat or the changes in supply and demand, that typically what people are doing are imaging the before and after situations and comparing them. They're not running movies.

As a matter of fact, we tried to build a visual display for a computer screen on the relativity thing and maybe this was just our bad design, but when we tried it out on subjects they did better at understanding without the visual display than with it. The movement didn't help them a bit. Maybe if we built a before and after picture, maybe it would have done.

• *It's interesting because certainly presumably you have to rely on people's introspective reports for . . .*
Well no the trick is not to rely on people's introspective reports. Let's suppose I ask you, what's 7 plus 3? Was that an introspective report'?

• *No.*
No, because among other reasons you can't fool yourself or anybody else and get the right answer right?

• *No.*
So our strategy on that score has been to explore the limits of what inferences you can draw with visual imagery and if a person draws the correct inference, then he must have been able to image it, because if he couldn't image it, he couldn't draw the inference. So you give tasks. You don't ask people to say what they think they're doing with their eyes, you give them tasks and see whether they can answer them. I just gave a talk down at the ABA over the weekend on this . . . I don't use overhead projectors, so wanting to illustrate a talk on visual imagery, I just used the mind's eye of my audience. So I gave them tasks. 'You've got a rectangle that's twice as wide as it is high. You drop a line from the top to the bottom bisecting it you've two figures.' I ask them 'What are those figures?' They said 'squares'. 'You draw a diagonal from the north-west to the south-east corner of the rectangle. Does that intersect the vertical line you drew?' They all said yes. I said, 'how do you know?' 'We saw it.' I said, 'Can you prove that they intersect? Can you give me a geometric proof?' 'No.' Then I said, 'I'm going to draw a diagonal from the north-east corner of the eastern square to the south-west corner of that square'. To an American audience – I say from Bangor, Maine to New Orleans. 'Does that diagonal of the square intersect with the diagonal of the rectangle that you drew before?' 'Yeah', about 80 per cent of them said it did. By this time, 20 per cent had dropped out. 'Now draw the mid-point of the shorter diagonal, the one in the square marks the mid-point of it somewhere around Nashville. Is the intersection or the two diagonals below or above that mid-point'. Half the audience said 'below'. 'Which is longer, the segment from the mid-point down to that intersection or the segment from the intersection down to New Orleans?' About 30 per cent,

with a certain hesitation, said, 'The segment down to New Orleans.' Most of the rest were not voting by this time. 'So how much bigger?' Four answers two to one.

- *So you kind of eliminate people's wrong answers . . .*
No, you begin to get – by the way, I've done that with a dozen audiences now and the percentages are remarkably reliable. I should run an honest experiment on it.

- *I was going to ask you, in this kind of task it's clear what you're doing, but to come back to one of the things you talk about in terms of problem solving, there are people who are obviously think that the individual images that we have are very particular and that therefore it seems you're cutting yourself off from a potentially rich source of data.*
Which source?

- *Well, say what I've just told you about the difference between the two ways. Somebody else might have a much more . . .*
Well, firstly, we're very much interested in that and that's why we do so much critical analysis. This is the way we get data. This is a thesis on economics and then what we do is we try to see in enormous detail how that can be explained by the computer program the candidate's written which does this. And here is one of the kinds of summary tables showing the match between – I don't even know what this one is – I'll have to think about that for a minute and interpret it. But you know we go from this and the computer program, we put them side by side and really examine in painful detail, I think 'painful' is the right word, how they match with each other. So we believe in studying individual subjects but the trick is that you've got to study people, study anything, in a way which is objective, reproducible. Another lab has to be able to get the same results and not take our word for it. We can't go through the disaster that introspection went through at the turn of the century, when what introspection you got depended on whose lab you were in. So we're very sensitive to the need to produce objective data that can be made public.

- *You talked in your autobiography about Humphreys on thinking. Did you gain anything from that and the Wurzburg studies?*
Yes. Seltz was right on the right track. He had the misfortune first of all of living before computers and secondly of being finished off by the Nazis, but we can now by hindsight see that he had a very good conception of a processor that was completely unlike the general problem solver.

• *One of the things that some of the people I've interviewed have said is that for them the psychology kind of comes alive when they write about it. In a way it's like, you know that famous phrase of E.M. Forster, the novelist: 'How do I know what I think till I see what I say?' Is that true for you?*

Well it's certainly true in writing that often – sometimes it depends, sit down and write off ten or twenty pages. But, of course when you're writing or speaking, you don't know what words are going to come out until they're there. . . . But I think where psychology comes alive for me actually, is in looking at behaviour, particularly verbal protocols. Really understanding what goes on in a verbal protocol is a moment of insight. And I get so impatient with the students who absorb the current methodology, running experiments, carefully designed, putting the numbers which are probably already in the computer – because that's the way they ran the experiment – into some statistical package and cranking off chi squares and thinking that they've learned something about behaviour. So I send them back and say: 'All right, look at the actual behaviour, look at the actual data and tell me what you see, and if you can convince me you've seen something there then maybe later on I'll look at your statistics.'

• *I did my PhD without any statistics at all.*

Good for you. You'd have a hell of a time over here.

• *You obviously must have followed a current quite new, in a sense, interest in consciousness. Do you think we are getting anywhere near where we can begin to develop models of consciousness?*

Why not? A flip answer to that would be to say: Well, we have all these programs that are doing things, that people are doing when they're solving problems. All we have to decide is which parts of the behaviour of those programs is accessible to reporting and which isn't. And we'll call that boundary, 'the boundary of consciousness'. Now we might not really be permanently satisfied with that because there's also something in consciousness having to do with self-modelling. When they modelled the world which includes the self – I don't know, maybe you don't have it in England, the ads with a particular cleaning powder that was widely used in households here. It had a picture of somebody looking in the mirror – so you may want to have something like that in your model. But I don't see any reason why we shouldn't be researching on that.

• *In terms of a public beyond your immediate scientific peers the thing that kind of grabbed people's attention there was the chess-playing program. Where are they now? Can they beat anybody, apart from Bobby Fisher?*

No, not anybody. There are probably still – most grand masters can be. It's well known and you can demonstrate it that Karpov and Kasparov can't handle as much information as a program. But I don't regard them as particularly interesting, except in vindicating my 1957 judgement that chess programs would be real champions in ten years. I can't vindicate the judgement quite any more. But what I was interested in was what the NSS program that I built ten years ago was aimed at and a more recent program later that . . . was to do it in a humanoid fashion. And these programs, Hi-Tech and Deep-Thought both of the best programs are on this campus. So in terms of getting anybody to take seriously the task of building a chess-playing program that would play very good chess the way a person does, I find the history of the last 35 years disappointing. The only attempts at that I know of are about five or six in number, two of them my own, so that doesn't count. Jacques de Trie in France had only one go at it one time and one other program in this country.

• *That brings me to – and I'm sure it's a criticism you've often heard – that for all the stress on computer intelligence, we still don't have a computer that can do half the things a six-year-old child can. One professor at Stanford said to me: "Well send me a computer intelligence that's interesting. If you tell a computer, like you could do a six-year-old, 'Fix me a cup of coffee', it can't do it."*
Well, it depends on six-year-olds – maybe you have different six-year-olds in England.

• *I'm merely quoting his . . .*
Well, what they can do depends on what they know, just like a six-year-old and by and large computers are sensorially deprived. They have very little access to the real world either through sense organs, or through instruction to the richness of that sensory world. We have here a lot of robotics going on . . . and one of the things we have is a project called Nav Lab which is an autonomous vehicle. For certain legal reasons we always have a driver in the driver's seat but this guy really isn't supposed to touch. Nav Lab has now reached the point where it can operate at 45 or 50 miles per hour on the Brooklyn highway. So I don't know. Is that harder or easier than making a cup of coffee?

• *It's very interesting. Now I would have thought that's a rather good counter to sceptics.*
I don't deny for a bit that there's some real tough problems. The way I like to put it is, when we started this game, we thought that the eyes and the hands were going to be easy to simulate but these deep-thinking parts of the brain were going to be hard to simulate. Well it's turned out to be exactly the other way

around. But if we had thought a little bit about the fact that deep thinking is a product of the last million years of evolution and the eyes and hands are a product of the last 400 million years of evolution maybe we wouldn't have been so surprised. The thing that does the professorial thinking is very new and jerry-built. A thing that grasps for objects from the world outside or drives a car is fine-tuned over 400 million years. Most of the mammals do as well as we do on these things. They're different to some extent. So it's been a tough struggle to find out how the system extracts visual information from the environment and turns it into objects and an internal map of what's going on. We're just beginning to get there. It turns out to be terribly hard to do the kind of manipulation that a structure of bones does for equivalent strength – steel is simply too heavy. Some of the robots we build in there, if they take a swing at you, you really know you've been hit if you survive. So it turned out to be a big task but I don't mean to seem to be making anything mystical about it.

• *One of the things you said in your autobiography was that one of the pleasures of science was 'catching glimpses of new patterns'. Is that the most exciting thing for you?*
I think so. Seeing phenomena and then saying: How did that come about? What's the pattern here? What's governing it?

• *And one of the things that I certainly have found sometimes is that many psychologists believe their theories apply to all human beings apart from themselves. I mean are you comfortable with the idea that your head – that your brain is a kind of problem-solving computer?*
Sure. What else can it be? What would really be scary would be to have a brain like some of the free-will types, who, when they're pressed to explain free will start introducing quantum uncertainty. I don't want a lot of quantum uncertainty or other things like that rattling around in my head. I'd rather have the things that I do, caused.

• *So this doesn't cause you existential angst?*
Sure. Existential angst I guess goes with the species but I don't attribute it to that cause.

• *But for my final question, you said in the book that you use the metaphor of a maze and I'd like, if you don't mind, to try and ask you to visualize that maze because from a psychologist's point – I mean I've just spent a lot of time in labs where there are endless T-mazes and sometimes slightly more complicated T-mazes, and I presume you don't mean a T-maze?*

No, I don't mean a T-maze. When I visualize it it branches much more like a tree and quite irregularly and maybe because of my chess studies I know where it had more than a hundred branches. No, it's a kind of a free form one of the early – who's the Dutchman who painted very stylized trees? And you can go back to his early paintings and find the actual tree . . .

• *I'm not good on paintings – I'm sorry.*
My trees are more like real trees.

• *And finally, does it surprise you, because you talk of the boy in the book, do you think the boy would be surprised if he saw the man now?*
I don't know. I find it hard to put myself in the boy's place. He always wanted to do something, discover something. I don't know; do kids ever really visualize what adult life is like, what career they'd like? I don't think so. They see adults. It's a hard question.

• *Not all questions have answers. Well, thank you very, very much.*

Chapter 10: Burrhus Skinner

Burrhus Skinner died in 1990. He was perhaps the last psychologist to really command a world audience which is why I believe it is useful to still include him in this edition. He dominated psychological theory from 1945 to 1970, at a time when the discipline was much less fragmented than it is today.

I have only made some small additions to the original introduction to the interview. Whatever psychologists thought of Burrhus Skinner's work, he became something of a legend. His less technical books such as *Walden Two* (1948), *Science and Human Behaviour* (1953) and *Beyond Freedom and Dignity* (1972) caught the popular and journalistic imagination. Few psychologists get the ultimate American accolade, being featured on the cover of *Time* magazine. Skinner achieved it. He helped develop a number of techniques of 'behaviour modication'. 'Behaviour modification', based on sound principles of Skinnerian conditioning, has become nearly as popular in the USA as psychoanalysis. It is still being used with delinquents, with the mentally handicapped, with autistic children and with other people whose behaviour is considered in some way inadequate. Even weight watchers use it. In *Walden Two*, Skinner described a perfect and harmonious community. To achieve this new utopia, one had to use the kind of conditioning and reinforcement that Skinner made famous. He always had something of the social reformer in him.

Skinner's evangelical strain upset many psychologists. They saw him as a man who was more interested in publicity than in experiments. Skinner's *Beyond Freedom and Dignity* was an instant best-seller. In the 1960s and '70s, that damned it. His autobiography, *Particulars of My Life* (1976), also attracted much attention. Because of all the publicity, Skinner acquired an image. It was impossible to interview him without being aware of it. In 1977, I wrote: "He looks a small man. His head seems a little large for his body. It looms out of it so that he has the aspect of an elder, one of the wise in some science-fiction epic. He looks intently through you at times". This detached intensity suited the image of a man seeking to change the way we think of ourselves. He headed one of the sections in *Science and Hunan Behaviour*, 'Man a machine'. He went on to say: "Behaviour is a primary characteristic of living things. We almost identify it with life itself" (p. 45). The polemical heading 'Man a machine' suggests, of course, that many psychologists will deny such a mechanical view. They cower, Skinner implied, behind the myths of free will. But what was controversial about Skinner was not so much his view that human beings were very superior machines but his views on what made the machine run.

Skinner dismissed all the baggage of consciousness, all feelings, all motives, all intentions as, at best, by-products. We attribute to the mysterious inner man the reasons for behaviour that we are unable to explain otherwise. He suggested it was all much simpler – in theory at least. What determines how a person behaves is the past history of the organism. Where Freud argued that one's motives are central to what one is, Skinner dismissed as irrelevant anything except actions. For there can be no behaviour without action. In Skinner's view it was, of course, fitting that such a psychology should come out of America, heartland of action where Schwarzenegger now rules California.

Since most of us think of ourselves as being somehow rooted in the stream of our consciousness, Skinner's views seem dehumanizing. He appeared to downgrade what we think of as our unique human qualities. To be free to choose what we want to do, to act because of our feelings, to be intimately aware of ourselves through our consciousness seem essential to being human. All this was an illusion, and a dangerous illusion, said Skinner. It threatened our future. We had to learn to control ourselves better, by which he meant to control our behaviour better.

Skinner's great discovery was a new kind of conditioning which allowed him to shape behaviour just as a sculptor shapes clay. In the 1930s, he found that if he placed a rat or a pigeon in a cage, he could train that animal to do any number of things. The process was simple though it must have needed enormous patience till he built the machines needed to provide the rewards and punishments. If, for instance. Skinner saw that the pigeon raised its head high sometimes, he would then reward it each time that it lifted its head. Later, he would only reward the pigeon with a pellet of food if the bird managed to get its head above a particular height. Skinner found he could nudge the animal along in this way till it frequently raised its head above its 'natural' level. With rats, Skinner did the same kind of things. A rat was placed in a cage with a lever and a slot through which a pellet could fall. It is this apparatus that has come to be called a Skinner box. At first, Skinner rewarded the rat every time it made the least movement towards the lever. Then, the rat had to get to within a foot of the lever for him to dish up a pellet. Then, the rat had to come within six inches. Nudge, nudge, closer and closer till Skinner would only reward the animal was when it stood just by the lever.

Then the rat had to do more. It didn't get a bite till it pressed the lever.

Skinner's 'shaping' of behaviour is a precise and meticulous process. You reward each bit, each segment of behaviour that brings the animal nearer to the final action you want it to accomplish. It is like an elaborate, very precisely measured dance.

By such means, Skinner taught pigeons to peck at keys and at balls so that they could play a primitive form of table tennis with two birds pecking shots at one another. He also trained a dog to open a door and three pigeons to guide a missile. This may sound incredible. Skinner devised, in fact, a plan known as Project Pigeon. The Pentagon thought it essential to counter the V1 s and V2s Hitler was developing. The trouble was that the guidance systems for the primitive missiles that existed were yet more primitive. Bring on the pigeons, said Skinner. If they could be taught to play table tennis, they could be taught to guide a missile. All you had to do was to teach them to peck at something like a map strapped into the nose of the missile. The pigeons pecked at a symbol that stayed in the centre of the map as long as the missile stayed on course. If it veered off course, the symbol moved to the left or the right. The pigeon's peck also then moved. This provided information to the servo-mechanism which enabled the missile to steer itself back on course. By using certain schedules of reinforcement, Skinner could guarantee these pigeons would go on pecking till they dropped dead. (They did, of course, drop dead when the missile exploded.) Various tests showed that this was a practicable scheme. At first Skinner was annoyed by the ignorant scepticism of defence administrators – they asked him, among other things, if he didn't love animals – but he got backing in the end. Project Pigeon, however, was abandoned in favour of the development of the atom bomb. When the Manhattan Project got going, the pigeon missiles were grounded.

Bizarre as this tale might seem, it shows Skinner could achieve exquisitely accurate control. He did in a very analytical way what good animal trainers have done for centuries. It was this that lent him the slightly sinister air that many writers attributed to him. For Skinner's psychology makes it possible to control not just animals but also people.

Skinner always complained about a few small details that were misused, to reinforce this idea of him as a macabre power-hungry individual. It was rumoured that he and his wife brought up their daughter in a Skinner box. It was not remotely the kind of cage the Skinner box is. He built a special crib for his baby daughter. He was always fond of building gadgets. Second, critics often blamed him for the techniques of persuasion used in the film *Clockwork Orange*. Those techniques depended on vicious punishments. In the film, every time the boy hero had a thought, a desire, an urge that was forbidden because it was anti-social, he was punished. Electrodes fired pain in his brain. The psycho-boffins in

Kubrick's film could, leaping across decades of research no one has managed to do yet, tell when the boy was thinking forbidden *thoughts*. They then zapped the pain centres of his brain. He soon learned that it was better not to be punished. To be unpunished, he had to think no evil *thoughts*. And so, he didn't.

Skinner said that people *thought* he advocated more and more refined punishments, even though he had spent his whole career since *Walden Two* attempting to use science to make punishments unnecessary. It is an interesting misrepresentation.

For a man supposedly so hard and mechanistic, it was ironic to come across Skinner pottering on his lawn in a beautifully wooded and select suburb of Boston. In his Bermuda shorts and tennis shoes, he seemed the model of the relaxed, successful American living the good materialist life. A harpsichord dominated the living room. The walls were crammed with etchings and colourful doodles. Sipping Scotch by his swimming pool, the problems of 1971 America seemed miles away. He seemed leisurely, unpressed for time. He talked gladly about why he thought American society was breaking down. Later in the 1970s, I found Skinner much less relaxed. He politely explained that he had nearly not given me a second interview because he felt he only had the time left to him to do so much. He could no longer fritter away time. He insisted on an interview much shorter than I would have wished. It was only when he talked about what he was believed to believe that he seemed eager to make points. If you discover you have written a gospel, you want people to interpret it correctly. He was bothered because he felt he was not properly understood. "I have made constant efforts to clarify my position", he said then, "over the last thirty-two years but I am still dismissed as a Watsonian behaviourist." He felt as annoyed in 1977 by that, as he was in 1971.

When Skinner went to Harvard in 1929, he had already read Pavlov and J.B. Watson. And though it was Watson who influenced the thinking behind the experiments, it was Pavlov who had the more immediate influence. Skinner went to work on the reflex. In the interview, he explains how he became dissatisfied with it. His concept of the *operant* came from his critique of the *reflex*. The distinction between Skinner's operant and the reflex is easily glossed over, especially if one is interested in the social applications of his work. The main difference is that in operant conditioning you examine and utilize the consequences that a particular behaviour generates. In *Science and Human Behaviour*, Skinner explained this as follows (pp. 64–5):

"We may make an event contingent upon the behaviour without identifying or being able to identify, a prior stimulus. We did not alter the environments of the pigeon to *elicit* the upward movement of the head. It is probably impossible to show that any single stimulus invariably precedes this movement. Behaviour of this sort may come under the control of stimuli but the relation is not one of elicitation. The term 'response' is, therefore, not wholly appropriate but is so well established that we shall use it in the following discussion.

"A response which has already occurred cannot, of course, be predicted or controlled. We can only predict that similar responses will occur in the future. The unit of a predictive science is, therefore, not a response but a class of responses. The word 'operant' will be used to describe that class. The term emphasises the fact that the behaviour operates upon the environment to generate consequences. The consequences define the properties with respect to which the responses are called similar."

Many of the key points in Skinner's psychology stemmed from this definition. First, it is behaviour and its consequences that matter. Unless there is an action or a response that "operates" on the environment, there is nothing worth studying. Some people thought that Skinner actually denied the existence of thoughts and feelings which are not made public and which cannot be publicly verified. In fact, he never denied we have feelings or thoughts. He just denied these feelings and thoughts had any central role. Once, men were so arrogant as to believe the Earth was the centre of the universe. They resisted fiercely the ideas of Copernicus that displaced them from this central spot. It is equally human arrogance to insist we have feelings, intentions and purposes which we know through introspection and which make us do things. In *Beyond Freedom and Dignity*, Skinner used a quotation from Voltaire to summarize the folly of such arrogance. "When I can do what I want to do", said the author of *Candide*, "there's my liberty for me but I can't help wanting what I do want." There's the rub.

It is the key point. Skinner claimed that you can explain actions not in terms of inner feelings and intentions but in terms of past history – and this history is one of external actions. I can't help what I do want because of what has happened to me in the past. The consequences of my past actions have shaped and, in fact, determined the pattern of my response now. I have no choice. It would be inaccurate to say that I did this because I felt such and such or thought such and such. Skinner accepted that our actions may be accompanied by these inner rituals, but they are merely epiphenomena, by-products. The stream of consciousness, that supremely human flow and rush of ideas, impressions and moods, has nothing to do with what life is really about – behaviour.

In *Beyond Freedom and Dignity*, Skinner set out to analyse the resistance to his ideas. "The mentalists", as he called them, refuse to see how circular their ideas are. If you say that a person ran away because he was afraid, you are not saying anything useful about why he ran away. If he had not run away, you would not have known fear was his state of mind. If a person says that he hit you because he was angry, Skinner would look at the context in which he hit you. Suppose you had, in fact, just hit him. The fact for Skinner was that he hit you because you hit him or because, an hour ago, he had been insulted by his boss. Inner events do not provide causes of actions. Looking for the answers to motivation inside the head is looking in the wrong place.

Some fairly radical consequences follow from this and, in *Beyond Freedom and Dignity*, Skinner looked at them. If I have no choice, I am not free. I can deserve no blame if I happen to be anti-social: but I can take no credit if I happen to be a genius. It is the environment that did it to me. Skinner claimed that it was this insight that made him such a critic of punishment. It is not merited and very often it is ineffective. But much of that book is devoted to an attack on "the literature of freedom". Since the Greeks, people have in their arrogance cherished the dream that they are free.

They have defined this freedom as something mysterious, uniquely human. At its most poignant, it is perhaps the freedom to die with a certain dignity. Viktor E. Frankl in his account of life in Nazi concentration camps goes so far as to rebuke many inmates there for failing to assert their freedom by the manner of their death. But many did succeed.

Skinner claimed that we have deluded ourselves as to what it means to 'feel free'. This isn't some ecstatic, mysterious inner state. You feel free when you have escaped from conditions you wanted to avoid. Freedom is the avoidance of painful conditions. In *Beyond Freedom and Dignity*, he wrote (p. 37):

> "Almost all living things act to free themselves from harmful contacts. A kind of freedom is achieved by the relatively simple forms of behaviour called reflexes. A person sneezes and frees his respiratory passages from irritating substances …. More elaborate forms of behaviour have similar effects. When confined, people struggle ('in rage') and break free. When in danger, they flee from or attack its source. Behaviour of this sort presumably evolved because of its survival value: it is as much part of what we call the human genetic endowment as breathing, sweating or digesting food. And, through conditioning similar behaviour may be acquired with respect to novel objects which could have played no part in evolution. These are no doubt minor instances of the struggle to be free but they are significant. We do not attribute them to any love of freedom; they are simply forms of behaviour which have proved useful in reducing various threats to the individual and hence to the species in the course of evolution."

The mistaken view is that freedom is a possession. "A person escapes from or destroys the power of a controller in order to feel free and once he feels free and can do what he desires, no further action is recommended", Skinner added (p. 37).

He went on to accuse those who are responsible – if, of course, they can be fairly said to be responsible for anything – for "the literature of freedom". It is not quite clear what this literature is. It sounds political. Recall Rousseau: "Man is born free, yet everywhere he is in chains." But it is more than political. *Hamlet* without free will is as worthless a dramatic proposition as *Hamlet* without the prince. Macbeth becomes ridiculous if he does not have the choice to kill or not to kill. The whole of literature almost is the literature of freedom and popular literature even more so. In Tolkien, it is the choices the hobbits make that turn them into heroes. Skinner's anger at literature is interesting, as he once had had literary ambitions of his own.

Skinner singled out for special blame those who used the slogans of freedom to obstruct reform. He argued it was possible to change many penal practices for the better. Operant conditioning offered practical solutions to educational and remedial problems. But all these benefits are fought all the way in the name of freedom. (Eysenck too became an angry old man when he attacked the Home Office for not being interested in his work on how a better diet made prisoners less violent.) But those who practise the "literature of freedom" prefer to snuggle up with their illusions. They hope to prevent the kinds of reforms Skinnerian techniques could offer in education and penology and they do so because they claim such improvements would be new and sinister forms of control.

It is apt that Skinner attacked Noam Chomsky, the linguist. Chomsky made his reputation in two quite separate fields. He is regarded as one of the greatest linguists of the 20th century: he also happens to be a radical political activist. Chomsky also does not believe that the environment and the history of a child account for the fact that normal children in all cultures have learned how to speak by the age of five and, so, mastered an incredibly complex set of rules. He will be able to generate original sentences and to understand sentences he has never heard before. Chomsky argues that only some inherited organization in the brain that is specifically destined to acquire language can explain how the infant learns to speak. It doesn't depend on what happens in the environment.

Skinner regarded such a view as anathema. In *Science and Human Behaviour*, he anticipated the view that he was to set out in full in *Verbal Behaviour* (1957). He wrote: "Verbal behaviour always involves social reinforcement and derives its characteristic properties from this fact." For Chomsky, verbal behaviour – and he would shudder at the way Skinner felt obliged to pin the label of *behaviour* on language – is part of our biological specialization. It is unique to humans. It seems to require some inherited schema, something akin to the rationalist philosophers' theory of innate ideas. The history of a particular organism may marginally affect how well it speaks, but this environmental effect is minute. When Skinner published *Verbal Behaviour*, Chomsky gave it a murderous review. Skinner believed the book was his most important, because it bridged the gap between explaining relatively simple behaviours and complex ones. Skinner tried to explain how children learn language purely in terms of what language they are exposed to and what language behaviour is reinforced. Skinner felt the book had never been adequately appreciated. Skinner was bitter about that and the latest research suggests Chomsky is not as right as was once believed.

Chomsky and Skinner also disagreed about issues of social control. Chomsky saw Skinner as a man whose ideas made it respectable for the state to exercise power over individuals. Skinner denied that it was his aim. He argued men are controlled but we prefer the controls to be less conspicuous. If a man has a burning desire that stems from his childhood history, he is not really choosing to have it. There is no inner man who has the choice to decide not to do that. Childhood history, childhood reinforcements, make us what we are though we hate to admit it because it makes us powerless.

Skinner believed that one of the reasons for this is that if a society were intelligently designed, people could take neither the credit nor the blame for their actions. They would not deserve anything. Conventionally we praise great deeds and great souls, but, for Skinner, there is nothing to praise. The deeds and the souls are the product of contingencies of reinforcement. Skinner did not mind the fact that this sounds soulless. He argued, tellingly, that this free and autonomous man has ravaged the planet, massacred his fellow humans and shows no sign of being able to live in constructive peace.

But radical thinkers like Chomsky always suspected Skinner of really finding ways to enshrine the status quo. Dire warnings against permissiveness burst through. Though Skinner often said he was opposed to punishment, he warned against dropping out and sex and drugs as an alternative to a fruitful social life. He said in *Beyond Freedom and Dignity* (p. 117):

> "When the control exercised by others is thus evaded or destroyed only the personal reinforcers are left. The individual turns to immediate gratification, possibly through sex or drugs. If he does not need to find food, shelter and safety, little behaviour will be generated. His condition is then described by saying that he is suffering from a lack of values."

Two assumptions here are worth noting. Without the need to make money – for what else are finding food, shelter and safety about in a capitalist society? – there will be little behaviour. It is not difficult to see one could add something like 'that is socially acceptable or useful'. For those who rebelled against the whole ethos of America in the late 1960s did not suddenly stop doing things; they stopped behaving themselves. The authoritarian "Behave yourself" is very apt here. The rebels of films like *The Graduate* and *Easy Rider* could still think, feel and act. But, according to Skinner, it would seem they were generating only little behaviour. Little behaviour, it might be thought, means little behaviour of the kind American society as established in 1977 would like to see. Second, Skinner called this a "lack of values". He went on to explain why the word 'values' is inappropriate. But he clearly did not even consider the possibility that the protest of the late 1960s stemmed from a rejection of existing values for better ones. A critique of the existing values seems out of the question. "Permissiveness", Skinner wrote, "is not however a policy. It is the abandonment of policy and its apparent advantages are illusory" (1972, p. 85). Permissiveness is the soft option.

Skinner argued the emptiness of protest, and the reasons behind protest. It is not surprising, therefore, that his techniques of 'behaviour modification' should arouse the suspicions of the left and liberals. Sometimes, they can see the usefulness of using behaviour modification in very limited ways. A social worker in New Jersey explained to me that she detested Skinner till she came across a patient who could not urinate or defecate except in his own home. As the man was in business, this quirk was a threat to his career: American business is always on the move. The client went to a 'behaviour modification' therapist after a psychoanalyst had told him that it would take at least a year to get to the root of his problem. Skinnerian conditioning cured the man in three weeks. Skinner would have argued that this is a typical instance of where the "technology of behaviour", as he liked to call it, is of real benefit. His opponents would argue that such a case was too simple and too comic. The client wanted to be cured of his peripatetic constipation. He was not being forced to conform to society's ideas of what he should be like in any serious way.

I never had any doubts that Skinner was sincere in his belief that he was arguing for a positive improvement in educational and penal practice. Interviewing him before 1984, he sniped that Orwell's book had justified a lot of inactivity. Psychology had to face the fact that there is great resistance to using it to reform anything at all.

Skinner, in the interview, went some way to explaining his precise position on some issues. I came away thinking that he had more reason for being aggrieved on the issue of feelings and less on the issue of control. On feelings, he shifted his ground. It was not always clear if feelings were not causes and did not need to be studied at all, or if feelings should be studied, as Watson had done, from a behaviouristic standpoint. The behaviourist view would be that feelings exist and may even matter, but that they are not causes.

Skinner always said he did not want to see an authoritarian society but little in the interview suggested that he had really appreciated the uses to which his views could be put.

• *Why did you become a psychologist?*
That's a long story. When I was in college, I wanted to be a writer. I majored in English. I had no psychology. And, between my junior and my senior years, I

went to a small school of English in Vermont. One of the figures backing that school was Robert Frost. He came there for a day or two and I was introduced to him. We had lunch together and he asked me to send him some of my stuff. The next fall I sent him three short stories and he wrote me a very encouraging letter which appears in *The Collected Letters of Robert Frost*, although the editor was not able to identify the Mr Skinner involved. This decided me. I was going to be a writer.

I took a year living at home which was a miserable failure. I didn't produce anything of any value whatsoever. And then, some friend of mine said: 'Well, after all, science is the art of the 20th century.' So I thought I'd be a scientist. What scientific background had I had? I had thought of biology at college but I decided I was going to be a psychologist. I had read Watson and then I got hold of Pavlov and I came to Harvard fully expecting to find a department which was completely behaviouristic. But, of course, I found nothing of the sort.

But that was how I got into it. I turned from the kind of interest in human behaviour that the novelist has to the kind that the scientist would have. I turned bitterly against literature. I heard that Chesterton had said of a character of Thackeray's, 'Thackeray didn't know it but she drank.' In other words, Thackeray had managed to portray an alcoholic woman without knowing she was alcoholic. It seemed to me that was true of someone like Dostoevsky who could portray marvellous people because they were all parts of Dostoevsky really without his understanding it at all. I was very bitter about my failure in literature and I was sure that writers never really understood anything. And that was why I turned to psychology.

• *Professor McClelland suggested to me that many psychologists of your generation went into the field as a reaction against religion and fundamentalist moral positions. Was that true for you?*
He's got me in the wrong generation. It was a generation or two before. The people who in the 1890s went into psychology had often been ministers or studied for the ministry. I think that is true. There was some of that, I suppose, in Watson and there was some of it in me. I was raised a Presbyterian but I gave that up before I went to college. I don't believe I was following Jeremy Bentham in trying to get over my fear of spooks which he acquired from the nursemaid who told him ghost stories. No, I don't think that would be true of me.

• *What were the major early influences on your work?*
Accident primarily. I've developed that theme in a paper. I had read Watson and Pavlov before coming to Harvard. Then, I met a graduate student, Fred Keller. He knew standard behaviourist arguments and lingo. I had some

contact with Walter Hunter, one of the original behaviourists, who came to give a seminar. I don't believe I got much from Hunter. I got some general physiology from Crozier who had an influence on me of sorts. He left me to do my own thing but he turned my attention to the organism as a whole. I started off being interested in reflexes, in Pavlov, Sherrington, in Magnus and postural reflexes. But Jacques Loeb had developed the concept of the organism as a whole. If you deal with the organism as a whole, you can't deal with organs in isolation. What is the organism as a whole doing? He's behaving in space, in an outside world. You're no longer interested in what's going on inside, in a gland or in a muscle. Loeb could only find a tropism as orienting behaviour in space. I turned to the reflex but I moved from a section of the leg and a Sherrington preparation to the whole organism. The first apparatuses I developed which were very close to ethology were concerned with the reflex behaviour of the total organism.

• *Did you ever meet Watson?*
No, and I don't know anyone who did. He had already left the field by that time. He had been kicked out of Johns Hopkins for moral turpitude. Today, no one would think twice about it but he had an affair with his assistant and married her eventually when his wife divorced him. For a year or two, he was reduced, I think, to selling rubber boots in Louisiana. Then he got into advertising and emerged as a very important executive. The only psychologist that I know who kept contact with Watson was Lashley. He came to Harvard in the middle thirties and I believe that he only came after consulting with Watson.

• *What organisms did you work with first on the reflex, animals or humans?*
The first animal was the squirrel, three baby squirrels. I had already done experiments with the squirrels in Harvard Yard, hanging peanuts on a string from a branch and watching a squirrel pull on the string to get the peanuts up. I was thinking of Kohler's *Mentality of Apes*. I was going to do *The Mentality of Squirrels*. I kept those squirrels around as pets for a long time but I went to work with rats. And baby rats at first because they showed all the postural reflexes in Magnus's book. I studied the behaviour of a rat that was running down a straightway on a very delicate platform. I would sound a click and the rat would come to a dead stop. I would get a very good measure of that stop, very much like Sherrington's torsion wire myograph in responding to a single muscle. I was trying to get the response of the whole rat as Sherrington had got the response of a muscle. That was my thinking at the time. From that, just by accident, I got into reinforcement and the operant area.

- *What particular accident was it that led to that?*

I had my rats running down this alley and I would reinforce them with food. They would then go up a back alley before coming down again. I noticed that they would wait before starting and I began to time that wait and I found it was changing. So here was a change in the probability that a rat would go around that loop, so I set up a special apparatus to follow that change. In other words, I was looking at the rate at which a rat would respond under direct reinforcement and then, by accident, I got it on a cumulative curve and I found I was scheduling. I found that I was in.

- *How did you find you had to modify Pavlov to accommodate the findings you made?*

Pavlov remained a psychologist dealing with organs, not the organism as a whole. Moreover, he was dealing with the autonomous nervous system and with just about the only gland that would have worked. It's an amazing accident that he hit on it. It's very hard to find another gland that could be used. I did not think that efforts to use muscle preparations as with flexion of the leg, for example, were Pavlovian and I don't think so today either. You can't use tears. You probably could have used some other gastric secretions if you could get at them more easily. But I doubt that you could use urine or sweat. Salivation was it. As a matter of fact, though I've only just thought of it now, you might say that Pavlov was a specialist in conditioned salivation.

- *When you began your research, was there still much controversy about a behavioural approach or had that battle been fought and won in the 1920s?*

Well, I can't say it was won. My colleagues among the graduate students at Harvard, with the exception of Keller and, possibly, of Charles Trueblood who dropped out of psychology shortly afterwards, were all interested in Titchenerian psychology. They studied lifted weights, thermal sensitivity, absolute judgement and so on. One of them had spent a year in Germany with the Gestalt psychologists studying the phenomenon. They were all mentalists of the first order. I wouldn't say that behaviourism won its place at that time at all.

- *How did you come to develop the concept of the operant?*

I was very strongly moved at first to think in terms of the reflex. I separated it from physiology in my thesis, in accord with the burgeoning positivistic movement of the time. I read Bridgman. (I was the second psychologist to cite Bridgman. Harry M. Johnson was ahead of me on that.) I read Mach, Poincaré and the people who led up to the Vienna Circle. I never followed them. I don't think they were on the right track but I was looking for the observations upon which one bases concepts. My thesis contended that the reflex was not a physiological device. Sherrington never saw a synapse. The reflex was a statement of the relationship between stimulus and response. That was the beginning.

I developed this further in another paper on the generic nature of stimulus and response. I was moving in the direction of the operant. But it was Konorsky and Miller who, when I first published my papers on lever pressing in the rat, sent me a copy of a paper they were submitting to the *Journal of General Psychology*. Preparing a reply, I realized how I had moved away from a reflex formulation and, also, how I differed from Konorsky and Miller. They had taken an ordinary reflex and added a consequence. You shock a foot, the leg flexes and the flexion produces food. This was in addition to a Pavlovian formula and they felt it was similar to what I had done. My objection was that, by using a reflex, shock-flexion, they killed the whole thing. You would have to find in nature stimuli which were correlated with consequences whether the reflex occurred or not, since the flexion was producing the food.

It occurred to me that you have to have relative freedom from stimulus control in an operant to get the effect of reinforcement. That was our difference then and that is the difference now. It was in my reply to Konorsky and Miller that I first used the word 'operant'. By the time I came to write *The Behaviour of Organisms*, the concept was fairly clear. Most people feel that I distinguish between the autonomic and the skeletal nervous systems and assign the autonomic to respondent or Pavlovian conditioning. When I tried myself to condition an autonomic response as an operant, I failed. I got what looked like it but there turned out to be a mediating response, as there almost always is, unless you knock a man out with curare – which you can't do

• *Much of your work started out as animal work. How securely do you think it can be applied to human beings?*
Well, by the end of the war, it had not been applied at all, with one or two exceptions. I think Fred Keller did something with one of his children. But then I wrote *Walden Two*, which was a wild guess about how this could be applied to the design of a culture and, slowly, the research moved into the human field.

By 1953, I had published a book, *Science and Human Behaviour*, in which I talked about the place of the operant in religion, government, education, economics, psychotherapy and so on. Then the whole programmed instruction movement came along very quickly. Then behaviour therapy developed. Ogden Lindsay and I were, in fact, the first to use the term 'behaviour therapy'. We did the first work using operant conditioning with psychotics at the Metropolitan State Hospital. Behaviour modification also came in and, meanwhile, a great deal of laboratory work was being done with human subjects. There's no question in my mind that it works well with any species, any vertebrate species at least.

• *Some of your critics have argued that while you can control the contingencies of reinforcement for an animal very exactly, the same doesn't go for Man. Though you are showing something that can be made to happen, it isn't how those things normally do happen. Do you see any justice in such criticism? You have a similar problem in medicine.*

If you have a really sick person, you take him to a hospital because there you can handle things properly and make sure he gets the medicine at the time he wants it. You're not quite sure he'll take it when he is out in the world at large. Of course, you can arrange conditions much more precisely in the laboratory. On the other hand, it will work in the world at large, if it is being applied. The achievements of behaviour modification to date are quite dramatic.

• *But presumably you don't just want to modify behaviour. I understand your work to be trying to explain how we have come to do certain things and, even, to feel certain feelings.*

Yes, I would say there are three things that can be done in the world at large through an understanding of behavioural processes. One, we can use them to predict what people will do in given circumstances. Two, if we can arrange the circumstances, we can control behaviour. Three, we can use it to interpret behaviour. This is very important and it is an aspect of it that is easily misjudged.

• *In what way?*

Interpretation isn't guesswork, it isn't theory, it isn't metascience. It's what the astronomer does when he interprets information from outer space as, say, a black hole. He doesn't know. But from what he knows about the behaviour of matter, when it is under his control, he can make some guesses about what is going on when it is not. We can make some guesses about what is happening in, let us say, a family where there is a behaviour problem with a child. We can make better guesses by looking at the contingencies of reinforcement that are visible than the psychoanalyst who turns to theory and starts talking about the relation of the son to his mother. We can point to more relevant things and we're more likely to suggest effective changes.

• *Do you foresee a study that will map the whole reinforcement history of a person?*

That's out of the question for anyone. Psychoanalysts themselves sometimes try to reconstruct a life history. And a good psychoanalyst doesn't, of course. No, I

think you have to accept the fact that human behaviour is extremely complicated and you do what you can. I have never claimed that I have solutions to all
the problems in the world. I have solutions to very few, alas.

• *You seem to have a very ambivalent opinion of Freud, if I may say so. You're
obviously critical but you seem to me to be far kinder about him than many
other psychologists. Can you explain why?*
I think Freud made some very important discoveries and, also, that he brought
attention to discoveries which had been made by other people. We have
changed as a result. We no longer believe in accident, in whim, in caprice. There
are reasons why you forget appointments, for instance. I don't think he always
gave the right reasons but I accept his determinism. I think his great mistake was
to invent the mental apparatus, as he called it, a fantastic creation out of
German will psychology. It was a tragedy. If he had organized his facts without
reference to three personalities of ego, super-ego and id, without reference to the
topography or geography of the mind, the conscious, pre-conscious and unconscious, he would have made much greater progress but he wouldn't have
attracted so much attention. There's no question that there is fascination in this
theoretical stuff. It gives a sense of profundity, of depth. Psychoanalysts love the
word depth. It also means that Skinner is on the surface. They're more profound. I don't think his therapy has been the success psychoanalysts think it has.
Eysenck is perhaps a little extreme on this but not too much so.

• *Your opinion of the mental apparatus leads me to another criticism, certainly of European psychologists, and that is that your work is the ultimate in
the tendency of American psychology to study action rather than thought. Is
that fair?*
It's probably a by-product of the peculiar environment that Americans came
into in moving here from Europe. You could act here. You could go places.

There were all sorts of things you could do, as I am realizing as I write in my
autobiography about my childhood days. And Americans have been men of
action rather than of contemplation. It is largely an environmental difference,
I'm sure. It's certainly not due to character – whatever that may mean. But it is
important because, to my mind, cognitive psychology is an appeal to ignorance.
It is putting explanatory entities of one kind or another inside the organism –
things associated with thinking, reasoning, intuition. I want to get at the environmental manifestation of the behaviour which is attributed to these inner
thought processes. When you do that, you take a step forward because if you
explain behaviour in terms of what a person is thinking, you then have to
explain that thinking. You have a whole new problem.

- *If you ever achieve a final explanation of behaviour, as it were, would you then feel you should attack thinking or do you believe it is just an unimportant by-product?*

I'm very much concerned with the problem of thinking. I have a book coming out in the spring which has a great deal about the problem of thinking. I think that behaviourism makes the greatest possible contribution to an analysis of thinking.

- *I must confess I find that surprising.*

The reason is that we are trying to get at the external manifestations of that behaviour attributed to thinking. I make a distinction between behaviour which is shaped by contingencies, and behaviour which is generated when people follow rules extracted from those contingencies. And rational behaviour involves the giving of reasons where the reasons are statements about contingencies. I can deal with rational behaviour very well. It's very different from contingency-shaped behaviour. Rational behaviour is also contingency-shaped but it is so at one remove. We learn to extract rules and we have to be given reasons for following them.

- *Can you also deal with creativity on this model?*

That is another one of those 'soporific virtues'. How do you account for the fact that a child can utter sentences it has never heard? Why? Because it possesses some cognitive rules of grammar. And how do you know that? Because it emits sentences it has never heard before. That passes for solid thinking nowadays among linguists.

- *Do you think then that creativity is an artificial concept?*

No, creativity is simply the production of novelty, of original forms. You have precisely the same problems with operant behaviour that Darwin faced in evolution. Natural selection and operant conditioning are very similar. Both move the concept of a prior design to an *a posteriori ex post facto* selection. Both move purpose from before to after. This explains origination. The key word of *The Origin of Species* is 'origin'. The environment of the child who is learning to speak selects behaviour and it has the same creative function as the environment in natural selection. The child comes up with novel combinations. There are reasons for this which I set out in my book *Verbal Behaviour*. As a result, the child will emit novel verbal responses. You say it is due to creativity. I say that is creativity.

- *Your book* Verbal Behaviour, *in fact, stirred up tremendous controversy. Why do you think that was?*

I think it is my most important book. It's the missing link between the animal research and the human field. But its importance is one thing. The linguists have missed it so long now because they do not understand an operant analysis. They don't feel at home in it. They can't get into the book and it frightens them. But there is now some growing interest in the book even though it is so far away from traditional linguistics (which is almost totally mentalistic) that it doesn't appeal. (As a matter of fact, it hardly is linguistics.) Verbal behaviour is not what linguists talk about, they talk about verbal communities. I have a small appendix at the end of my book on linguistics and I think that's where it belongs. There are no specialists in verbal behaviour now. There are a few courses being given using my book but there is no person calling himself a linguist or a psycholinguist who specializes in the field, important though it is.

• *To what extent did Chomsky's famous and hostile review contribute to this neglect?*
Linguists have taken it very seriously. They take Chomsky very seriously. I didn't even read that review for ten years. Then, my students told me that I should and I did. I have never read his long attack on *Beyond Freedom and Dignity.* He's an emotional person who, for some reason, is outraged by whatever I write. I don't know how to explain it. When I'm often asked: 'Why is Chomsky mad at you?' I don't know why. Well, if he's right, I'm wrong and if I'm right, he's wrong, but I can view that with equanimity. It seems he can't.

• *Another field of some controversy has been ethology. You have said that some of your first work was along ethological lines and that you are puzzled by how people react to some of your work, arguing that you deny an importance to genetic endowment.*
I don't know where they get that. There is, of course, Watson's famous remark that he could take any child and make him any kind of person. But he said that he was exaggerating and he certainly was. I have never known any behaviourist, with one exception, who has denied the very considerable role of genetic endowment. I do question what it is. The work done on imprinting by a student of mine, Neal Petersen, showed that what was inherited was not the duckling's tendency to follow the mother but a tendency to be reinforced by reducing the distance between it and the mother or mother-object. It is not behaviour that is inherited but a capacity to be made aware of it by the verbal community that says, 'Why did you do that?', 'What are you going to do next?' Consciousness is imposed on the unconscious rather than the unconscious being produced by driving conscious material to the repressed depths.

• *Do you see any value in second-level needs, like for achievement and affiliation? Are they motivating in any way?*
I don't like the word motivating. You feel the need for something and there is a need in the sense of a want. You need food in the sense that food is wanting. But that is a condition in which, because of the history of the species, some kinds of things are likely to be reinforcing. I don't think people 'need to be reinforced'. They *are* reinforced. That is all you can say.

• *You make a firm distinction between what psychologists and what physiologists should do. Why?*
It's again the question of the organism as a whole. The behaviour of the individual in the environment in which he lives is not going to be analysed by instruments that get inside that organism. It's on the outside that the behaviour takes place. Changes occur inside, and the omniscient physiologist may eventually tell us what they are. At the moment he can't tell us very much. I said in 1938 that I knew of no physiological fact that threw any light on behaviour, and I still don't. Take hormones. What do we know about hormones and behaviour? We know we can change the extent to which sexual contact is reinforcing by giving hormones. That doesn't tell us about the deprivations that build normal sexual behaviour, or about satiation, about generalization to other behaviours. We still have the problems we had in the first place – about the extent to which a person is reinforced by sexual contact and what it does to him.

• *Because of this stand you have come to be regarded as a psychologist of the empty organism. Is that fair?*
That's not my phrase. I've always acknowledged the importance of what goes on inside the organism. You would have to be a fool not to. But I leave that to the physiologist. I don't want to meddle. I want to help, and a good clear statement of behaviour gives the physiologist his assignment.

• *You have also not been well understood in that many people think you advocate more punishment.*
I would like to see no punishment at all. I have never had anything to do with aversion therapy, though when I was in England, a year ago, I saw they were blaming *Clockwork Orange* on me. I have been so bitterly against punishment that some of my colleagues have been trying to psychoanalyse me to find out why. Did my father beat me? (Actually he didn't.) I don't think you can get rid of punishing contingencies. You can suddenly become permissive. We have to find alternatives to punishment.

• *If we may turn to* Beyond Freedom and Dignity. *There, you turn your attention to what you call 'autonomous man', that rather dangerous homunculus
within us who thinks himself free to act. Do you think we cling to that idea of
ourselves?*
We certainly do. The whole history of the struggle for freedom, and I accept that
struggle as having made great strides in human progress, has led us to believe we
are masters of all we survey. But that's not true. We are what we are because of
our history. We like to believe we can choose, we can act, and it's true that we
can if we overlook what determines how we act in our past history. We believe
we are responsible for our past achievements though we like it less when we're
held responsible if we do something wrong. Then society is at fault. In the long
run, I don't believe a person is either free or responsible. However, I want a
world where people feel free as they have never felt before. I want a world in
which people are under positive reinforcement instead of aversive control, in
which people achieve more than ever before. I want people to feel tremendously
worthy. (The word 'dignity' isn't quite what I want. The French word *'digne',* is
closer perhaps.) But that doesn't mean they originate anything. The awful thing
about the present obsession with the individual and his immediate gratification
is that we are paying no attention to the future. That's the theme of *Beyond
Freedom and Dignity.* By all means let's have freedom and achievement but they
mustn't over-ride the need to plan for the future.

• *But doesn't that leave you in a contradictory position? You want people to feel
free and yet you say freedom doesn't exist. Aren't you offering an illusion of freedom?*
I don't call it an illusion. It's a feeling. If I'm holding a gun at your head and I
say give me ten dollars, you're not free. But if I just say give me ten dollars and
you're a nice guy and give them to me, you say you're free to do so. There are
reasons why you give me ten dollars. Possibly you hope to get something from
me in return, or you may have been given a large sum of money, a thousand
dollars, and you don't know what to do with it. So you give me ten dollars.
There are reasons why you give them to me even if I'm not holding a gun to
your head, and you feel free in doing it. You don't feel free when I'm holding a
gun at your head. This is a very important difference and I'm as much concerned as anyone to free people from punitive coercion. I wouldn't call that an
illusion. You feel free. You have a feeling which is associated with positive reinforcement which is very different from a feeling associated with coercive
control. And you call it freedom. That's OK.

• *But what, on your model, is that feeling, that feeling of freedom? That seems
a very crucial question, as you deny the validity of feelings. . .*

I don't deny that. That's another misunderstanding. I think the behaviourists are ahead of the field in analysing feelings. I wrote a paper just before I wrote *Walden Two* that is, I think, extremely important. It explains how a person can be taught to describe private events within his body. It is something that Wittgenstein missed completely. He could never see how you could describe a private event. For him, the statement 'I am in pain' was nothing but a cry of pain. In that paper, I described how the verbal environment can teach a person to describe the state of his own body. We will call it feelings or introspections, in spite of the fact that the verbal community has no information about it. I have no hesitation in saying I feel my own body, I feel happy, I feel tired, I feel exhausted, I feel cheerful. But I don't behave in any way *because* of my feelings. That's the main point. Feelings are by-products of behaviour. The mistake people make is to take them as causes.

- *So feelings are epiphenomena?*
I wouldn't say that either. Feelings are not causes but that doesn't mean they're epiphenomena. If I kick you on the shins, you may be inclined to hit me and you will also feel angry. Now the kick on the shins creates the probability that you will hit me and also creates that state of your body you call anger. You feel angry. Now what's epiphenomenal about that? But suppose I then ask you, 'Why did you hit me?' and you say, 'Well, I felt mad at you.' That's not right. You hit me because I kicked you on the shins. You didn't hit me because you felt mad. But both, the anger and the hitting, are the products of a single cause.

- *Would it be fair to say, then, that feelings can be consequences but not causes?*
That's exactly it. They are collateral products. They are states of the body associated with behaviour, some of which can be felt. I make the point in the paper I recently gave at Oxford. Feelings are bad evidence and not very important to the physiologist for they don't get at the important mediating mechanisms.

- *Just as feelings are by-products, you seem to argue that consciousness is a by-product. You have said that awareness is imposed on us by society.*
All behaviour is unconscious to begin with. You behave even though you aren't aware of why you're behaving. But you can be made aware of it by the verbal community that says, 'Why did you do that?', 'What are you going to do next?' That is imposed on the unconscious rather than the unconscious being produced by driving conscious material to the repressed depths.

- *Your work is being put into practice in many ways in this country (the USA). Isn't there a danger that, if you design the culture you want, control will be exercised over people's lives but they won't be aware of it?*

There's certainly a danger and that's why I spend so much of my time explaining how people can be controlled. If you sequestered it, if you said let's not talk about it, there would be 'controllers' who'd snap it up and have a field day. No, I want everyone to be aware of how he is controlled. We are all controlled now. A friend of mine returned from China and said: 'You'd love it there, people are so controlled.' What do you think happens there? People are just as much controlled in America as they are in China but the control isn't as conspicuous, that's all. We are absolutely one hundred per cent controlled in America.

• *But who will design the culture? What will you reinforce? What will you not reinforce?*
A great many people will be designing it. Teachers will be teaching better. Psychotherapists will be helping people more effectively. Industry will be arranging more effective incentive systems which make people not only work better but also enjoy what they are doing. Governments will be able to govern without having too many policemen about. These are the changes that will be made. No one person will emerge as the controller.

• *In your writings you have quoted both Hull and La Mettrie, saying that Man is a machine. At the same time, I believe, one of the reasons why you express an occasional doubt over being called a behaviourist is that it seems to imply not only that Man is a machine but that he should be treated mechanically.*
It depends on what you think a machine is. If you're thinking of a 19th-century machine, a push-pull collection of levers, that's not what I think Man is. A man is a mechanism at the molecular level, a biochemical machine. That's all it comes down to. Miniaturization should have given us some idea of how far down a machine may go. When I say that Man is a machine, I mean that, as far as I know, the whole thing is an orderly physical system. It's certainly not a 19th-century machine with push-pull causality and that is an important difference.

It would be presumptuous to attempt a complete critique of Skinner's position in a few pages. Some interesting points, however, emerged from my interviews. First, Skinner clearly believed that he was a pioneer waging a lonely battle against the autonomous human. He insisted that we cling to this inner homunculus out of arrogance and ignorance. In *Beyond Freedom and Dignity*, he wrote: "Unable to understand how or why the person we see behaves the way he does, we attribute his behaviour to a person we cannot see, whose behaviour we cannot explain either but about whom we are not inclined to ask questions" (p. 19).

Ruthlessly, Skinner pursued his condemnation of the autonomous human, a creation of Greek psychology. He goes on: "He [autonomous man] initiates, originates and creates and, in doing so he remains, as he was for the Greeks, divine. We say that he is autonomous and so far as the science of behaviour is concerned, that means miraculous" (op. cit.).

It seems important to set these insights into context. Skinner's autonomous man does not differ much from Gilbert Ryle's "ghost in the machine". In *The Concept of Mind* (1949), Ryle elegantly bundled this ghost into oblivion. As a philosopher, Ryle wanted to show how misleading it was to talk about feelings, intentions, motives and purposes as private states accessible only to the individual who possessed them. Skinner went much further, though, in a series of directions that are perhaps more confusing than is generally realized.

Skinner moved all causes outside the body and outside the organism. It is what has happened to you, the external consequences of what you have done in the past, that make you behave the way you do now. A person is what he or she has done and what has been done to them. In the interview, Skinner rejected the view that he was a psychologist of the empty organism. He pointed out many defects in physiological psychology. But to point these out does not indicate what role there was in his own thinking for what goes on inside the organism. To say that the stream of consciousness is an irrelevance is one thing; to say the bloodstream is irrelevant is very different. Many internal factors affect behaviour. Why is one person angry one day when faced with a certain situation and not angry another day? There is evidence from Eysenck that people inherit different susceptibilities to the processes of conditioning. A philosopher like Ryle can ignore these factors for they do not affect the way we talk about things. But they certainly affect the ideas that should guide our research.

Till the mid-1970s, Skinner contributed to a climate where questions about thinking and feeling weren't seen as being at the heart of psychology. Skinner chuckled when he said it would surprise people to discover he had feelings and admitted it. He had been misrepresented. His point was that his feelings, the flotsam of his mind, did not make him act the way he did. If he had no feelings, he would act the same way. This seems a gross assumption. In 1977, Skinner's revelation that he was at work on an analysis of thinking did little to reassure. *Thinking Behaviour* never saw the light of day, however.

Moreover, Skinner admitted that the history of any human being is so complex that it would be impossible to trace the incredible chain of reinforcements that made him behave the way that he did. Although the principles Skinner argued applied to situations as intimate as falling in love, choosing one's friends and relating with one's children, it was beyond the wit of humans to account in detail for the reinforcements that led to a particular event. This is unsatisfactory. It left Skinner claiming he could make certain things happen in very structured and artificial situations. He used this to prove that, in fact, behaviour in all situations is caused in a similar way. Yet, he could not account in detail for real-life behaviour in many such situations because real life is too complex, the chain of events is too long. In his experiments Skinner forced behaviour to happen and to be caused in particular ways which might not be the way they normally do occur. It is a criticism that he did not really meet in the interview.

The precise position Skinner adopted on feelings is, actually, harder to pin down than one might expect. In *Beyond Freedom and Dignity* (p. 19), he wrote of William James's theory that it is our actions that cause our feelings and not, as is usually assumed, the other way round. In other words, what we feel when we feel afraid is our behaviour – the very behaviour which in the traditional view expresses the feeling and is explained by it. But no explanation has been given as to why we run away *and* feel afraid.

The interesting point here is that Skinner came close to saying that psychology should look at why we feel afraid as well as at why we run away. If he did not stress the relative triviality of feelings and how unimportant they are in the scheme of behaviour, he might have encouraged a more complete analysis of what happens when we do run away and feel afraid. He might also have made it reasonable to look at why, sometimes, we feel afraid but do not run away. We behave quite often, after all, in a way that clashes with our feelings and intentions. We do not always do the things that we think we want to do. But various factors are probably involved in this. The situation, the way we perceive the situation, what we want to get out of it, what we want to show ourselves as, are as likely involved as not. If these things sound vague, I can, at least, reply that Skinner also was vague. He did admit that it is not usually possible to trace out the history that has led a person to a particular action at a particular time. By his concentration on overt behaviour, he was not taking all the data into account. He wrote, at times, of "inconspicuous behaviours". These also need to be understood.

Even being generous, I have to say Skinner failed to appreciate some of the social dangers of behaviour modification. He claimed that since he wrote *Walden Two*, he had tried to educate people to give them insight into the techniques that are used to control them. *Walden Two* was the one book that he wrote quickly under pressure, and perhaps fervour, of inspiration. Skinner denied that he had a sinister aim; he did not want to become Big Brother. Though he seemed to me quite sincere in his way and did not sound as if he personally wanted to redesign the world, he was seeking a particular kind of culture and he was rather blind to the dangers involved. His plans required parents, schools and the government to co-ordinate and reinforce a similar kind of behaviour. The obvious danger of such a scheme is that it will be designed by those in power.

Work in behaviour modification is still popular. It can a useful technique. It deals efficiently with phobias, for instance. But it hasn't managed to deliver the large-scale social improvements *Walden Two* hinted at. It failed to do that and Skinner never quite admitted that this very partial success (though important in terms of alleviating human suffering) did actually cause serious theoretical problems. 1984 came – and went – and Skinner was an old man by then, but his psychology remained highly influential – and still is, despite the cognitive revolution.

In his autobiography Skinner listed virtually every event that seemed to have happened to him. Despite this comprehensiveness and despite the fact that he admitted to having feelings, Skinner seemed to hesitate to record what these events made him feel, even on such occasions as when his mother washed out his mouth with soap and water to punish him. At least Skinner was consistent in his portrait of himself: *Particulars of My Life* smuggled in little ordinary emotion or consciousness – it is a list and little else. Skinner saw life in terms of action, not of reflection. It is no accident that it is in America, the land that extols action and the man of action, that he was most influential.

Chapter 11: Deborah Tannen

I first interviewed Deborah Tannen in a London hotel in 1991 shortly after her book *You Just Don't Understand* became a best seller. Tannen offered something the classic feminist texts of the '60s and '70s, even going back to Simone de Beauvoir's *The Second Sex*, did not – something that looked like serious scientific evidence. I was there to talk to her for the *New Scientist*.

Twelve years later I get out of a taxi on the edge of the campus at Georgetown University in Washington DC. The campus buzzes with freshmen and women, pretty girls on mobile phones, self-serious young men. Posters advertise every lobby you could dream of – Irish groups, Middle Eastern supporters of Palestine, auditions for the balletically challenged and the Republicans who sport a dull picture of Bill Clinton with the tag line "He lied". Youthful energy fizzes. It reflects, Tannen explains later, a key change at Georgetown. It was a Catholic school but in the recent past it has become eclectic. When Tannen first went there, every dean was a Catholic. Now there are five who are not.

I make my way into the Edward Walsh Centre. Tannen works in the Intercultural Center which specialises in foreign languages and linguistics. She has changed the time of our interview from 3 to 2.30 without explaining why. Her secretary brings me to a small, very neutral room. I usually like to comment on the décor psychologists work in – Flavell with the pictures of Piaget, Frankl with pictures of himself – to get a sense of their personality. But there is nothing you can hang the smallest story on; you can tell nothing from her cramped office.

Tannen is a tall handsome woman with curly hair and a friendly smile. She is much more relaxed than she was in 1991. The first thing she does is explain why she changed the time of the interview – the Soviet dissident Nathan Scharansky has come to address the Jewish Society on the crisis in the Middle East. She wants to listen to him. I am very welcome to join her. As I made a film about dissidents who were incarcerated in Soviet psychiatric asylums, I am very keen.

Tannen has had an unlikely career. As she explains in the interview, she was always interested in writing. She took two degrees in English before she went on a linguistics course because she wanted to do something more "intellectually challenging." Most linguistics are highly technical but this course was focused on the use of language in everyday life or socio-linguistics.

For me the phrase the use of language in everyday life brings back my undergraduate days. When I studied philosophy and psychology, the philosophy of ordinary language was all the rage. Great minds like J.L. Austin, the author of *How to do Things with Words*, picked and nit picked language to bits seeking to find well . . . not the real meaning since the essence of ordinary language psychology was that there was no real meaning, no essences, nothing fundamental but the fine distinctions in the way we use words. The aim of philosophy was to free us from metaphysical delusions. The way the philosophers did this would have been familiar to Aristotle. They sat and thought, they did not go out and see how people actually used the words at a bus stop or in a pub. Hell no, they pondered in their ivory towers. No one has suggested that this might be one of the reasons ordinary language philosophy has gone out of fashion especially as we know now there is no one correct use of words. Listen to a 1950s radio programme and see how language has shifted – particularly English which was once shiff and pukka but is now looser, multi-cultural. Trinidad English ain't that of the Queen.

Tannen is a little more objective and has been known to get out of her armchair. She examines the psychodynamics of language, the patterns in how men and women speak to each other. Her first book relied on many examples from her first marriage – to a Greek she met when she left the United States after she had finished her first degree. In one book she tells a strange story of how he became furious when the toilet paper came out the wrong way from the holder!

This is what is interesting about her position. Usually psychologists believe that language is something "you see through" to the deeper meanings within. Freud's *Psychopathology of Everyday Life* was about how slips of the tongue revealed what was really going on in the mind. But while Tannen does not deny that in relationships it matters if you share tasks such as taking the garbage out, words are not quite "all we have" but a good part of it. Language is constitutive of relationships, as she puts it more formally. She insists she is not a psychologist.

Tannen was disappointed by the reception of her first book, *That's not What I Meant*. People were not jumping up and down at her insights but the sections on men and women were extremely well received. As she explains that experience led her to write *You Just Don't Understand*. The book examined in sometimes funny details the different ways men and women talk to each other – and how we often miss. Men tend to see conversations as ways of solving problems; women just like talking because it creates intimacy. Men also hate not knowing and Tannen discovered a new social phenomenon – the fact that men hate asking directions perhaps because to ask is to show you need to be dependent and so can dent the male image. The hunter gatherer in 5000 BC presumably did not ask whether he had to turn left or right to find where the nearest woolly mammoth was and that still affects us today. As I write this I can't help wondering if the real predecessor for Tannen was not the great American humourist James Thurber with his vignettes of how the American female and American male never really understood each other.

You Just Don't Understand became an instant best seller but it was also eventually attacked rather bitterly by feminist writers. Those attacks influenced the direction Tannen's work took. She began to study how Western culture promotes arguments. We do not seek to resolve disputes she believes but we revel in the language of thrust and parry. The House of Commons in Britain is the perfect example with the two main parties facing each other like prize fighters. *The Argument Culture* focused on rows in media and politics and came to the unsurprising conclusion that the more we polarise positions, the less we understand. Back in the 1970s John Birt, later director general of the BBC, was one of the authors of *A Bias Against Understanding* which made similar points about British TV culture which encouraged people to snipe at each other on screen. The sound bite culture of today shows how much Birt failed. Tannen published her book in 1998 and blasted the press, politicians, lawyers and even the education systems, ambitious targets. As she comments in the interview, many in the press agree with her but her book has not changed anything.

If *The Argument Culture* offered arguments against arguing, the other book Tannen published in the wake of *You Just Don't Understand* is perhaps her most scientific to date. Tannen decided to study how people talk at work and gave tape recorders to a number of participant observers as she calls them.

After that she had a hankering to return to relationships and that led to "I only say that because I love you." Some of the dialogues she records have a feel of a Woody Allen movie. A daughter is cooking Thanksgiving Dinner. Her mother is watching in the kitchen and she can't open her mouth without criticising her turkey, her stuffing, her apron. She wants her daughter to cook the perfect dinner and if she criticises "It's all because I love you." A lot of this rang true with me as with other aspects of Tannen's work. My Jewish mother used to nag me to stand straight for much the same reason. "It is not all about Jewish families," Tannen insists but if you are Jewish it is very hard not to see the humour. Tannen is now collecting all kinds of material about mothers and daughters. She does not have children but she is a daughter, she smiled, and she had managed to write about men and women "while being only one of those."

In one respect, however, she has reacted very much against her Jewish background. She said she never felt guilty and that hers was a "rhetoric of good intentions."

It is this mix of real life data and a certain eye for drama that makes Tannen's work so interesting. She did even write a play and it was presented together with that of a black woman writer. She was appalled though when the theatre tried to publicise the show as a confrontation between the black and the Jew who were going to box it out with dialogue.

In the introduction, I mentioned the love of power that psychologists have had. I find it interesting that just as Sandra Bem was attacked by feminists even though she thought her work was broadly supportive, Tannen also found herself attacked. Even though *You Just Don't Understand* dissected the way men talked, hardly held us up in a golden light and emphasised how much women hated being lectured by know-all macho types, Tannen got, as she puts it, "slammed". And it hurt her.

• *How did you become interested in linguistic behaviour?*
I was always interested in words and language. I wrote stories and poems. I was a literary type, on the board of the literary magazine in college. I was also very much a creature of the 60s so when I graduated from college I had no career goals. I worked for a short time, saved my money and went to Europe on a one-way ticket, so my only goal was to be outside the United States. I ended up in Greece teaching English there. And that's when I first became aware of the field of linguistics. Then I came back to the United States and I got a master's degree in English. My first husband was Greek and that's what I write about in my book, *That's not What I Meant.* I went on to get a Masters in English for no particular reason but I had that experience of teaching English as a foreign language. Then I got as job teaching writing at the community college level and this brings me to the age of 29. I was bored, I wanted to do something intellectually challenging again and I thought of English because that was what my BA and MA were in but it somehow seemed… When I was working for my masters I'd seen a poster for a linguistics institute and I thought that's interesting. My Greek husband went back to Greece and I found myself with a little more flexibility and so I went to a summer institute. I was lucky the institute was devoted to linguistics in context because so much linguistics is more technical and abstract and I don't think that would have interested me.

• *What is linguistics in context?*
The patterning of language in everyday life so it was a view of language very much like analysing literature. It was like analysing a work of fiction in everyday conversations. I took courses from Robert Lakoff on gender and language, on communication styles which I later developed into conversational styles. Then we had a whole barrage of blackboards rolled into the lecture hall and each one

was a transcribed phone conversation. It showed a pattern of how people ended conversations. It became a paper called 'Opening Up Closure' on how people opened up ending a conversation. And it just won me over that you could analyse everyday stuff in this way.

• *It's a bit different from Chomsky.*
He's not interested in gender at all.

• *As a man I've certainly been told I can end conversations abruptly.*
My father says 'well it was nice talking to you.' Even though there was nothing leading up to it. (She laughs.)

• *It's not exactly a meta message.*
No well it is a meta message but it's a very simple one. My parents were from Poland and Russia and they're still alive – 92 and 95. I actually wrote a play about my father and his going back to Poland and his relationship with Judaism.

• *So how did your interest in linguistics develop?*
So for that first course on Lakoff I wrote a paper called 'Communication mix in and mix up' about my Greek husband and I used… It was my first public thing and it led to my master's thesis and really from there to my dissertation on New York and California conversational styles.

• *What did that study find?*
The text of dinner conversation and the New Yorkers gave a short pause or no pause at all and that's a way of showing enthusiasm and the interesting thing is the creator (of the pause) is not just the one who begins talking but also the one who stops talking encouraged by the overlap. That was the seed of all that came after. For me I did not most certainly think of myself as a gender specialist. For me it was conversational style and general interest in language. The other area that I worked in was comparing written and spoken language and I edited books on that.

• *When you wrote the first books… when you made those discoveries it's interesting that you were providing a scientific proof of some the complaints feminist writers like Greer had been making.*
It's interesting because as I say the gender was not really my way into the subject. That's not what I intended in my first book for the general audience. That was the book that will change the world, open everyone's eyes and people will realise that the things they thought were personality, that were psychology led, could be

simply understood as conversational style – as style. Language is normally something we look through when actually language is the thing that we make impressions of each other through. So when the book didn't have that kind of effect, I scaled back, I thought OK that is not how it is. You just write books, you do your work and eventually someone might notice. So I was quite unprepared for the impact *You Just Don't Understand* would have. I was surprised that was the one that would get into everyone's imagination. I was quite . . . but had I been writing in the field of gender I would have realised how controversial that statements in it were but to me it was all just a sub-section of conversational style.

- *You were not part of the feminist debate?*
I never was, though I always saw myself personally as a feminist. I was influenced by the fact that it was the late '60/'70s. I went to consciousness-raising groups when I was at Berkeley.

- *Not many consciousness-raising groups in Greece I would imagine.*
In Greece I was oblivious. I was there from '66 to '68 and I was teaching and I was 20 years old and I was very excited to be living in a different country from the United States. I wasn't thinking at all. It was when I got back from Greece . . . it was all very personal. I never thought of my research supporting feminist positions. I always had the goal of understanding human beings and improving the world and improving intercultural relationships . . .

- *Bem was very hurt when feminists reacted very strongly to her work on psychological androgyny, work which showed that men who did female tasks and women who were adept at male tasks were psychologically healthier. So what did she get slammed for?*
It was because there was some value to masculinity.

- *But the men who did well at female tasks also did better.*
It didn't matter. There was something good about masculinity.

Oh dear, you know that's why I wrote *The Argument Culture*. I was subjected to that too and I was also very hurt by becoming a bête noire to the feminists. First of all they should know I'm a good person, I think.

- *The rabbi blessed you?*
Just because I'm human. I think that those who grew up in academic world sometimes think, 'well I'm in a highly contentious field', but linguistics is not that. So I was not prepared. In Berkeley when you went into a conference room, they said that's very interesting and this is another perspective you might like to

have thought of. Berkeley is not like Brown or MIT or Harvard where you give a talk and you're attacked and you have to parry. I didn't have any experience of it. I think it's a combination of my own personality, of having been to Berkeley which was a very different academic culture and my age. I was already 30 when I started grad school, I was 35 when I did the PhD, 45 when the book came out. I'd already pretty much formed who I was and I had not had that experience.

• *I come out of a British culture – in Oxford and the House of Commons – you attack and have to defend. And there is a belief that the clash of opposites allows you to test the arguments of the other side.*
Yes, yes and because I'm Jewish I know that Talmudic tradition, the position that argument is a way of thinking, that poking holes is a way of exploring but the personal experience of being attacked was new to me. And I was very, very hurt. It took me about two years. These attacks didn't come right away and I believe that was because I wasn't so much on the radar screen of the gender specialists. But when *You Just Don't Understand* got all that attention I was treated very kindly by the press and Elaine Showalter, who is a good friend, said I had a charmed life because the press did not go for me as it went for her. But after one or two years I realised I was a person to position yourself against. You could start out by saying Tannen said this and she's outrageous. Whenever you do that, you're going to misrepresent what the person is saying so I was surprised to find I was being misrepresented. I also talked about this in the introduction to *Gender and Discourse*. My work was right out of the tradition of the anthropologist John Gompertz about the style of each group and how when they talk to each other they don't understand each other because they don't share the same style.

• *How do you record the use of language?*
Some of it comes from my family but not all. It's amazing people think it is all Jewish I would call it some combination of participant observation and case study approach. It is of course totally different from the scientific approach when you have hypothesis and you test your hypothesis and you use a random sample. I sometimes refer to it as a ethnographic method but clearly it's not an ethnography as an anthropologist would call it, where you go out and observe a culture for a year and write it up. It's ethnographic in that I try to describe the patterns I see.

• *Do you use a tape recorder?*
I do and I don't, but not in a very systematic way except for the book *Talking from 9 to 5* where I gave my participants a tape recorder and they took it away for a week. I had people record everything they said at work and I had it transcribed. We had four females record what they said so that would be one

extreme of deliberateness in my recording. Most of the time I would just pick it up, people tell me, I observe, I read things, I experience.

• *Do you see yourself as a psychologist?*
The extent to which I'm a psychologist? Once I had a big fight. I had a rather highly strung editor and she said 'this a book is amazing, it's going to be a best seller.' And then she called me up and said we're going to have to change the title *How conservational style affects relationships.* We're going to have to call it the *New Psychology of Language.*

• *What a bad title.*
I said you can't do that. I'm not a psychologist. My whole reason for writing this book is to get people to pay attention to language and not to psychology. She said 'the book is going to bomb, I've done enough work on this'. So I went into a panic and I tried to think of other titles and then she called back and said all right . . . well go ahead. But the book is put in the psychology section, all my books are in the psychology section because there is no linguistics section and people who are interested in these phenomena tend to read psychology books.

• *It seems that what you are saying can be seen as over-extending the importance of language.*
Anything you study you blow out of proportion because you study it. By putting it under the microscope you blow it up so you can see it and then hopefully you put back in perspective when you take the slide out of the microscope.

• *I have certainly been guilty of some of the scenarios between men and women you describe.*
I never say guilty.

• *You think that language is a determining factor in relationships?*
I wouldn't say determining but I would say it's inextricable from other aspects of a relationship. A phrase I use often is that conversational style is not something extra like the frosting on a cake, it's the stuff of which the cake is made. Language is constitutive of relationships because how else do you express the relationship. Action matters, of course.

Whether you pick up the garbage, whether you bring someone a cup of coffee in the morning, whether you are physically there. But inextricably it's talk – so you can't, as a lot of people assume, say it's what you do, what you think, what you feel; words are a basis the way I look at it, it's all created by language and through talk. So think of typical conventions. A woman saying what happened during the day and a man offering to fix it. And she says, I don't want solutions, I want you to listen. And at some level this is how a relationship is because it is created through that kind of talk. That's what creates the intimacy, that's what expresses the intimacy. Of course you care about each other but it creates the intimacy to know certain things about each other and knowing the details of each other's life is in itself constitutive of intimacy.

• *One of the ways in which your findings seem to fit in with many feminists' arguments is that they have been taken as saying that men are bad listeners. Would you go along with that thesis?*
No. You'll never catch me saying men are bad at anything. I hesitate to quote myself again but mine is a rhetoric of good intentions. That doesn't mean I'm so naïve that I think nobody has intentions. No. I just think we need some error corrections because I feel we are so inclined to look for bad intentions. I say let's assume good intentions and go from there though later we may have to say different. And you can be a bad listener by sitting quietly, you can be a bad listener by talking along, you can be a good listener by sitting quietly and you can be a good listener. What I feel strongly is that you can't line up a way of talking as good or bad.

• *Have people taken up your work as a way of changing discourse? Are there courses in Tannen language modification?*
I wish there were. I frequently get letters asking if I see private patients. I don't. Or do I know someone who does my kind of work and I have to say, but I know many therapists have their clients read my book and incorporate it.

• *You've never been tempted to do that?*
I don't think it's my forte.

• *I once made a film in which I got seven stiff-upper lipped British to role reversal, with the men acting women and the woman acting men.*
I'd love to see it.

• *Do you have any interest in doing that kind of thing?*
Probably not. I was a consultant once in a documentary where they took two people and tried to see how they could change and they had me do the language but I don't think I did very well.

• *What response did you get to* The Argument Culture?
I got a very good response from the press which surprised me because I thought that . . . most of the press were accepting. I was invited to speak at various jour-

nalists groups and they said right on, we agree, it's been bothering us too. But they didn't do anything about it. I got slammed in the *New York Review of Books* and that was an example of a feminist attack because they thought of me as a feminist because of *You Just Don't Understand.*

- *There is a lot of politics in the book?*

There is a lot of politics and a lot of press. The first draft of the book started with education and then I did press and politics. I did the law and medicine too but I didn't have enough material on medicine and the book was too long. The editors said I should start with the press because that is what most people think arguments are about.

- *Has it had an effect?*

I don't think it's had an effect on action but I think it's had some effect on conceptions. There is a organisation on the press which has adopted *The Argument Culture* and talks about its ideas but in terms of how people behave now.

- *When did you form the ambition of changing people?*

I don't know changing people was ever my conscious goal but raising awareness was. So if the question is when did you decide you wanted speak beyond academia to the world at large then I can go way back to grad school when I remember telling a fellow grad student and talking about how we both had these fantasies of going on talk shows.

I was aware very early on that the average person was interested in the kind of thing I was doing and I would often end up at a cocktail party with a group talking about New York Style or LA style or gender. I would often end up talking with group of women who complained not that the man never brought you a cup of coffee but that they're always lecturing you.

- *I identify with that one. I remember people lecturing me that I lectured them, I probably have done so plenty.*

You paid for your whole race. I love Jane Tomkins who claimed that feminist debates were sometimes like the shoot-out in a Western. The good guy has to destroy the bad guy.

- *Is this department unusual in its context on language in everyday life?*

It is unusual in that people study language in context. Typically you would only find one such person in a linguistics department but here we have four and sometimes five. It's as very good environment in which to work.

• *Are you surprised by what you have ended up doing?*
Oh, yes, yes. I was surprised by the reaction and I never in my wildest dreams did I think I would become the gender lady. It's not what I saw as my area of expertise. I also never expected the level of effect it has had. *Why Don't Men Ask for Directions* has become part of the culture and that did come from *You Just Don't Understand.* No one talked about that before. And the book came out and that was what everybody wanted to talk about and that example caught people's imaginations.

• *Your books are full of homely examples?*
I think a lot of the pride that I take is that one thing I always felt I was good at was writing and writing was always what I did and part of what I've done in my books is to write vignettes like doing a short story.

• *A number of psychologists have told me that the subject really comes alive when they write it up.*
So I'm not unique in that . . .

• *What are you working on now?*
I've just decided that my next book will be on mothers and daughters and I intend to focus on their conversations. So much has been written on mothers and daughters but I want to zero in on their conversations. Partly, every book has run out of the one before. That's not what I meant that was my word to the world but it was the gender chapter that got so much attention so that went to *You Just Don't Understand,* the attacks started to brew just then but people said I needed to do something about work so I did *9 to 5* but *The Argument Culture* was really a reaction to the way the gender books had got attacked. And then I really wanted to get back to personal relationships and I wrote just say that because I love you and the chapter on mothers got most attention. People talked about the book as if it was just about mothers.

I am now planning to write on mothers and daughters and when anyone tells me a story about mothers and daughters, I'm thinking is this something I can use. And if it is I write it down straightaway.

That was the end of the formal interview. Tannen looked at her watch and said it was time to go and hear Nathan Scharansky. There is an interesting link between Tannen's work and his defence of Israel. We hurried across the campus and Tannen had to vouch for me when we were questioned by security men at the entrance to the hall. We walked into a room of less than 80 students. Scharansky was in full flow explaining the Israeli position. He spoke with the moral authority of a man who had been imprisoned by KGB because of his political beliefs. He had done years in the cells because he believed in democracy and he argued there would be no solution to the Arab Israeli conflict till Arab countries were democratic.

Scharansky spoke of his mentor the physicist Andre Sakharov who came to hate the old Soviet regime. Both men had implored Kissinger not to do a deal with the Russians until they were democratic. Scharansky had a magnificent insight. In the cells where the KGB held him, he had to take himself very seriously to survive. He is a short stubby man who can puff himself up. Every move in the battle of wills between Scharansky and the Soviets would affect the future of world history. But, de-puffing himself, Scharansky said he had to laugh as well and take himself not that seriously.

What struck me most was that the language Scharansky used did not matter that much. In the Middle East, the argument culture has become a bomb and suicide culture. In Georgetown, however, Scharansky was preaching to the converted. I found it very sad that there seemed to be not one Arab student who had come to listen to a man who was a liberal hero and risked his life for freedom. But now that man is representing a country that is bitterly divided and, certainly, not the 'beacon to the nations' it once was. However much you modify the way you talk so that an audience can get your meaning, you have to have that audience there in the first place to get your message across. I said goodbye to Professor Tannen but the irony is we had sat through an hour which showed all too clearly that studies of language cannot help when the arguments between cultures are so bad, different groups won't even speak to each other.

Chapter 12: Niko Tinbergen

Not many psychologists have won the Nobel Prize. In 1972 Niko Tinbergen shared it with his close friend Konrad Lorenz and Karl von Frisch.

As a student, I attended some of Tinbergen's lectures so I expected his house in Oxford to be filled with birds and fishes, gulls and sticklebacks; he'd be observing them day and night. The birds wouldn't be in the house, of course, as he always stressed the need to observe animals in their natural habitat.

Tinbergen established a reputation as one of the first ethologists, a pioneer, with Konrad Lorenz, of a new approach to the study of animal behaviour. This was not the result of any theoretical preconceptions but simply, he says, a revolt by young zoologists against the dead animal. "We felt no guidance and returned to psychological texts but found little relevance to the things we saw. We turned to McDougall and felt that's not the scientific way of looking at animal movements", he told me.

Tinbergen is not a flamboyant man. No greylag geese flap around him, as I imagined they always did around Lorenz. He sits in his living room which is decorated with primitive art heads and an Arctic photograph, in an anorak, and he looks all kitted out to go bird-watching. But he is not, in fact, at all divorced from reality. His pursuits, like bird-watching, may be solitary, and he sometimes has a rather distant and elusive smile, but then he snaps back with a sharp remark. Despite his long stay in Oxford, he has remained very Dutch. He says "eye" (not like a German, please note) rather more often than yes. Like many Dutch men and women, he is amazed to find himself hailed as a model of tolerance.

His tolerance extends to those who criticise his own work. Once or twice, having flayed an academic adversary in conversation, he retracts: "No, that's rather unkind". I had the feeling that he sees himself as slightly beyond demolishing opponents with glee.

The early ethologists were often bird watchers and aquarists. "We found forerunners in Charles Otis Whitman and Julian Huxley who looked, as Darwin did, at behavioural patterns that were common to species". He quotes Lorenz's saying, that ethologist's should consider behaviour like one looks at organs – it is an organ. "The exercise has been to deal with animals' behaviour like the more concrete topics in biology were dealt with, asking the normal questions in biology, but about animals' behaviours."

When I was writing in the 1970s, it was easy to forget how novel the approach of the ethologists was in the 1930s and 1940s. American psychology was rat obsessed, the study of the life and times of laboratory animals. They were not observed: they were experimented on.

One of the fundamental points the ethologists made was that one should study the whole life-cycle of species – a fine one was done on Cichlid fish – which implied, of course, that observation should precede experiment. At the time that was novel. Further, in the 1930s the orthodoxy was that nothing was innate, everything was learnt. Creatures were a *tabula rasa* for learning theories to dazzle and impose upon. The ethologists, Tinbergen and Lorenz foremost, maintained much was innate. "We were a bit rash, I think, in the emphasis we placed on the innate but it was part of our reaction to psychologists then," Tinbergen explains. But this strong anti-nurture, anti-environment line did, at least, start a critical dialogue between Continental ethologists and some American psychologists.

In 1956, Lorenz came to Holland and invited Tinbergen back to Austria to spend a couple of months with him. He is remarkably frank about his relationship with Lorenz. "We supplemented each other. I was more a verifier, an experimenter, whereas he had a ray of light at first sight." He was inspirational to Tinbergen while, on the other hand, "he held experimentation in high regard." There is an echo in Tinbergen's voice that suggests almost too high regard. But, until the war forced Lorenz into the German Army and Tinbergen into (eventually) a hostage camp in Holland, they collaborated and wrote a great deal to each other.

After the war, Tinbergen decided that they would not have any success in introducing their observational approach into the English-speaking world unless one of them settled there. Professor Alistair Hardy at Oxford had a job going; so Tinbergen took it. He was allowed by the Dutch government to take only 35 guilders out of the country – plus his family. He discovered that there was already some similar British work. "Thorpe was already working at Cambridge on birds, for example." But Tinbergen's arrival in the English-speaking academic world did provide a great impetus.

Ethology suggested a number of very important concepts like imprinting, displacement activities (which occur when two incompatible behaviour systems are aroused in an animal) and innate releasing mechanisms. These mechanisms have to be triggered in an animal by outside stimuli, often another's behaviour pattern, like the correct wiggles in a stickleback's mating dance. Tinbergen's own work on gulls and sticklebacks is one of the classics of that period, as it broke down the elements of behaviour that had to occur, in their proper sequence, so that a full behaviour pattern could take place. It was like dissecting a *pas de deux,* showing how animals did communicate.

> "But now you can't really talk about ethologists any more. We learnt a great deal from the American psychologists who criticised us and they also came to see the value of the sort of evidence we had. Now, for example, you have two zoologists teaching here at the Institute of Experimental Psychology and plenty of psychologists have developed an interest in animals other than the white rat. There's been mutual traffic."

In the traffic, ethology has lost its ideological frontiers, its pioneer aloofness that it needed to survive when Lorenz, Tinbergen and the others were just a tiny group of "insiders", as he terms it. Clearly, the most important contribution made by the ethologists was that they rediscovered observation in the life sciences.

> "We placed a tremendous emphasis on observation. Observation is a creative act and we have been in hanger of skipping the whole observational phase. When you observe, when we observe, we are hypothesizing all the time. We think in terms of evolution, in terms of natural selection. Those behaviours, those animals, that failed... well... they're not with us any more."

A man had recently asked him what were the rules when he observed, what was the grammar. And he found he couldn't answer the question. He compared the situation to a primitive tribe that can speak its language perfectly well but couldn't begin to analyse its grammar. The tribe didn't know the rules that could be extracted from their speech. The same goes for observation. Good ethologists know how to do it, but they can't self-consciously dissect how or why. You can't, for example, teach all pupils how to observe. You could almost say, either they've got it or they haven't. It surprises him, too, how easy it is to miss things. "I've been observing gulls for 40 years and, last year, I went with a student and he pointed something out to me that I'd missed. Suddenly I said, 'you're right Joe, gulls always do that'." But I'd never noticed it.

Observation is an individual thing, more individual perhaps than many life scientists would like to admit. It's ironic, too, how little study has been made of observation. Observing observation does sound a little like one of Russell's paradoxes but it isn't paradoxical at all. Any philosophy of the behavioural sciences will have to face the problem of what happens when scientists do observe – what they bring to observation, what they select from it. It's just wrong to assume it's a replication of the impersonal (allegedly) observation of the physical sciences.

The 1960s saw many extrapolations from ethology to humans. Desmond Morris's *Naked Ape* (1967), Lorenz's *On Aggression* (1966), Ardrey's *The Territorial Imperative* (1967) set a trend. Tinbergen also began to be interested in humans but in a much more specific, much less grand way. He and his wife became interested in the subject of autistic children and how they can communicate. He told me,

> "I have begun to feel that maybe I was a little asocial through my life with my animals. And then Oxford started a new faculty of human sciences and so I have had to try and teach animal behaviour in a way that it can be used in the study of Man. Then – another accident – I was roped in a few years ago by a couple who were studying autistic children. I didn't feel I could help them much, but then it dawned on my wife and me that everything we've heard described about autistic children we have seen, at some time, in normal children. As autistic children don't speak, understanding them must be based on expression and movement. These sorts of movement and expressions had been seen in animals. Many of these children live in perpetual conflict between hyper-anxiety and frustrated social longing."

Tinbergen and his wife developed a new hypothesis which emphasizes the environmental causes of autism. In the late 1960, this clashed with the orthodox view that saw autism wholly genetic or organic. Tinbergen didn't want to claim too much because he was afraid to raise false hopes. He also worried that some parents might feel that they had caused their child's condition.

When I interviewed him in 1972, Tinbergen was absorbed in his work on autism but much of our talk dwelt rather on the past. He felt he had reached the stage when a scientist must resign himself to doing research by proxy, suggesting new fields to students and then not interfering too much. "I say to a student, and I know enough to say it with conviction, that here is a wonderful subject, but then I must leave the development of the subject to him".

He day-dreamed about how he might use ten years without a single administrative chore. Despite that, he has also become deeply interested in popularizing the study of animal behaviour.

"I couldn't make up my mind whether to be a photographer or a biologist when I was young", he explains. And so it is no surprise that he enjoys filming – and has been very successful at it. His film, made with Hugh Falkus, *Signals for Survival*, won an Italia Prize film award and he has supervised the making of 13 animal films which were shown on the BBC and other TV networks round the world. "We've seen that people are interested not just in pretty-pretty pictures but in a story. They want to know how the African elephant lives and to the limited extent that we know, why it lives in the way that it does."

He had had a hard time with TV, with final cuts of films being shown without consultation, and he had become a little cynical about TV. (I can only imagine what he'd have said of shows like *Big Brother* which purport to study human behaviour in the raw!) He consoled himself with the fact that whatever TV executives might do to his material, the films would still be vital for the teaching of animal behaviour. So the TV pays for it.

It is easy now for a scientist to latch on to one issue and carve his career and livelihood out of the one nook. You expect Tinbergen to be the ethologist, less flamboyant than Lorenz but with a one-track "let's just eyeball the animals" mind. Lorenz, he says, tersely admits that he is a preacher now. He has been rather disappointed because he feels many psychologists and psychiatrists haven't understood really what he is getting at. Tinbergen, less flamboyant, seems not at all one-dimensional. He has gone beyond ethology, not yet having satisfied himself that it has been fully incorporated in the behavioural sciences. Now, Tinbergen looks forward both to popularizing animal behaviour studies and to applying them in very specific human areas. Will he be writing his own *Naked Ape*? (What about *The Naked Zoologist* as a title?) He says he feels that a weakness of both Morris and Lorenz, whose works he admires, was that they didn't reveal the methods they used. "They didn't expose either the power or the limitation of their methods." And that, he thinks, might be worth doing. In his life, he has had occasion to adapt animal knowledge to human behaviour in a light way.

Having meandered through many topics before, during and after lunch, I asked if there's anything else he wanted to say. Another smile. "An interview, to use a grand word, is your creation." He wouldn't impose on me. His wife, though, said with a quite surprising insistence that he should tell what happened to him in Canada a year or so before. He was on a lecture tour and was trailed by Maoist students who heckled him 3000 miles from Montreal to Vancouver, breaking up a lecture. They brought out a pamphlet suggesting he was a fascist, because he published one article in a German periodical at the beginning of the war. "They never said, of course, that he, like all the other staff at Leyden, resigned because the Germans sacked the Jewish professors and that he spent two years as a hostage in a German camp, not a concentration camp but bad enough," his wife insisted.

There is a moment's silence. The quiet pleasant interview has been changed. She almost apologised for her intensity. So did he. I really didn't see why. Few things can be nastier than to be called a fascist who cooperated with Germans. But the display of passion, of personal passion about himself as a person, was obviously not something Tinbergen liked.

• *How did you become interested in the study of animal behaviour?*
Having as a boy taken delight in observing wild animals – along my native seashores, in the rich Dutch sand dunes and coastal marshes, in the little aquaria I kept in the back garden – I was not happy with simply dissecting dead animals,

or showing that my spit, in a test tube, did something to starch. I was interested, just as a hunter is, in what intact animals did. To get professional advice, I turned to psychology textbooks, but found that they offered little help – the things I saw were just not discussed there.

- *When you looked to the psychology textbooks, what did you find there and how did it affect you?*

At first I went to what was then modern American psychology – a less dogmatic but more method-obsessed form of behaviourism. It was only much later that I discovered the early papers of Watson and Lashley, who together did some quite interesting field work on birds. McDougall did for a time appeal to us, but although he discussed behaviour in a wide context, we soon became disillusioned with his essentially vitalistic attitude. We had a strong urge to observe closely what animals did when coping with their natural environment. I dare say there was a great deal of intuitive projection of self in these early studies, and we were vaguely aware of that, and tried desperately to be 'objective' about animal behaviour. This made us react over-violently against such pioneers as Portielje, Buytendijk and Bierens de Haan. Nowadays we are less ashamed to admit that a certain amount of identifying oneself with the animal, of screening into its skin, does often guide one's intuition. It's at the verifying stage that one has to be wary of relying too much on one's intuition.

- *What were the major influences on you and who did the group of ethologists in the 1930s consist of?*

The early ethologists – Darwin of course, later Heinroth, Huxley, and then the great reviver of ethology, Konrad Lorenz – were all naturalists. After I had published some of my early studies, on the homing of wasps, on the everyday life of the hobby, on the mutual signalling of sticklebacks, I got in touch with Lorenz. Lorenz considered Heinroth as his revered teacher. But Heinroth had a curious attitude of refusing to theorise. In his papers, one can read a great deal between the lines, but even when giving a beautifully organised lecture, packed with new facts, he would end by saying, 'Well, the moral you can of course draw yourselves'. Lorenz – psychiatrist, zoologist, philosopher – was the man who designed a theoretical framework; one can now hardly imagine what a tremendous impact his early papers made. The translations of his papers have come too late to bring this out. Lorenz invited me to come and work for a time with him, and the four months spent with him in Altenberg have been of decisive importance for me. He showed me the value of observation as a method and *he* felt an undue admiration for my knack of experimenting. After my return to Holland we kept up a busy correspondence.

• *Does observation play a crucial role?*
Yes – although, as I said, we did experiment a great deal, we spent most of our time patiently watching, interfering as little as possible with what the animals did. The watching was so fascinating because one *interpreted* all the time; and one also compared the animals' behaviour with what went on in the environment, either as likely causes of behaviour, or as likely effects – such as the effects of their 'displays' on conspecifics. Medawar, and also Lorenz himself, have since broken a lance in favour of such 'creative observation' as a legitimate, indeed indispensable, scientific method. I myself have also learned a great deal from what I like to call natural experiments – seeing for instance what events in the environment set off a reaction in an animal. Strictly speaking no more than a correlation, but one on which one could build a little hypothesis. It has often been said – most clearly by Frank Beach in America – that in its haste to step into the 20th century, psychology has skipped the observational phase. To have made 'inspired observation' respectable again in the behavioural sciences is, I believe, a positive achievement of ethology.

• *Did the early ethologists attempt to describe the whole life-cycle of particular species?*
That is true – at least we attempted it. In the thirties a number of 'ethograms' were published. We realise now how schematic they were, but they helped us in seeing the wood and not merely the toad.

• *After all these years devoted to the observation of animals, do you have a clear idea of what you are doing when you observe?*
That is an interesting point. When my wife and I recently applied some of the observational and interpretative methods of animal ethology to the behaviour of children, we came in contact with many psychiatrists, to whom our approach was entirely alien. And one of them asked at a given moment, 'What is the *grammar* of what you do?' I could not really answer him, and realized that we had paid too little attention to analysing our own procedures. Of course the use of the word 'grammar' was not quite helpful – it made one think of the rules of language which linguists *extract* from their study of language, not of the unconscious rules which people apply when they speak. The fact that even now so much in our selective observation is intuitive makes this type of observing so difficult to teach. And since our teaching has not yet developed very far, one has to rely in educating one's students very much on their gifts, and one finds it very difficult to develop good observational powers in a student who is not a born observer. One can provide a few rules of course, such as: 'describe movements rather than use catchwords', 'ask yourself what made him do this or that?', 'ask what could be the

survival value – if any – of this or that', but how very personal one is in unconsciously attaching value to certain aspects of behaviour becomes clear every time one observes the same scene jointly with a graduate. Two persons see quite different things. Often, of course, I can call a pupil's attention to events he has overlooked. But quite often a new collaborator calls *my* attention to quite obvious things, of which I have to admit at once: 'You're right – I've seen it time and again, but I have not *registered.*' Very humiliating, but a very salutary experience.

• *Do you think that the process of observation itself might be worth studying?*
I certainly do. And in a primitive way, we all are trying to do it all the time. But it offers all the difficulties of a system (the brain) studying itself – and the system is, of course, incredibly complicated. What is particularly worrying is to experience in oneself how strongly one's own expectations, even one's non-rational moods, can colour and even distort what the senses report – quite a long way towards hallucination. That's why we must record on film on tape, etc, so that one can submit the material to a number of observers.

• *Does observation depend on experience?*
Yes and no. I have found that very often pupils come up with a profusion of ideas, of which they cannot quite assess the validity because lack of experience prevents them from knowing evidence that refutes many of them. The role of the experienced man is then to marshal this evidence, and to demolish. But also to jump up on some occasions and say enthusiastically, '*That's* it! *That* you must follow up. It fits with this and this and this – a splendid idea!' It was in this way that Martin Moynihan 'discovered', and I helped working out, the important concept of 'appeasement signals'.

• *What were the main problems of the early ethologists?*
Apart from putting the emphasis on observation, there was the emphasis on 'innateness' of much behaviour – more correctly (as we often put it now) the considerable genetic contribution to the 'programming' of an animal's behaviour machinery. Early ethology also broadened our insight into social behaviour. Perhaps one could put it most generally by saying that we learned to see behaviour as the outcome of natural selection. That's where we owe so much to the pioneering work of Julian Huxley, who as a young man showed, in his famous paper on grebes, the courage of his convictions when these were not at all popular.

• *Much of your work has been experimental, has it not?*
Yes, and that is still the work I love most. I am sure that Lorenz is right when he says that I am a hunter at heart – my interest in an animal intensifies at once

when I see it in its own environment, whereas in a zoo it bores me stiff. And I am irresistibly drawn to animals that elude one, which one has to outwit. Yet, I don't regret at all the time spent in laboratory studies, nor the time spent with birds that are easy to study, such as the gulls. There the challenge comes from a more subtle way of 'outwitting' – something of the nature of: 'to know what you are up to, and why – better than you know it yourself.' It was one of the great experiences in my life when I could help putting the Serengeti Research Institute on its feet, join my pupils there in their work, marvel at what then seemed the Garden of Eden, now a most gruelling demonstration of 'nature red in tooth and claw'. Apart from all that, it's the beauty of unspoilt habitats that fascinates me.

• *Was it difficult to find a receptive audience for your theories in the 1930s?*
Yes and no. To make clear to psychologists what we were after was very difficult – partly because they were themselves busy with fascinating problems, and because our techniques were in many respects very crude and unsophisticated compared with theirs; partly because we were still working so intuitively and finally because we were abysmally ignorant of what they did. Zoologists responded much more readily, although our early 'physiologising' – in some respects naïve, in others too wild – put off most neurophysiologists. On the whole it has been an uphill struggle, and this I think explains our aggressiveness, mixed with arrogance, in those early days. My younger friends still say that I am far too much of a missionary. Gradually I have learnt some tact and, I hope, some humility, but once a missionary, always a missionary.

• *What were your relations with Lorenz like?*
One in which we mutually supplemented and stimulated each other. He was and still is the man with vision; I am the more pedestrian verifier. And because we are such close friends, we always gave our best when we disagreed with each other. Naturally, when we both became involved with increasing responsibilities, locally, nationally and internationally, there simply was no time any more for correspondence, and hardly any for a relaxed half-day a year.

• *How did the Second World War affect the development of ethology?*
At once, after the invasion of the Low Countries, contact between German and Dutch scientists began to suffer – with censorship operating it was impossible to correspond fruitfully. At first we could continue with research and could write up and many scientists on both sides tried to keep scientific contact going. A few years ago I was bitterly reproached by some Canadian Maoists for having published in the *Zeitschrift für Tierpsychologie* in 1942. But Lorenz was drafted;

my university clashed with the German authorities and I ended up in a hostage camp. Not as bad as a concentration camp, but not exactly a picnic. Unknown to me, Lorenz was assumed missing, presumed killed at the battle of Witebsk, and was not released until 1947. Neither of us will ever forget our meeting at Bill Thorpe's house in Cambridge. Friendships with many Germans have weathered the Nazi storm. Research ground to a halt halfway through the war, but a surprising number of gifted youngsters joined us soon afterwards. Living under Nazi occupation taught us a great deal about human behaviour – normal, sick and heroic.

• *Is it still possible to speak of the ethologists as one group?*
Not really – national trends have developed so that German ethology is now rather different from Anglo-American ethology; and many borderline fiends, between ethology and neurophysiology, genetics, ecology, animal and human psychology, are being, so to speak, invaded from both sides. Some of our closest colleagues are psychologists by original training, and many psychology departments now employ zoologists on their staff. Here in Oxford, zoology and psychology share the same building. And of course ethologists now begin to look seriously at human behaviour – think of Lorenz himself, and of course of my very gifted pupil, Desmond Morris. It was a source of great satisfaction to me when he decided to return to Oxford as his base.

• *Were you following in Lorenz's footsteps in seeking to study Man?*
To a certain extent, yes. I have been late in taking the plunge, but my social conscience finally caught up with me. But I am doing it my own way – I can't claim to have the vision, or the flamboyance, of Lorenz and Morris. Although I admire their work very much, there is something missing in their more widely known works *On Aggression* and *The Naked Ape*. I feel that we will have to explain the methods more fully that we consider of potential value to the study of Man, including their limitations. And this is where I believe I can still make a useful contribution. And since I joined Professor Pringle and Dr Halsey in their work on behalf of the newly founded finals course on the human sciences, I had, of course, an extra spur to think about ethology's potential.

Then, by accident, my wife and I joined forces in one particular area where ethological methods could be fruitfully employed. Many years ago, Drs John and Corinne Hutt had asked me for advice with their studies of autistic children. For a long time I felt I could not be of much use to them. But when, a few years ago, they pointed to similarities in the behaviour of autistic children, and of normal children under certain conditions, my wife – who has an enormous fund of knowledge of children – made me look at the whole problem more closely. We found that we could 'cash in' on our lifelong studies of social behaviour in animals and by careful study of the situations in which normal children showed, let us say, 'autistoid' behaviour, we arrived at a hypothesis, a dual hypothesis really: we concluded that many autists suffer from a severe emotional conflict, in which fear blocked affiliation and other socialization. and also exploratory learning; and we were forced to conclude that the social environment, including parents, often has much more to do with causing the disturbance than is generally acknowledged. Having the sad fate of these severely damaged children in mind, we decided to publish our ideas, with a description of our methods, before we could marshal as much evidence as we could have wished. Our entry into the world of psychiatric research and psychotherapy gave us many cold showers, but also a surprising amount of support. It is still too early to say to what extent we are right, but research and therapy are profiting from this exercise, if only by being forced to have another look.

• *Can one easily apply ethological ideas to the study of Man?*
To certain areas, yes. For instance to problems of non-verbal communication; and to children's behaviour. Here the application of ethological methods, by Corinne Hutt, and by Nick Blurton Jones in London (who recently edited a very valuable collection of studies by a variety of workers) seems to me to have great promise. But I do think that psychiatry, and those responsible for medical research, still vastly underrate what ethology can contribute. But tile application of primarily ethological methods can't be stopped – ideas have no frontiers – and although I shall not be able to do much of this kind of research myself, I am looking forward greatly to the planned close collaboration with Professor Jerome Bruner, who has just joined us.

   Of course in a minor, incidental way I could not help looking at my own children with the eyes of an ethologist. When one of my children began to yawn compulsively when our family doctor came to see her, he said, 'she seems to be very tired' and I had to explain to him that she was merely scared stiff – it is a very common 'displacement activity' such as scratching, or biting your nails when under slight stress. And speaking of nail biting: one of our children started biting his nails when he was still not quite a toddler. I remembered that female birds often eat anything hard and white when they have just laid eggs, and that my wife was a bad 'processor' of calcium, a defect that he might well have inherited, and (with the puzzled approval of our very research-minded doctor) we smuggled extra calcium into his diet. A wild gamble, but it paid off: the nail biting stopped promptly and never came back. Most doctors will even now laugh this kind of thing off, but then the medical training is not, of course, tailored to research, and certainly not to genuine biological thinking.

• *Does that mean that you have abandoned research with animals?*
At my age, and with so many different types of involvements, one inevitably does research increasingly 'by proxy' – by interacting with students and colleagues by suggesting, criticising, enthusing, creating opportunities and so on. What I shall do when I retire I still don't quite know. It will certainly involve a kind of reappraisal, of finding my priorities. Some of my old books badly need a face-lift; I should also like to continue my work on behalf of educational and documentary films – a fascinating new method of mass communication which is still evolving very rapidly.

• *What kinds of films?*
Making good films that tell a story – rather than 'wildlife spectaculars' which drown the viewer with ever flashier, even more dramatic 'glimpses' – has become possible for us teachers since the explosion of TV. The BBC has given Hugh Falkus and myself some fine opportunities. But we find, with several TV companies here and abroad, that they still lag behind the rapid evolution of public interest. 'Pretty-pretty' pictures have their place, but an increasing number of people want a film to tell a real story, and to tell it clearly. One often meets with a very opinionated attitude in producers or with people who dare not experiment for fear of losing out in the rat-race for promotion, and such TV producers interfere much more with the integrity of the man who makes the film than a publisher ever does with the author's integrity. To make our type of film successfully one also needs more time than is given to the usual documentary, and one needs a closely integrated team of cameraman, scientific expert and script writer, not to speak of a director. So now, after having completed a series of films *on* animal behaviour that will appear on TV soon, we have decided to be a little more independent. This became possible when we received outside support without strings attached. And what we are, of course, really after is not the occasional TV showing, but full and regular use of our films in teaching and entertainment, and of reading material as well. We want to continue 'multi-media publication', as we achieved it with *Signals for Survival:* TV programmes, film copies and a little book.

• *Do you think that ethology has been successful enough to allow it to go out of business, as it were?*
As an isolated discipline it may go 'out of business' the way a small shopkeeper may be swallowed up by a supermarket. But as an integral facet of the behavioural sciences it's only just coming into its own. I am more optimistic than Lorenz, who sometimes feels that outsiders and colleagues in other disciplines somehow always manage to get hold of the wrong end of the stick, and misapply our work. The main reason why I think that ethology will become very

influential even in the study of Man is that ethology puts the amazing phenomenon of 'adaptedness' – the characteristic of living things – in the centre of its attention, and that what threatens mankind at the moment, and will threaten it for a long time to come, is disadaptation. Most people still think of the evolution of human society as 'progress', and have no idea at all of the frightening precariousness of living – which for our species is *more* precarious than for animals. And with a surprising blend of optimism, complacency and arrogance even many biologists still believe that our behavioural admissability can easily match the rapid changes that are taking place in our society. But this is very doubtful.

• *What is the solution?*

Whoever claims to know that is either a crank or a scoundrel. We shall have to mobilize all our intellectual resources to even begin a proper study of Man as an animal species – as a unique species who is the guinea pig in what one could call an experiment of Nature. For our type of evolution, the 'cultural' or 'psychosocial' evolution, there simply is no precedent in the history of life; we have not a single example to go by – not even one that tells us how *not* to proceed.

• *Is Man in danger of arresting his biological make-up?*

You could put it like that, but it's a rather negative statement. Man should take a 'cold look' at himself, and brace himself for some unpleasant discoveries. We shall need all the optimism we are capable of, lest we throw up our hands in despair. And a desperate man loses what little understanding he may have had, and can't explore.

• *How has your role as a man who teaches about animal behaviour affected your career?*

It has, if only because our field is now so popular that one can't confine oneself to teaching one's specialist students. One has to write and communicate in other ways, such as through TV and educational films. And of course for every teacher there comes a time when he has to hand over, when he has to admit that he can't quite follow any more what a very bright new generation is doing. And the present generation of young behaviour students are a bright lot. Just as well, for society will soon be clamouring for them.

Niko Tinbergen died in 1988.

Chapter 13: Philip Zimbardo

I have always loved the Officer Krupky song in *West Side Story*. In that song the teenage thugs make fun of the liberals in social work who say they are depraved because they're deprived. Stephen Sondheim's lyrics make the teenagers not just savvy but well up with their Freuds. After our interview, I left Philip Zimbardo singing that song.

With most psychologists the question of how you started usually gets an answer which centres on what they were interested in when they began university. In some cases, as we have seen, people only gravitated to psychology in their late 20s or later. So I was quite unprepared for Zimbardo's answer which almost burst out of him. He is, as far as I know, the only person who was destined to be a psychologist from the age of six. In the interview he gives a gripping account of growing up in a New York that made *West Side Story* seem tame. He became a psychologist in the South Bronx gangs and was probably called Brains Zimbardo.

He is a tall man with a pointed beard and a creased face. He would make a good 60-year-old Christ. He is still very fit and was a good athlete in his youth once he had survived a bad health scare.

Zimbardo explains how he had to fight to become a psychologist. There was no tradition of education in his Sicilian family and it shows that the local Don Corleone was a poor talent spotter because he should have recruited Zimbardo when he was a smart teenager. Zimbardo put himself through college, discovered psychology and did so well that he got an assistantship at Yale. Not usually a place for smart kids from the Bronx.

In the interview Zimbardo describes how he initially worked on rats but he was so full of energy he had to out-do all the other rat psychologists. He ended up with the largest rat colony in Yale and, after the death of his supervisor, continued his research. But he had always been interested in how groups behave and in who becomes the leader of the gang. He was soon involved in social psychology and in the arguments that ranged round cognitive dissonance theory. Leon Festinger developed in the 1950s a counter intuitive theory which went against traditional notions that rewards motivate people. Festinger argued that we come to love what we suffer for. Zimbardo did his PhD trying to test that theory.

After an unhappy spell in New York, Zimbardo came to Stanford. It was here that he hit the headlines as a result of the Stanford prison experiment. The idea was very simple. You randomly divide a group into prisoners and guards and see what happens. What did happen was frightening. On the morning of the second day, the prisoners rebelled. What should have been a game – an early version of *Big Brother* – became deadly earnest. The guards felt that they had to teach the prisoners a lesson and violence broke out. The experiment had to be stopped because subjects were getting hurt physically and emotionally. Zimbardo argues that is what happens to real prisoners. He describes it in great detail in the interview. For him it shows the power of the situation where one group has power over another. In some circumstances, personality does not matter.

He is also a man who has a real sense of drama and it showed in the way he described his famous prison experiment. He also describes how he worked with the Palo Alto police and persuaded them to arrest the students who were going to be prisoners. As a result, there was a real suspension of disbelief and the middle class students who were banged up felt it was really happening to them. Hollywood has now picked up the film rights and the writer of the *Usual Suspects* is writing the script of the experiment. Zimbardo is very excited by the prospect. He is also very angry about the BBC's recent replication of his experiment and explains why in the interview.

By a strange quirk of fate, Zimbardo was at school in New York with Stanley Milgram who did as controversial an experiment in the late '60s. Milgram showed that ordinary, seemingly nice people were perfectly willing to administer what they believed were electric shocks to human beings who were failing to learn maths properly. Milgram showed that we all have a tendency to obey those we think are in authority. Zimbardo showed that those in authority easily abuse their power. It is a very dark combination of studies and, Zimbardo laments, you could not do these experiments today because of fear of lawsuits.

Zimbardo went on to study shyness in great detail and became president of the American Psychological Society. He saw me in his small ante-room which has two slightly surreal drawings of him and a picture of his family. Family remains very important to him. As we sat, I got a sense of how busy his life is as there were constant interruptions as students wanted to see him. He was very courteous to them and to me because I did not quite finish all the questions I wanted to ask him and he replied to them by email. But he is also quite sensitive. Tannen told me she had not realised who he was when she was at Stanford and he did not appreciate that.

He remains for me the most original and perhaps the most driven of all the psychologists I talked to.

• *How did you become a psychologist?*
Oh I am a psychologist by nurture. I can trace it back to several experiences from early childhood – one when I was five and a half, the others just through adolescence. The early life experience was when I developed a contagious disease, whooping cough and double pneumonia. My family was poor, uneducated Sicilian. This was 1939 and all children with contagious diseases were sent to a hospital in New York City called The Willard Parker Hospital for Contagious diseases. Which meant there was this huge ward with children with every contagious disease for which there was no treatment and we lay in the bed all day. I was there for six months from five and a half to when I was just over six.

• *What was the ward like?*
What it meant was that the nurses wore masks, they could do nothing for you and children died. There was this conspiracy of denial. Nobody could say that anyone was dying though really at some level everybody knew that if you woke up and the bed next to you was empty. You'd ask the nurse where did Billy go and you were told he went home. Somehow it was strange they always went home in the middle of the night. So it was at this early age I coping with fear and the fear was palpable. Then in those days it was the philosophy of the hospitals to emotionally break the connexion between children and families and to replace or reassign that to the staff. One of the ways they did that was to limit visiting hours to one day a week on Sunday afternoon and you only got to see your parents for two hours. And this hospital is very difficult to get to. No poor parents had telephones. There was no phone on the ward so if your parents couldn't come, you didn't know and you just waited. Sunday passed and you had no visitors. And there could be a number of reasons. I was there from December to April so it was winter in New York. My parents would have to walk five blocks to the subway, take two subways and then walk five blocks. I was five an a half, I had a brother who was four and a baby and one of my siblings had polio.

• *So they had a lot on their plates and sometimes presumably children were not well enough to see parents?*
There times when they came and you were in an oxygen tent and when they came you were behind a huge glass wall so that you talked on a kind of phone. So I learned to deal with fear. And no one slept at night because you did nothing all day and people were crying. So it was very interesting and you had to be self

reliant. Practically you had to deal with the nurses. Parents had no function at all except that my father was called in the middle of the night to give me a blood transfusion and I still remember lying side by side with the loop going between us. [Zimbardo demonstrated the loop with large gestures.] The only way you could get in touch was by telegram. But also I learned to ingratiate myself with the nurses because they were the key to power, the key to an extra sugar, an extra pat of butter, an extra piece of bread.

• *It sounds quite Dickensian? And you were six?*
I learned about the psychology of fear, the psychology of denial, being aware at some level that these kids were dying but saying 'OK I'm here, what do I have to do to survive?' The thing with the other kids was how threatening they are, how powerful they are, creative they are too. And then you want the other kids to like you. I used to make up stories. I still remember some of them. One was something like these are not beds but boats we're in and we're going down the Nile so it was for me almost the start of being a leader, coming up with creative ideas.

Also I learned to read and write before I went to school – mostly it was comic books. The only things we had to read in the hospital were comic books. You passed them round, you asked the older kids what does this mean? So I took away all these positives. I'd like to add just one quick aside.

• *Please.*
For years, at least once a year, I had this dream of wrinkled sheets. I called it the mystery of the wrinkled sheets. It was this dream fragment of looking into a room and the bed was all messed up and dirty. No one was in it. But someone would come in and put fresh sheets on. And I'd know when I woke up because I'd be sweaty. And it never made sense. And I told my family about it. I only became aware of it a few years ago when I had a student who was dying of AIDS and I was acting as father surrogate. He got worse and then better and then there was a period when he was getting better when the director of the hospital said that we need his bed and he had to come home. As if he had a home. So I'm trying to find him a place and I can't do it, I tell the director of the hospital, I'm sorry. And just then I noticed that the patient in the next room was not there. It was an AIDS ward and I said, 'Oh good the patient is not there so Lonnie doesn't have to move. I believe that is a bed.' And the moment I said that I was struck with this guilt. I'm happy that this man has died and then Lonnie does not have to move. And then the whole thing becomes clear. Wrinkled sheets mean a child is in the bed but clean sheets mean a child is dead.

And the connexion after all these years must have been the guilt because I must have said, aside from the terrible awareness that someone has just died, a child, a friend, it means you could be next. There was no treatment but there is also the feeling it's terrible but better him than me and better him than Lonnie. And I'm saying this after 55 years of having the dream. But if you don't tell people about the connexion with the hospital, a connexion I never made, it doesn't make sense. Then I knew what it meant and I never had the dream again.

• *Do you find it strange as a psychologist that you could never work it out?*
Yes. I mentioned it to other people; I even mentioned it to other psychologists who did not get it. But if you don't have the pre-story of how I was in the hospital and my experience there, you don't know . . . All of that prepared me to live in my mind, to be interested in behaviour. The second thing was growing up in the ghetto on the South Bronx. Children lived totally in a world of their own, quite apart from adults. It's hard to imagine now. Your apartment was where you ate and slept. The rest of the time you were out on the street because you lived on the streets everyday when it wasn't freezing. We played on the streets for hours and hours.

• *What were you like when you came out of the hospital?*
I was very very sickly, consumptive – that was the expression those days. I got beaten up by these bad kids and also they thought I was Jewish because I was skinny and had blue eyes. Well they beat me up for weeks on end until one day my mother said to the janitor's son, Charlie, 'could you take him to Church' and Charlie said 'no, he's a Jew.' My mother said 'no he's a Catholic, we're Italians' and Charlie replied 'he can't be because we've been beating him because he's Jewish'.

And I didn't understand why people would want to beat me. I was such a nice kid. Then it was again learning street smarts and the psychology of survival. How do you survive on the street when you are a skinny little kid and big kids want to beat the shit out of you for no good reason? So how do you align yourself with power without becoming compliant, without getting a dangerous situation? A lot of those kids on the street ended up getting arrested or killed. So how do you move up from being an obedient good follower because it was clear to me then that I wanted to run the show?

• *You knew that then?*
Oh sure I knew that then.

• *And before you went into hospital?*
No before I went into hospital I was a simple good little kid. What is wonderful about being in the street is that you have this array, this distribution of talent

and of strengths. Being in hospital, being fixed . . . I have just thought about this minute, you know . . . being fixed encouraged me to be a very good observer. There was no physical movement, you're stuck in this bed and the world passes you by . . . a world of nurses and other kids . . . And when I was out of there I'd be looking out of the window of my tenement and seeing how kids play down below. And you'd see who dominates, who takes over, what kind of thing motivates. There was another thing. Nobody had money and we didn't have toys. There would be marble season and we just had a lot of games. And it was the kid who came up with the game when the other game was wearing thin, just getting boring and who said how about this . . . It was clear to me that breaking the boredom by coming up with something interesting to do, which is what I sometimes did, was the way. And then people said, 'Hey Zim what shall we do?' So I began to move into a leadership position not because of my physical strength but because of smarts.

• *And that has had a long lasting effect?*
My sense is that this prepared me to become a psychologist because that was what I was doing. There was another way I was training to be a psychologist. My parents had a rough marriage and I was like my mother's confidante. I would at an early age deal with her feelings, her stress, her feelings of helplessness, having four kids and no money – and my father was out of work. So here I am as young adolescent giving psychotherapy to my mother, saying it'll be OK, look at it this way. That's a very long answer to your question of what made me a psychologist.

• *It's also a most interesting answer. What happened at the end of your teens? Were you the first person from your family to go to college?*
I was the first one from my family to finish high school. My mother didn't go past elementary school or junior high school. Same thing with my father. And then for southern Italians education had no place in their life. Northern Italians was very different but they never emigrated. Southern Italians emigrated because they were poor but there was no history of education, of education being the way up. Education was something you had to do, so I had to fight to go to college and then I had to fight to go to grad school.

• *What was the attitude when you went to college?*
My father said that since you're not bringing money in, you can't take money out. I was self supporting. I worked at the St Joseph's theatre on 44th Street as a concession boy checking hats and coats, selling chocolates, 'Oh sir would you like a programme for the show'. That meant I lived in the Bronx and I com-

muted three hours a day. At my college I was captain of the track team and president of the class. Then every night on the way home I would stop at the St Joseph, work from 7 pm to 11 pm and get home by 11.30 pm. Then I'd do my homework or whatever and set out the next day. Saturday it was 12 to 12 at the theatre because there was a matinee. Essentially I used to work all the time and it was all wonderful. It was showbiz even if you were just checking hats.

• *So you had to work very hard?*
I became a leader, captain of the team, president of the class. I had all the right non-verbal instincts. You sit at the front of the class, and you sit at the head of the table.

• *And then what was college like?*
Yes I went to college and there was a subject called psychology and I was so excited by it until I took the course. I got a C. I graduated with honours. It was a terrible course, a terrible teacher, terrible everything. I didn't take another psychology course until my senior year. I took every sociology and anthropology course and then I realised that sociology asked really big questions but they never had an answer. But psychology in the 1950s were asking boring and trivial questions. But they had all these tools and all these mechanisms for providing answers to them. I thought all I had to do was to ask the right questions, the more interesting questions. So I switched to psychology. I also took experimental psychology at the urging of a dear friend of mine who was a psychology major but who needed a partner for experiments he had to do. He knew I would work so I took the course. I loved experiments.

• *And what happened to your friend?*
He became a sociologist. And then I went to Yale in 1959. My undergraduate psychology was limited in fact to one year. In 1959 Yale was still the centre of behaviourism. Clark Hull had recently died but there was still Frank Logan, Frank Beech. It was rats. Pigeons were at Harvard. It was still the heyday of Hull. My advisor was Carl Hovland. I got there and I was interested in race relations as I'd already done research on the dynamics of prejudice between blacks and Puerto Ricans which was one of the first studies of prejudice between ethnic groups. I had also done some work on patterns of self-segregation in the cafeteria and a third study was looking at the lack of appeal of political parties to Puerto Ricans who were coming into New York. And what did I get when I got to Yale? I got rats. I'm running rats. I ran rats until at one time I had the biggest rat colony at Yale. I had 250 rats.

• *And you managed that?*
Yes I managed that. It was incredibly hard work but I was always a hard worker.
And Yale was simpler than New York. I had a bike to get to the apartment. I had
just one thing to do.

• *So you had abandoned showbiz by then?*
I abandoned showbiz for the time being. Then I moved in my third year back to
my love of social psychology. For me too Yale was my residential college. It was
like starting college all over again because in New York I had been commuting
to Brooklyn College. I loved it though New Haven was dull and boring

• *You were obviously close to your family.*
The great thing about Yale was that it was an hour and a half away so I would
come home once a month. We have a strong Italian family and there's always a
sense that you want to be as close to the family as possible. So one of the things at
Yale is that it's like a candy store. Here are all these famous people and I want to
work with as many different people as possible. And the ethos is to publish. I did
work with Carl Hovland and Frank Beech. I did work with Seymour Sarason.

• *And did you do that in a canny 'it will help my career' way?*
I never thought of a career. Even now I live one year at a time. Someone asked me
how I would describe my career path and I said *boostraphooical* which is the path
oxen take when they are crossing a field. But at Yale you had all these resources and
you had all these famous people and all you had to do was say 'I'm interested in
working with you' and they would say 'yes'. So in fact I had a sense of working not
with one person – but with a whole set of people. Each person can give you something, some people are good at designing experiments, some are good at explaining complex ideas, some in translating ideas. So my sense is where is all this getting
me? It was clear incidentally that you had to publish and present at meetings. At
conference all the graduate students presented. But I had a problem and it was that
that I was poorly trained as an undergraduate so I was way over my head and I was
never good enough at maths but you know in my third year I organised a symposium and I had Harry Harlow as my discussant as we were doing something on
exploratory curiosity. The guy who I worked for with the rats was K.C. Mont-
gomery who committed suicide the second year I was there. I said to the grant-
giving body give me the grant because I have all this stuff going and it would be a
shame not to pursue all this material; and they gave me the $38,000 grant.

• *That must have been a fortune then?*
Yes, they had a faculty member supervise it.

• *How did you get back from the rats to social psychology?*
A guy called Bob Cohn. All my teachers had just come out of the Second World War and they had come out of grad school and then there was a whole cadre of these guys starting out as associate professors. All were idealistic, all were excited about applying psychology to real problems . . . I got involved with the rats and as they say you love the things you suffer for and one day as a graduate I had become the co-author of a paper in *Science* and I was doing some statistics and I was feeling high. The article had been accepted for *Science*. And Bob Cohn turns up and I start describing the rat study and he says, 'it sounds interesting. Could you do me a favour? Could you look out of the window and see what's going on there?'

[Zimbardo turns to show me what he did and acts out what Bob said to him.] 'There are some people there. Could you describe them', he says. I described them. 'Any idea what they're talking about', he asks. He keeps asking questions and I'm getting a little irritated. And he finally says, 'let me ask you a blunt question. Which do you find more interesting? People or rats?' I said people are obviously more complex. He said, 'that's what you should be studying – not rats. You come from the Bronx. From your background that's what you should be studying. Any one of these guys here could study rats. Coming from the Bronx you want to exterminate rats, you don't want to make them smart.' And then he said I'm teaching a course next term. And I did it. Brehm had been a student and Leon Festinger is sending his manuscript on cognitive dissonance which is being published at the end of the year. It's not just hot off the press, it's hot off the typewriter. And it was so stimulating because everything in behaviourism is so rational, you give a rat more pellets and he presses the bar harder. And here was dissonance theory saying just the opposite. The more the reward, the less behaviour, the less the reward the more behaviour! It was just so intoxicating. I did my dissertation comparing a dissonance prediction with a standard Yale attitude one and dissonance won. I was hooked on dissonance. I wrote a book on dissonance and the cognitive control of motivation. It was, I think, the first time the term was used.

• *And after you left Yale?*
I went to New York and I was teaching ten courses a year, mostly to large classes for $6000. I also taught summer courses to make ends meet. I realised too that if I didn't do any research I'd never get out of New York.

• *How did the prison experiment develop?*
A weekend simulation provided such dramatic effects in ordinary college students and the answer was that the simulations can become all too real. It became

a prison run by psychologists and not an experiment. And so it was a very profound experience. And the reason it worked and most people take this for granted but the most dramatic part was the arrest of the 'prisoners' by the Palo Alto police. It could never happen now because of potential lawsuits. But again it was street smarts.

• *Your youth again?*
I worked a deal with the captain of the local police department because during the students strike the university called the police on to the campus because students were disrupting things. I helped arrange town-gown co-operation so that students rode in the police cars and the cops went into the dormitories. Then I went to the new chief of police and I said I want to continue this relationship and I'm thinking of doing this experiment, so how about having some of your rookies act some of the prisoners so they get the experience of what that's like. And he said great idea. And then I said we'd actually like some of you guys to arrest people who are going to be prisoners as that would make it more realistic. Because you want people's freedom taken away from them. That is what happens in prison. You are signed in by these people in uniform.

• *As you may know the English psychologist Rom Harre is very critical of Milgram's study because it was in Yale and so people would know somehow people would not really be hurt and so he claimed it was unrealistic?*
Yes, Milgram's subjects were in that situation for 30 minutes. My study was not real but people were there day and night as if you really are a prisoner. As in really good drama, the boundary between reality and illusion gets shaken. You knew you had not really committed any offence, any felony, but you're handcuffed, there are police cars with lights, neighbours looking in and then you're taken to the real Palo Alto police station. Men fingerprint you, they book you. For middle-class college kids, you're feeling guilty. How many times did you steal things from stores? How many times did you masturbate? All the little things you did which violated social norms and which you are now going to be punished for. So the guilt is real even though it is not connected to what the cops said or did. So though people knew it was not real, what was dramatic was the way it started and then the tension just builds up because people are living in the prison day and night. No one expected what happened. The kids who are prisoners assume they are going to sit in cells and read books and play the guitar and stuff. I assumed something like that too. And the turning point was when the prisoners rebelled on the second morning and that changed the dynamic. The guards said these guys are dangerous, they embarrassed us and we have to show them who is boss. And that switched the whole thing. Then it became pure power as in prison because in

real prisons, prisoners have no power. Then power became an aphrodisiac. And the prisoners were broken and the guards would do worse and worse things.

• *So the recent BBC replication was a nonsense?*
Total nonsense.

• *What is your more considered perhaps view of the BBC replication of your prison experiment?*
The BBC pseudo replication has only the most superficial resemblance to the original experiment. It is a made for TV pseudo experiment with more demand characteristics than any study ever done, with phoney random assignment that guaranteed the prisoners were big burly types tattoos and other distinguishing features that the BBC cameras focused on repeatedly – when the prison role should have imposed anonymity and dehumanisation. Also the head guard was a millionaire businessman who was always concerned about his image after the study was over and constantly sucked up to the inmates. So in the end the prisoners ran the show and the guards were their playthings. Maybe that is how prisons are run in England, not so in the US or most other nations. I could go on endlessly about the waste of money or time. But suffice to say that when the filming was over and the cast shown previews, the prisoners did not like the way they appeared so they insisted that it was recut. And it was. So what the audience sees is hardly on line reality TV but rehashed, reshaped unreality TV. The British social psychologists in charge knew as much about prisons as I knew about the Queen Mother's toilet habits – nothing.

• *You are angry about it?*
It made me angry for two reasons. It wasted millions of dollars and it could have been done so much better. It was an experiment on a prison run by prisoners. I don't believe there was random assignment either. Jean Genet writes about prisons, lots of prisoners have written about prison well. The first thing you document is that these are normal middle class college students who have done nothing wrong and are put in a prison. And this is 1971. These kids are civil rights activists, they protest against the Vietnam War, they are peaceniks and now you put them in a uniform and you've got the guards acting as Nazis. And you've got people who are having emotional breakdowns. The other thing is that we gave them batteries of psychological tests and so we said at the beginning not only are these kids ordinary normal kids but we can say they are psychologically normal and healthy. So any changes you see are brought about by the weekend experiment. It could not be pathology they brought in with them. So the fact is that we separated the pathology of the participants from the pathology of the

situation. Milgram and my research are really book ends of the power of the situation. His research studied how much power an individual can wield when there is a dominant individual in a white coat telling him to do something while mine is about how belonging to a group changes your behaviour.

• *How did your work on shyness develop?*
In 1972, a year after the Stanford Prison Experiment, I was teaching about the experiment and used the metaphor of shyness as a silent self-imposed prisoner with the shy person internalising both the prisoner and the guard roles, where the guard limits the basic freedoms of the prisoner self and the prisoner often silently rebels but eventually gives in and surrenders both freedoms and self esteem. Students in that class indicated they wanted to know more about shyness so I started a no credit seminar for shy students and we began exploring the concept with surveys, interviews and research – which expanded into a formal Stanford project with grants and cross-cultural research and in 1977 with the start of an experimental clinic to study shyness in depth and to use what we knew to help shy people.

• *Were there any repercussions from the prison experiment?*
There were no negative repercussions legally or otherwise. There were many positive consequences in terms of how many of the people in the research were significantly changed.

• *You spoke about the power of the situation. Do you see that as a very pessimistic thing in terms of political hope for a better world?*
Not at all. It means you have to understand the nature of situational power in order to avoid it or change it. The alternative is to focus on evil people and to kill them. We have run that play to death and nothing changes.

• *How do we avoid the power of the situation?*
We are all products of the roles we play in multiple situations. He is now the interrogator, the torturer but send him to Palm Springs with a beautiful woman and lots of cash and he will be a hedonist enjoying sensual pleasures.

   Do you know my book on torture? We interviewed many former Brazilian torturers and death squad executioners and our verdict was that none of them were pathological but they were all products of intense situational indoctrination.

• *You have also written about cults? What makes them attractive?*
They provide instant family, social support, personal recognition, an illusion of stability, a place, role, job, high-sounding values, an escape from the demands of

society, a simpler existence, free from crime, social security – all wonderful but mostly all illusory and filled with lies and deceptions since many cult members end up as beggars or recruiters not really knowing what they're doing. I wrote an article in the *APA Monitor*, 'The cults are coming'.

• *What was it like being President of the American Psychological Association?*
Wonderful in many ways, extensive travel to spread the psychology gospel and a chance to develop a new initiative that will demonstrate how psychological research and practice makes a real difference.

• *Lastly it seems to me that psychology has not fulfilled the idealism of some of those especially after the Second World war who wanted it to change the world for the better. Do you agree or not – and how can we change that?*
After World War Two, psychologists were filled with enthusiasm for doing good and working internationally but they had to publish to get promoted or they'd perish so they became conservative and tentative and focused narrowly on projects that were readily doable and publishable. But it is changing now with the infusion of new female blood and brains. Women want a psychology filled with meaning overflowing with using knowledge for social good and dealing with the emergent problems facing nations world wide and I believe that as psychology becomes more relevant with female psychologists leading the way we will return to the idealism that flourished after World War Two.

Chapter 14: Unfinal Conclusions

I started on what has been a riveting journey through contemporary psychology soon after I left Oxford. A number of magazines, such as the *New Scientist* and the Paris-based *Psychologie* were interested in the careers and thoughts of psychologists because it seemed important to cover different theories of human nature. So over the course of the last 25 years I have interviewed 37 of the world's 'important' behavioural scientists – some more than once. As I said in the Introduction, in this latest version I have kept interviews with those who seem historically most important together with some of those who have done very interesting work recently. I have had to leave out a number of brilliant researchers or the book would be thicker than a phone directory. Among those I have not included in this book are the late Michael Argyle who was a leader in social psychology, the therapist Karl Menninger, Patricia Churchland who has developed theories of artificial intelligence, Donald Broadbent who was the first psychologist to be elected to the Royal Society, Thomas Szasz the great critic of psychiatry, and J.B. Rhine who put parapsychology on the map with his studies of some men who had what seemed to be real gift for telepathy. I also have left out the French neuroscientist Michel Jouvet who discovered paradoxical sleep and Liam Hudson who wrote two important books, *Contrary Imaginations* and *The Cult of the Fact*. I give this list because my unfinal conclusions do draw on what I learned in these other interviews.

One of the most striking things is the sheer variety of views on what makes human beings tick. The behavioural sciences are mixed and many. Historically they were extremely ambitious. As Zimbardo notes when he went to Yale in 1951, there were behaviourists who really believed they could produce equations which explained all learning, all motivation, all human endeavour and much else besides. And often psychologists hoped to change the world for the better. That ambition has not been wholly lost though it is a little muted these days.

In the first two editions of this book I was mainly aiming to reach academic audiences and so my conclusions dealt with a number of technical issues – such as the different approaches to methodology, the question of how much you can learn about human behaviour in the laboratory, why too much psychology concentrates on abnormal behaviour and what kind of science psychology is if it is a science at all. As all students know, the convention in the learned journals is that one reports results of experiments and if there was only one chance in a hundred or fifty that a certain correlation would occur by accident, that is a fact. That remains an important issue because it means there is such a focus on prediction.

Over the past 25 years some of these issues have been if not resolved, at least, become less pressing. For example, there is far more work than ever before outside the laboratory and more interest in normal behaviour. The introduction of cheap video cameras has made it much easier for psychologists to record and observe long sequences of normal, natural human behaviour. On the whole we film children and young children more than adults but nevertheless psychology is no longer mainly a lab-based science. Deborah Tannen, for example, has used participant observation as a key method in her work especially in her study of how men and women talk at work. The methods of psychology are more eclectic than ever before – and I did argue the need for that back in 1977.

The question of what kind of science psychology is has not really been resolved however because in the interviews it is clear that 'romantics' like Laing and Frankl still remain influential against hard experimental scientists. Psychology has mushroomed and octopussed – a discipline that octopusses must surely spread tentacles all over the place – so much in the last 25 years that I begin to wonder if this debate will ever be resolved. The enormous success of self-help psychology, telling people how to find their inner self and so become better lovers, tennis players, gourmet cooks and parents, suggests that there will always be a market for romantic psychology. I am sorry to introduce the word *market* but psychology is among many things an intellectual bazaar where all sorts of persons sell their wares. That trend is most obvious in therapy. Viktor Frankl was a little ambivalent about the humanist therapist Abraham Maslow whose theory of peak experiences remains influential. Maslow noted, "the first overarching Big Problem is to make the Good Person. We must have better human beings or it is quite possible we shall all be wiped out and even if not wiped out live in tension and anxiety as a species." The answer of course was to follow the methods of Maslow, which would lead one to more peak experiences, and to being 'fully illuminated' not to mention 'self actualised'. Currently Skinners are rather down on the Psych Stock Exchange and Zimbardos are up...

Like a bazaar, psychology is full of energy but of course psychology is more than just a market. I suspect I'd award the prize of most energetic psychologist of the last 25 years to Zimbardo with Eysenck close behind!

The less accidental psychologist

One clear sign of energy and evolution is that psychology is big business in the health and education professions. In the first version of this book I noted that many of those I talked to had become psychologists by accident. As psychology has become more and more a career with a set structure, thousands of undergraduates study it because they want to work at it, fewer go into it by accident or mistakes. Luckily to keep life interesting, there are still exceptions like Deborah Tannen who became a linguist by accident and then, also by accident, became the kind of linguist who studies behaviour rather than phonemes.

But there has been a price to pay. As it has become more an established subject psychology has also fragmented. A hundred sub-specialities have bloomed. There are journals devoted to mathematical psychology, moral psychology, political psychology, interior decoration psychology, sports psychology, consumer psychology and somewhere I expect there is the *Japanese Journal of Bicycling Psychology* with learned articles on how to condition subjects to pedal backwards. One consequence is that there are many trivial studies done just to add another publication to the vita. That is true of every other academic discipline but rather more serious is that there is a real risk that there will soon be no core of knowledge all psychologists share. Very few undergraduate courses spend much time on economic psychology, for example. Very few study language in context and what that reveals about human behaviour.

Without mastering such a common core, psychologists fret about publishing the kind of grand psychological theory of human nature that Freud, John B. Watson, Herbert Simon and Skinner attempted. Freud kept up with all the experimental psychology literature of his day; in the 1960s, Donald Broadbent, Skinner and Eysenck had a good sense of what therapists and psychiatrists were doing. But you would need to be a poly-polymath to understand the latest advances in genetics, the debates on hard versus soft models of artificial intelligence, and recent findings in brain research which affect how we respond, never mind work on social psychology.

Instead of grand visionaries, we have specialised visionaries like John Flavell who has developed important theories in a limited area. This fragmentation makes it perhaps all the more important for those who work in and are interested in the subject, to have some sense of the big ideas in areas other than those they are professionals in.

To produce grand theories you also need to be philosophically nimble

Psychology has unique problems because of the kind of subjects we study. Our subjects are not objects; they too are subjects – even subjects with free will.

Sometimes they have to be deceived for experiments to work; often they can guess what the experiment is really about. In physics there may be a theory of the formation, life and death of stars in splendid physico-chemical complexity but, at least, astronomers don't have to worry about what stars know and whether stars might be producing quirky data because they are having a bad stellar day and just want to show the arrogant experimenter that they know perfectly well what she or he is trying to get at. And it makes them laugh.

The giggling nebula . . . well no one has seen one of those yet.

It is this complexity of human beings that makes it hard for psychologists to be sure what they are doing and what it means. That is why it is so disappointing that there has not been much new work on the philosophy of psychology.

The philosophical work is needed because psychology has to explain three levels of behaviour – and how they interrelate. Why do all human beings behave in some ways like all other human beings? – everyone sleeps, everyone dreams, everyone eats? Many but not all of these questions are biological. Second, why do some human beings behave in some ways that others do not – why do particular groups of males ride motorbikes and take drugs while others do not? Why does everyone who does not suffer from colour blindness see the sun as golden and the sea as blue? Finally there have to be explanations at the individual level. Why does Zoe Jones always do well at maths, love garlic and worry about the fact that she wants to be meet a boy who is not too exciting, has freckles and whose skin smells of hay? And how do the personal characteristics of Zoe Jones make sense in terms of what we know of genetics, neurology and all the sciences that have some links with psychology?

I have written two biographies of psychologists – one of John B. Watson, the founder of behaviourism, and the other of the founder of humanistic therapy, Carl Rogers. I have some sense of how hard it is to do more than set down the facts about another human being. We still have to see psychologists attempt to write a detailed biography of an ordinary person and explain their life as a whole. The closest we get to that oddly are the stream of clinical reports written about people who are in trouble. In very important cases like those of the Guildford Four and serial killers like Harold Shipman, defence and prosecution often commission experts with radically different views to explain how and why they did what they did. I have occasionally seen some of these reports and many are very thorough. But from a scientific view, they are not part of the literature usually. Only a few details are read out in court. The main body of these reports remain confidential. It is ironic that while we publish much trivia, we cannot publish even in academic conferences some of the potentially richest case studies in psychology and psychiatry. As a result we have no way of checking whether we have methods which allow us to make sense of complex life histories. I can't see a way of changing that sadly.

Changes in theory

The two most important changes in psychology over the last 20 years have been the reintroduction of consciousness which behaviourism had outlawed and the rise of developmental psychology. No one now pretends, as Skinner tried to at his most provocative, that there is no need to study thoughts and feelings and Flavell has shown how very competent some very young children are at understanding the fact that other people have different ideas. It is possible to see how psychology will develop a more rounded view of human life but there is a long way to go. Any reader of learned journals who is not lulled by their peculiar conventions will remain depressed by too many studies with strange sounding titles that really seem to have little to do with life. The British psychologist Paul Kline suggested in *Psychology Exposed* that psychology's serious sounding predictions often turned out to be common sense dressed up as jargon. According to Eysenck, Kline was just having a bad day. According to Kline, Eysenck was just defending his all-too-inflexible ideas.

The power of psychologists

It must be said that humility does not come easily to psychologists. Physicists may gaze in awe at the wonders of the galaxy, zoologists may wax lyrical about the beauty of the gazelles and the cheetah in hot pursuit but I did not often find the behavioural scientists so entranced, astonished by how people behaved. Zimbardo came closest perhaps. This lack of humility reinforces the thesis powerfully put forward by the late Professor David McClelland of Harvard. He was interested in what motivates people to achieve economically and linked that to the Protestant work ethic. He highlighted the fact that many psychologists had deeply religious parents and claimed they reacted against this. They wanted psychology to be scientific and not to preach how one should behave. But McClelland took away from 40 years in psychology a more disturbing truth – psychologists loved power. That was why for much of the 20th century the battles between different schools of psychology were so intense. Skinner had to convince everyone that he was right. Chomsky had to convince everyone that Skinner was wrong. And it is unfair to single out these two. Frankl and Eysenck, for example, were just as intense. R.D. Laing was destroyed by the interview he gave to Anthony Clare, a fellow psychiatrist, on the radio when Clare got him to admit how much of a drink problem he had. Laing's enemies – and Clare was never one – seized on this and Laing was struck off the doctors' register.

McClelland suggested to me that each important psychologist wanted to convince us that their view of human nature was the only correct one. Either

Watson or Freud had to be right, for example. It could not be both of them. The supposedly wise and mature psychoanalysts were amongst the most bitter in their debates. Frankl described well how he had been excommunicated by Adler who had earlier walked out on the Freudians. Vienna had so many cafes because each psycho-group had to have its own place (with its own special cakes, I am tempted to say).

Far more serious than the Vienna squabbles it is well to remember that behavioural scientists who have managed to get real power have not covered themselves in glory. One of Goering's cousins was a psychotherapist and created an institute to help motivate young Nazis. The only expert in behavioural science to have held really high office so far was Radovan Karadic, a psychiatrist who is wanted for war crimes against Bosnia. He was ruthless, cruel and ordered tens of thousands of deaths. As far as I know he has not been condemned by professional bodies incidentally. It is perhaps just as well that psychologists do not get to wield any real power outside the academic world.

Why do psychologists need and love power so much? I did not get any of them to talk frankly about it, although Zimbardo is very interesting about how his struggles as a young child made him determined to use his intelligence to become a leader. McClelland suggested it was partly ego but also because what they were writing about felt so important to them. One of my aims in this book has also been to try to make some sense of the psychology of psychologists. Anne Roe (1953) produced a series of studies and found that psychologists tended to be hostile to their parents and not to withdraw away from personal relationships. Many were still angry at their parents 20 years, even 50 years on. Perhaps they love power to compensate for feeling powerless in their youth. There is a nice PhD study for a graduate who does not mind taking risks.

But this love of power also has a positive side. It is also clear that many psychologists want to influence the world for the better. Sandra Bem and Deborah Tannen are very open about this. Male psychologists were usually less frank but the interviews have shown how Skinner wanted to influence social policy while Chomsky has become a political activist; Herbert Simon wanted also to influence social policy and Frankl was at the heart of debates about the Holocaust; Eysenck battled against ideas of political correctness arguing that he had seen Nazis in action and students who called him a fascist had no idea what they were talking about. Zimbardo was politically active and clearly loved the political action surrounding his prison experiment. Just before Eysenck died, he was attacking the Home Office because it refused to follow up on nutritional research, which suggested that a better diet would reduce violence in prisons. Yet another example of the political class being unwilling to listen to scientific results.

It is sad that psychologists do so often fight over views of psychology. There have been those who believed that as more women became prominent in psychology that would change. I am not sure the facts bear that out. Two women psychologists have had much criticism to cope with are Bem and Tannen who have both been 'slammed', Tannen's word, by fellow feminists: I could not use some of Tannen's attack on one of her critics because it might have been considered libellous.

Love of power and making the impact with one's singular views is also harder given the eclectic nature of reported results over the last 25 years. That has forced most psychologists to be less ambitious and less dogmatic. Today we see a little less of the either-or attitude, either you are with me or you are against me, as fewer feel bold enough to try to explain the sweep of the complexities of what human beings get up to – and why.

In some ways psychologists have compensated by becoming media pundits, called in to comment on every last bauble of human behaviour as well as telling us how to live. Psychologists are the new priests. The death of God reported at the end of the 19th century by Nietzsche seems to have led to the birth of experts who can soundbite on anything the Six o'Clock News needs. As I have commented on the body language of contestants on *Big Brother* and re-designed environments for the BBC so that singles who don't feel they are having much luck improve their sex lives, I am not in a position to throw stones. Zimbardo was acid about the way the BBC re-ran his prison experiment. Far more psychologists than ever before enjoy the chance to explain what they think about issues of the day. This is hardly the same kind of power as developing a new theory of human nature which is a real discovery or a new synthesis. Still if you can't have the one you love, love the one you have and many psychologists do enjoy their brief 3-minute soundbite in the sun. It is a little bit of weak power.

I foresee incidentally that we are at the very start of a discipline in which the ageing baby boomers find out how to make the most of your 60s. How to have a good sex life for the over 80s is a tome I expect to write when I am 75 and which will keep me long after the state pension has become worthless.

The failures of psychology

Other realities have also softened the ideological bravado of psychologists. First it has become all too clear that psychology does not have the power to understand, let alone fix, many problems. I want to take three serious examples of this – the growth of child abuse which has been endlessly debated, the number of deaths caused by accidents in military training in the UK and the rise in the use of anti-depressants with children.

We do not really know if there is more child abuse than in the past or whether it is just reported more. What is now clear is that children who are physically, sexually or emotionally abused suffer and continue to suffer. Stephen Ceci has shown, however, that despite huge sums of money spent on counselling, many psychologists and linked professionals are still very poor at questioning young children sensitively about what has happened to them. The result is confusion about what really took place and more distress for youngsters. There has also been a complex and inconclusive debate about whether therapists actually make some patients fantasise they have been abused when they have not been.

I deliberately choose a very different second example – military psychology. The army, navy and air force use psychologists to help train recruits and also to make sure that the design of weapons – the man/machine interface – works. Donald Broadbent learned to do experiments while working for the RAF and improved the design of altimeters and other instruments which cut the number of aircraft accidents. Today the military use psychologists in a number of ways including helping devise training so that recruits learn how to handle weapons – including very sophisticated weapons – well. Despite this long tradition of using psychological research to help design equipment so that soldiers can use it properly in the heat of battles, some 2500 British service personnel died in military accidents during the 1990s. That is about 1 per cent of the number of soldiers in the UK. There are of course many different reasons for such tragic accidents but many reflect the fact that soldiers get confused by their instruments. Others have been due to deficiencies in training. There have been persistent problems of bullying recruits. This means that despite the greatest psychology industry in the world, the Pentagon sent soldiers into Iraq with very little sense of how different cultures behave and how to adapt to that.

A third example of the failure of psychology is that we have seen a huge rise in the use of anti-depressants with children because psychologists and psychiatrists cannot handle problems in behaviour in any other way. In addition they have not managed to find ways of training and teaching parents to cope with such difficult children.

The fact that it is harder and harder to master the main debates and new findings in the whole discipline and the fact that psychology has often failed to deliver promised insights means that in their secret souls – and they have them – serious psychologists get anxious. Who am I, given what we know, to do what I dreamed of doing, think up a theory that will explain so much? Some of those I interviewed did not feel that stark or humble but the failure to impose a theory like the Big Bang theory in cosmology continues to worry many behavioural scientists. Psychology is still a young science, they say. I ask when will it grow up?

Back to prediction

This was a problem that did bother a number of those I interviewed. Eysenck argued strongly psychologists knew so little about natural science that they could not see how different psychology had to be in its methods. Surprisingly for someone who argued so much for science, Eysenck felt that the traditional form of the experiment – you have a hypothesis, you work out how to test it, you make the formal predictions – was often a hindrance rather than a help. Theories had to be tested of course but psychology did not have to give in to the tyranny of predictions. Eysenck complained:

> "In psychology and indeed in most sciences where research is carried on at the edge of the unknown, weak rather than strong theories are the rule, and successful prediction is of greater importance than unsuccessful prediction: the former suggests important follow up investigations and leads to the conclusion that the theory, though not necessarily correct, may be leading in a promising direction, while the latter is open to many divergent explanations which did not necessarily imply a failure of the theory as implied by the major premiss."

Eysenck went on say, "Psychologists sometimes seem in danger of throwing out promising ideas of wide applicability through premature insistence on a degree of deductive and experimental rigour which is quite out of place in a young science just beginning the hard task of building up its foundations" (1970).

The psychology of psychologists and creativity

In the past psychologists seemed to find any attempt to link their lives and their work a little strange. That does seem to have changed but material on the psychology of psychologists remains very limited. Skinner, Simon and Eysenck did write autobiographies and Damasio does have a good deal to say about his personal journey in trying to make sense of Descartes and Spinoza.

I find this interesting because a number of psychologists claimed that the subject only really came alive for them when they were writing it. Tannen makes this point very strongly saying that she had always known she could write and that this is one of the aspects of the work that gives her the greatest pleasure. Skinner wanted to be a writer and in his youth sent poems to Robert Frost to comment. In the first edition of this book, Neal Miller and David McClelland commented on how much they liked writing. Two other psychologists, Henri Tajfel and Liam Hudson, argued like Tannen that they are most creative at psychology when they write it. Tajfel told me back in the 1970s:

"The only time I am ever creative is when I sit down at my desk and write the damn thing up . . . writing is of course the acid test because you come up against contradictions, weaknesses and so on that you haven't notice before . . . This is also the time when I really think, when I write."

Such admissions and confessions have interesting implications about the nature of psychology as a scientific enterprise, I think.

Karl Popper, the philosopher whose *The Logic of Scientific Discovery* was so influential, argued that logic has nothing to do with having new ideas and that "there is no such thing as a logical method of having new ideas or a logical reconstruction of this process." Popper was no I-am-always-logical-Dr-Spock (of *Star Trek*, not child care) and he saw flashes of irrational creativity as being crucial for scientists. They led up to experiments. Those flashes were the moment of insight when the great scientist realised what the key question was. Henri Poincare, the great French mathematician, talked of finding solutions in dreams. The unconscious mind was spluttering away doing the equations, seeing things from different perspectives, giving the ideas. That was inspiration, the perspiration was collecting the data. But does the unconscious mind work for psychologists? Probably not. I have to say perhaps because Freud hogged it all.

Anyhow individuals as different as Herbert Simon, Deborah Tannen and Liam Hudson appear to work in quite different way. Their creativity takes place after they have their results. They may no longer be armchair theorists but it is as they sit as at the keyboard, they get shafts of insight. Setting up the study, collecting the data, marshalling the result is not where the psychological action is. For many the action is in the writing up. This feels though I cannot prove it rather different from the Eureka moments of creativity in other sciences. As a science psychology is supposed to be above the quirks and prejudices of its practitioners but if psychologists psychologise most – and best – when they write, it might be because they are finally free of trying to be scientists and can "utter themselves", as Liam Hudson said. Unfortunately, or maybe fortunately if you don't believe psychology can ever be really a science like other sciences, these passages into the personal are not clearly labelled 'and this is where I become personal' but Conclusions or Discussion. I have at least called this chapter Unfinal Conclusions.

The puzzle is the personal. Writers reflect themselves in what they are – and they are supposed to do so. But psychologists want to be scientists and not artists or vague and woolly thinkers. Hell, they'll be lumped in with cultural studies next. And science is allegedly impersonal. Yet it is not so easy for the psychologist to be impersonal. The ideas a psychologist has about human nature must surely affect him or her as a person. I can hardly go about arguing that sex is one of the great motivators and peak experiences but not for me. Heavens no, moi is motivated by altogether more elevated drives such as helping humankind and collecting old postcards; I would not worry if my own sex life was as exciting as a wet afternoon in Margate. After the biography I wrote of John B. Watson, the founder of behaviourism, I wrote a radio play for Radio 3 in which I cross-examined Watson about why his theories of human behaviour in no way explained how he led his own life and responded to crisis. (Needless to say in my play Watson was stumped, apologised and promised to do better in his next life.) But this interplay between what a psychologist argues is human nature and the facts of their own life is very difficult ground because it threatens the idea that psychology is a science. Psychologists need to think about it, I would humbly suggest.

There is one final suggestion I should like to make. I have had the privilege of interviewing three Nobel laureates. Almost no psychologists win a Nobel because while there are prizes for economics and medicine, there is none for the behavioural sciences. There is no universally acknowledged Top Psychologist prize which commands any attention outside the profession. Psychology needs some such prize which could be awarded as easily to a developmental psychologist as to a social psychologist. I think it might provide a symbol of unity of the discipline.

I called this chapter 'Unfinal' Conclusions because I have tried to reflect the controversies in contemporary psychology. I'm not sure anyone can resolve them, but they matter – and they don't just matter to psychologists. We all want to understand ourselves and those other sometimes lovable, sometimes maddening people we share this small planet with. So far psychology has been less help in that than its ambitious founding fathers and mothers hoped. We need to give the discipline – and ourselves – a kick up the backside. "Could do a lot better" is probably a fair report on the state of art – science – speculation that is psychology today. I am very grateful to all those who agreed to be interviewed by me.

Bibliography

Bem, S. (1993) *The Lenses of Gender*. Yale University Press.

Borger, R. and Cioffi, F. (eds) (1970) *Explanation in the Behavioural Sciences*. Cambridge University Press.

Broadbent, D.E. (1961) *Behaviour*. Eyre and Spottiswoode.

Broadbent, D.E. (1974) *In Defence of Empirical Psychology*. Methuen.

Chein, I. (1972) *The Science of Behaviour and the Image of Man*. Tavistock Publications.

Chomsky, N. (1959) Review of Verbal Behaviour by B.F. Skinner. *Language* 35, 26–58.

Chomsky, N. (1957) *Syntactic Structures*. Mouton.

Chomsky, N. (1968) *Language and Mind*. Harcourt Brace and World.

Chomsky, N. (1996) *The Nature of Language and Mind*. Cambridge University Press.

Cohen, D. (1990) *Being a Man*. Routledge.

Cohen, D. (2000) *Carl Rogers: A Critical Biography*. Constable & Robinson.

Cohen, D. (2002) *How the Child's Mind Develops*. Routledge.

Cooper, D. (1967) *Psychiatry and anti-Psychiatry*. Tavistock Publications.

Cooper, D. (1972) *Death of the Family*. Penguin.

Damasio, A. (1994) *Descartes' Error: Emotion, Reason and the Human Brain*. Avon Books.

Damasio A. (2000) *The feeling of what happens*. Vintage.

Damasio, A. (2003) *Looking for Spinoza*. Random House.

Dennett, D. (1992) *Consciousness Explained*. Little, Brown.

Eysenck, H.J. (1952) The effects of psychotherapy and evaluation. *Journal of Consulting Psychology* 16 (5), 319–24.

Eysenck, H.J. (1953) *The Scientific Study of Personality*. Routledge & Kegan Paul.

Eysenck, H.J. (1964) *Crime and Personality*. Routledge & Kegan Paul.

Eysenck, H.J. (1967) *The Biological Basis of Personality*. University of Chicago Press.

Eysenck, H.J. (1986) *The Decline and Fall of the Freudian Empire*. Penguin.

Eysenck, H.J. (1990) *Rebel with a Cause*. W.H. Allen.

Flavell, J. (1964) *The Developmental Psychology of Jean Piaget*. Van Nostrand Reinhold.

Frankl, V. (1986) *The Doctor and the Soul*. Vintage.

Frankl, V. (1964) *Man's Search for Meaning: An Introduction to Logotherapy*. Hodder.

Freud, S. (1900; reprinted 1991) *The Interpretation of Dreams*. Penguin.

Freidenberg, E.Z. (1973) *Laing*. Fontana.

Holt, R.R. (1962) Individuality and generalisation in the psychology of personality. *Journal of Personality*. 30, 377–404.

Hudson, L. (1966) *Contrary Imaginations: A Psychological Study of the English Schoolboy.* Methuen.

Hudson, L. (1972) *The Cult of the Fact.* Jonathan Cape.

Kahneman, D. (2003) *Well Being.* Russell Sage Foundation.

Kahneman D. (2002) *Autobiography for Nobel Prize.* Swedish Academy of Sciences.

Kahneman D. and Tversky, A. (2000) *Choices, Values and Frames.* Cambridge University Press

Jordan, N. (1968) *Themes in Speculative Psychology.* Tavistock Publications.

Kendler, H.H. (1981) *A Science in Conflict.* Oxford University Press.

Kline, P. (1990) *Psychology Exposed.* Routledge.

Kuhn, T. (1962) *The Structure of Scientific Revolutions.* University of Chicago Press.

Laing, A. (1994) *R.D. Laing.* Peter Owen.

Laing, R.D. (1960) *The Divided Self.* Penguin.

Laing, R.D. (1967) *The Politics of Experience.* Penguin.

Laing, R.D. (1972) *Knots.* Penguin.

McClelland, D. (1973) The two faces of power, in D. McClelland and R.S. Steele (eds), *Readings in Human Motivation.* General Learning Press.

Mahoney, M. (1976) Seekers after truth. *Psychology Today,* April.

Maslow, A.M. (1973) *Farther Reaches of Human Nature.* Penguin.

Milgram, S. (1974) *Obedience to Authority: An Experimental View.* HarperCollins.

Polanyi, M. (1971) *Knowing and Being.* Routledge & Kegan Paul.

Popper, K. (1968) *The Logic of Scientific Discovery.* Hutchinson – originally published in German in 1934.

Richardson, K. (1989) *Understanding Psychology.* Open University Press.

Roe, A. (1953) A comparative psychological study of eminent psychologists and anthropologists and a comparision with biological and physical scientists. *Genetic Psychological Monographs* 67, no. 352.

Rosenberg, M. (1965) When dissonance fails. *Journal of Personality and Social Psychology* 1, 28.

Rowan, J. (1988) *Sub-personalities.* Routledge.

Ryle, G. (1949) *The Concept of Mind.* Hutchinson.

Shotter, J. (1975) *Images of Man.* Methuen.

Simon, H. (1991) *Models of my Life.* Basic Books.

Skinner, B.F. (1972) *Beyond Freedom and Dignity.* Jonathan Cape.

Spearman, P. (1927) *The Abilities of Man, their Nature and Measurement.* The Macmillan Company.

Szasz, T. (1960) The myth of mental illness. *American Psychologist* 15, 113–18.

Tannen, D. (1992) *You Just Don't Understand: Women and Men in Conversation.* Virago Press.

Tannen, D. (1998) *The Argument Culture: Moving from Debate to Dialogue.* Random House.

Tannen, D. (2003) *I Only Say This Because I Love You.* Virago Press.

Taylor, C. (1964) *The Explanation of Behaviour.* Routledge & Kegan Paul.

Zimbardo, P. and Huggins, M. (2002) *Violence Workers: Police Torturers and Murderers Reconstruct Brazilian Atrocities.* University of California Press.

Zimbardo, P. and Gerrig, R. (2002) *Psychology and Life.* Allyn and Bacon.